Robert,

Thanks for your work in humanism.

Herb

HERB SILVERMAN
Notary Public
State of South Carolina
Commission Expires June 7, 2017

ADVANCE PRAISE

"Herb Silverman's autobiography is not an anti-theological treatise. It is, however, a warm, deeply personal, and inspiring tale of one atheist's travels through life in one of America's most religion-drenched regions. Silverman 'plays well' with believers and nonbelievers who share this core belief: no government official dare treat a person as a second-class citizen because of what she or he believes about God, gods, or the non-existence of them."

Reverend Barry Lynn, Executive Director of Americans United for Separation of Church and State

"An entertaining and informative look at America's culture war from a writer who has been embedded in the front lines."

Steven Pinker, Harvard College Professor of Psychology, Harvard University, and author of *The Better Angels of Our Nature*

"Herb Silverman's lively history of an atheist raised as an Orthodox Jew fills a real gap in the literature of the 'New Atheism,' in that it describes the emergence of a creed based on human goodness without godliness in highly personal rather than abstract philosophical terms. In an account that will resonate with people raised in all faith traditions who have made the same journey, Silverman captures the essence of what it means to realize that you think differently from those around you—including the people who brought you into this world."

Susan Jacoby, author of *Freethinkers: A History of American Secularism*

"It isn't often that inveterate honesty and inviolable reasonableness are combined with such a sweet disposition and a wonderful sense of humor. Those who don't yet know Herb will find in this wonderfully entertaining tale of how he became a fighting atheist a man of true wit, true warmth, and true wisdom."

Rebecca Newberger Goldstein, author of *36 Arguments for the Existence of God: A Work of Fiction*

"Herb Silverman has long been one of the most important secularist activists in the United States. With this book, you'll find he is a wonderful storyteller as well. Herb's warm and thoughtful self-portrait shows what it can mean to be both Jewish and a Humanist. And his story of running for governor of South Carolina as an open atheist is laugh-out-loud funny and worth reading for anyone who ever loved and/or hated the bizarre but hopeful theater that is American political life."

Greg Epstein, Harvard Humanist Chaplain and author of *Good Without God*

"Dr. Silverman is certainly unique for Charleston, maybe even unique for anywhere. When he came down here as a fine math professor but a cultural fish out of water, he simply created a flood of reason in which his newly discovered fellow infidels could swim. Herb presents a rational and persuasive alternative to those of faith, both with his words and his behavior."

Judge Alex Sanders, Former President of the College of Charleston and Founder and President of the Charleston School of Law

"Iconoclastic atheist, humorist, and mathematician Herb Silverman takes you on an entertaining tour of his irreverent life, so far."

Wendy Kaminer, lawyer, social critic, and author of seven books

CANDIDATE
WITHOUT
A PRAYER

CANDIDATE
WITHOUT
A PRAYER

*An Autobiography of a Jewish Atheist
in the Bible Belt*

Herb Silverman

Foreword by Richard Dawkins

PITCHSTONE PUBLISHING
Charlottesville, Virginia

Pitchstone Publishing
Charlottesville, VA 22901

19 18 17 16 15 14 13 12 1 2 3 4 5

Library of Congress Cataloging-in-Publication Data

Silverman, Herb.
 Candidate without a prayer : an autobiography of a Jewish atheist in the Bible Belt
/ Herb Silverman ; foreword by Richard Dawkins.
    p. cm.
 Includes index.
 ISBN 978-0-9844932-8-9 (hardcover : alk. paper) — ISBN 978-0-9844932-9-6
(pbk. : alk. paper)
 1. Silverman, Herb. 2. Atheists—South Carolina—Biography. 3. Mathematics
teachers—South Carolina—Biography. I. Title. II. Title: Autobiography
of a Jewish atheist in the Bible Belt.
 BL2790.S55A3 2012
 211'.8092—dc23
 [B]
                          2011042928

Three essays in chapter 12 are modified versions of those that appeared as
"Silverman's Wager," *Free Inquiry* (Spring 2001): 45, "Kindergarten Questions
for God," *Secular Nation* (Third Quarter 2007): 20–21, and "God IS Great," *The
Humanist* (November–December 2007): 30–31.

To my stepdaughter, Lisa, a breast cancer survivor.
I doubt that any author could be more pleased and proud of your
following review: "I LOVE your book. I have been reading it for
the past two hours while sitting in this tiny waiting room filled with
women waiting for breast testing and I can't stop myself from
smiling and laughing. I think some of the others must find my
behavior peculiar. Perhaps a copy of this book should be
standard in oncology waiting rooms!"

CONTENTS

*The three conventional numbering systems are English, metric, and hotel floors. I've chosen hotel.

FOREWORD

If a man is going to publish his life story, he had best take the precaution of leading an interesting life first. Or at least of being a very funny writer or of lacing his pages with wittily unconventional wisdom. Or even of being just an exceptionally nice person. Fortunately, Herb Silverman ticks all these boxes, and more.

Not every autobiographer can begin his life with an amusing childhood supervised by amusing parents but, by Silverman's hilarious account, his mother was the mother of all Jewish mother jokes. And his story just goes on getting better, through adolescent encounters with girls to his career as an academic mathematician, then secular activist and his gentle and courteous puncturing of hypocrisy and illogicality whenever he finds it—which is pretty much every day in the life of a sensitive atheist. Silverman has the endearing capacity to laugh at himself and poke fun at his shortcomings. Boswell to his own Johnson, he quotes his own past sayings and writings, but with a conspicuous lack of the irritating self-regard that this might, in others, suggest.

Endearing pleasantries adorn every page. When his schoolfellows, asked to write an essay on a chosen U.S. president, selected the obvious ones like Washington and Lincoln, the young Herb chose John Adams. Why? For the sufficient reason that his family could afford only two volumes of the encyclopedia: A and B. "Were it not for the Adams family," Herb added, "it would have been considerably more difficult to justify why my favorite president was Chester A. Arthur or James Buchanan."

Later in life, he visited Israel and was standing by the River Jordan at John the Baptist's reputed *Stammtisch* when a young man approached and asked Herb to baptize him. Herb's "spiritual" demeanor had impressed him, and the beard and sandals reminded him of Jesus. The genial atheist unhesitatingly obliged, and no doubt did it beautifully.

Back in America, he has undertaken various political campaigns, losing them with his own distinctive panache as a means to winning a more timeless battle. The Constitution of South Carolina stipulated that no person could be eligible for the office of governor who denied the existence of "the" Supreme Being. That Herb's sole motive in running for governor was to test the legality of that prohibition is attested by the answer he gave when asked what would be his first action, if elected: "Demand a recount." I'm reminded of the paradoxical maxim that anybody who actively wants high office should be disqualified from holding it.

I once publicly criticized American atheists for tokenism (defacing banknotes, for example, in protest against the 1957 addition of "In God We Trust") when they should be going after what I saw as more important issues (like tax exemptions for fat-cat televangelists). I now realize that that particular criticism was misplaced (because ignorant people demonstrably *use* the banknote slogan as alleged *evidence* that the United States is a Christian foundation). One might still criticize token gestures like refusing to bow the head in prayer at university prize-giving ceremonies. But this criticism, too, receives a beautifully Silvermanian response. At one gathering when most eyes were closed and heads bowed in prayer, Herb reflected that his erect, open-eyed posture was the perfect dissenting gesture. It couldn't give offense because the sincerely devout wouldn't see it, while those not offended could catch each other's eyes and take reassurance from the company.

This last is an important point, as I have discovered when lecturing to surprisingly large but beleaguered audiences around the so-called (though overrated) Bible Belt. When people tell Herb Silverman he is the only atheist they know, he says, "No I'm not. You know hundreds. I'm the only one who has been public about it."

Silverman enjoys arguing—he might say it is a Jewish trait—and he takes a gentle delight in teasing his opponents. Persuaded to attend a Billy Graham rally, he characteristically went forward to be "saved." He was received by one of Billy Graham's underlings (vicars in the literal sense, I suppose), Pastor A. Pastor A discovered Silverman's Jewish background and handed him on to Pastor B, who had converted from Judaism. On hearing that Pastor B's parents were dead, Herb asked whether he relished the thought that, as Jews, they were roasting in hell. When Pastor B demurred, Herb simply summoned Pastor A over, and happily left the two of them to fight it out.

In an effort to convert him, Christian apologists might quote a verse like "I am the Way, the Truth, and the Light." Did they expect him to slap his forehead and say, "Gee, I never knew that. Now I'm a believer"? How many times have we all wanted to say something like that? Equally familiar, the media often refer to Silverman as an "admitted atheist" or a "self-confessed atheist." How do they feel when described as an "admitted Baptist" or a "self-confessed Catholic"? And the following is vintage Silverman:

> However, the oddest comments came from those who thought my not believing in a judging God meant I must feel free to rape, murder, and commit any atrocity I can get away with. I'd respond, "With an attitude like that, I hope you continue to believe in God."

He regularly horrifies "Bible-believing Christians" by showing them what is actually in the Bible. He happily accepts invitations to debate with religious apologists, usually Christian but, on one notable occasion, Jewish. Silverman's Orthodox opponent expressed religious objections to medical research on dead human bodies. He conceded to Herb that many lives had been saved by such medical research, but argued, "There are lots of *goyim* and animals available for such things." Wow, just wow, as young people say.

On another occasion Herb was pitted against a Christian apologist, a "philosopher" from an unknown "university," who seems to do nothing but travel the country from one debate to another. This full-time debater fatuously asserted that the resurrection of Jesus must be a historical fact because the disciples were prepared to die for their beliefs. Herb's answer was devastatingly succinct: "9/11."

Another moment to savor took place in the Oxford Union, in my own university, a debate for which Herb took the unprecedented step of hiring a (too large) tuxedo. The motion was that "American religion undermines American values." Herb well deserved his applause for the following:

> In the melting pot called America, we are one nation under the Constitution
> . . . but not one nation under God. Given how the religious right opposes
> the teaching of evolution or any scientific and social view that conflicts with

a literal interpretation of the Bible, we are really becoming one nation *under-educated*. And this is not an American value to be proud of.

Once, when debating with a Pastor Brown, Herb asked the pastor what he would do if God commanded him to kill a member of his family, as God had commanded Abraham: "Depending on your answer, I might move a bit farther away from you." He doubtless said it with such good humor that the pastor could not take offense—but was consequently all the more stuck for an answer.

Pastor Brown generalized the question to one of whether he was ever tempted to disobey God: "I'm sometimes tempted by women to cheat on my wife, but I resist because I know how much it would hurt Jesus." Herb Silverman's retort was almost too easy: "I'm sometimes tempted by women to cheat on my wife, Sharon, but I resist because I know how much it would hurt Sharon."

Herb and Sharon married late, and their love story is moving because it flies above mawkish sentimentality. By Herb's account the mystery is how she puts up with him, the answer being that he makes her laugh every day. It is a story both humorous and touching.

Herb Silverman is such a legendarily nice guy that he is the perfect mediator—albeit in his unambassadorial shorts and T-shirt (saying something like "Smile, there is no hell"). He loves fraternizing with those who wish to argue with him, perhaps because he wins the argument. He supported the Moonies when they were denied access to his campus, on the grounds that a university should hear all points of view (and in any case the Moonies are no more bonkers than other branches of Christianity, just more recently founded).

If a religious person says to an atheist (I can confirm that they often do), "I'll pray for you," Herb Silverman is too nice to use the reply that first occurs to him, "OK, I'll think for both of us." Instead, he says, "Thank you." He knows how to disagree without being disagreeable. Nowhere is this gift more necessary than when reconciling rival groups of atheists, agnostics, humanists, and freethinkers. "Herding cats" may be a cliché, but clichés can be true as well as tiresome. Herb Silverman is the cat herder beyond compare: quite possibly the only person in America who could amicably unite all factions of the nonbelieving community.

In this capacity he is the founder and president of the Secular Coalition for America: a union of ten member organizations including the American Atheists, American Ethical Union, American Humanist Association, Atheist Alliance of America, Camp Quest, Council for Secular Humanism, Institute for Humanist Studies, Military Association of Atheists and Freethinkers, Secular Student Alliance, and Society for Humanistic Judaism. Endorsed by an even larger number of organizations, and with an advisory board on which I have the honor to serve, the Secular Coalition runs the only lobby in Washington dedicated to secular causes, and its officers coordinate activities countrywide. But the driving force and guiding spirit of the Secular Coalition is the gentleman—in the best sense of the word—who is the author of this splendid and idiosyncratic book. Let me end with one of his most characteristic aphorisms: "Changing minds is one of my favorite things, including my own when the evidence warrants it."

RICHARD DAWKINS
OXFORD, ENGLAND

PREFACE

A rabbi delivered a moving sermon telling how we are nothing in this vast universe and that we must let God know we are appropriately humble. After the sermon, the assistant rabbi ran to the front of the congregation and yelled, "I am nothing!" Next the rabbi's wife ran up and shouted, "I am nothing!" The president of the congregation did the same. Then a newcomer ran up yelling, "I am nothing!" At that, an old congregant poked the man sitting next to him and complained, "So look who thinks *he's* nothing."

With the old congregant in mind, I held back writing this book until I finally felt comfortable with, "So look who thinks we want to read about *him!*" People mostly read about accomplished people—famous for doing very good or bad things. I'm mildly accomplished and very slightly famous. Although anyone who writes about himself must have a bit of an ego, mine isn't so big that I think everything about me is noteworthy.

When I was a graduate student in the 1960s, I occasionally took breaks from mathematics to write what I thought were clever stories. Then my roommate showed me a quote from Henry David Thoreau, "How vain it is to sit down to write when you have not stood up to live." So, prodded by Thoreau, I stopped my creative writing and focused on completing my PhD in mathematics. Now more than forty years later, I've written about a few of the times I stood up to live, about the times I couldn't or wouldn't, and about the times I stood up and should have remained seated.

I'm not trying to improve on the fine best sellers by the so-called Four Horsemen of Atheism (Richard Dawkins, Christopher Hitchens, Sam Harris, and Daniel Dennett). I don't disagree with their collective wisdom that God is both a delusion and not great, and that it would be nice if we could bring an end to faith by breaking the spell. Nor can I improve on the arguments in Rebecca Goldstein's clever book *36 Arguments for the Existence of God: A Work of Fiction*, or on Susan

Jacoby's comprehensive history, *Freethinkers*, or on Greg Epstein's insightful book with the obvious title that we can be *Good without God*. (Actually, I think we can be *better* without God.) Unlike recent books by atheists, this one is largely personal, with less emphasis on deep philosophical or scientific arguments.

I've been an atheist most of my life, but I've mainly identified as a mathematics professor. I don't have unrealistic expectations about my mathematical contributions. I recognize that my research has been respectable, but not significant enough to make much difference to the mathematical community. And it has had no impact on people outside the world of mathematics.

Though I've been actively engaged with mathematics considerably longer than with atheism, I feel that I'm making more of a contribution on the latter than I ever could on the former. I don't think that gaining respectability for atheists is the most important issue around. It's not even the most noteworthy civil rights struggle. If I had a magic wand, and believed in its efficacy, I'd probably first wave it to end world hunger. But there's not much I can do about that, so I don't do much beyond working on small community projects and contributing to worthwhile organizations.

Before committing to an action, I like to think about whether it will make a difference and to whom. Circumstances of my adult life in the Bible Belt turned me from apathetic atheist (as most atheists are) to passionate activist. It became my "calling," because I saw how I might make a significant difference in our culture. So I'm an accidental atheist activist rather than a purposeful philosopher or theologian. I'm more interested in "converting" people from apathy to activism than from theism to atheism.

My Orthodox Jewish background in Philadelphia where I grew up played into my life choices, so you'll hear about the family values on which I was raised, or, more accurately, the values on which my family attempted to raise me.

I find the South an interesting place to live, especially for a transplanted Yankee who occasionally secs bumper stickers such as, "If you don't like how we do things down here, go back up North." I sometimes don't like how they do things, but I love living in the heart of Dixie—where the "War of Northern Aggression" began. Change is needed, and there are many opportunities to affect change. And I ain't just whistlin' "Dixie."

I've written two mathematics books and more than one hundred mathematics research papers (don't worry, none are even mentioned in this book). I do include a couple of chapters about mathematics for those without a math background. I hope you find them enjoyable and enlightening. While mathematicians are less likely than the overall population to believe in deities, they are more likely to believe than scientists. One possible explanation is that some theoretical branches of mathematics (including the one in which I do research) have nothing to do with the real world. Mathematicians, like theologians, are free to make assumptions and construct their own imaginary little worlds based on these assumptions.

Most of my recent writings have appeared in humanist and atheist magazines. I'm also a regular contributor to "On Faith," an online forum about religion produced by the *Washington Post*. But this book is different because writing your life story is more like being a suicide bomber: you only get to do it once. In my math profession, I discovered that one of the best ways to learn a subject is to teach it. I also discovered that one of the best ways to learn about yourself is to write about yourself. Maybe after reading about my life, you'll be inspired to write about yours.

While I'm a serious person, I don't take myself too seriously. People (quite understandably) ask my wife, Sharon, why she not only puts up with me but also seems to like me, and she answers, "Because he makes me laugh a hundred times a day." If you don't laugh at least a hundred times while reading this book, blame Sharon, who told me you would.

Acknowledgments

First, I want to thank my wife, Sharon Fratepietro, who convinced and encouraged me to undertake this daunting project. She read every word of many drafts, including the final one, and deserves enormous credit for helping to decrease the quantity and increase the quality of this book. She also talked me into removing some (but not all) potentially embarrassing incidents. If you want to know, ask me privately.

I'd like to thank the following people who read early drafts and offered many constructive suggestions that I adopted: Andy Brack, Jack Censer, Elisabeth Cornwell, Richard Dawkins, George Erickson, Nancy Martin, Alex Moore, Dave Niose, Andy Thomson, Rob Wilder and the Taos writing group.

I feel doubly "blessed" to have had two fine editors who added valuable improvements to this book: Kurt Volkan, editor of Pitchstone Publishing (for the print version of this book), and Luis Granados, editor of the Humanist Press (for the e-book version). Not only have I had a terrific relationship with each of them, but they have cooperated wonderfully with each other because Kurt and Luis are committed to a movement as well as to business. Thank you both.

I must give thanks to all past and present activists who have made significant contributions to the Secular Coalition for America. I'm grateful to so many of you that it's difficult for me to name just a few. If I left you off the list below, you are in good company because I also don't mention such luminaries as Richard Dawkins, Daniel Dennett, Sam Harris, Christopher Hitchens, or Salman Rushdie.

Thanks to Lou Altman, Lou Appignani, Maggie Ardiente, Dan Barker and Annie Laurie Gaylor, Sasha Bartolf, Stuart Bechman, August Berkshire, Randy Best, Rob Boston, Lori Lipman Brown, August Brunsman, Ed Buckner, George W. Bush (unintended fundraiser for secularists), Marie Castle, Matt Cherry, Bonnie Cousens, Margaret Downey, Fred Edwords, Greg Epstein, Sean Faircloth, Nick Fish, Arnold Fishman, Bruce Flamm, Tom Flynn, Joe Foley, Mynga Futrell and

Paul Geisert, Jesse Galef, Rebecca Goldstein, Patty Gusikowski, Jeff Hawkins and Janet Strauss, Susan Jacoby, Larry Jones, Edwin Kagin, Wendy Kaminer, Woody Kaplan, Eliza Kashinsky, Bobbie Kirkhart, Amanda Knief, Nick Lee, Ron Lindsay, Mel Lipman, Hemant Mehta, Amanda Metskas, Shelley Mountjoy, Mike Newdow, Dave Niose, Massimo Pigliucci, Steven Pinker, Anthony Pinn, Steve Rade, Ellery Schempp, Mary Ellen Sikes, Dave Silverman, Ron Solomon, Roy Speckhardt, Todd Stiefel, Julia Sweeney, Jason Torpy, Steve Uhl, Warren Wolf, and Lauren Anderson Youngblood.

Finally, I'd like to thank all active participants in the secular movement who now number in the thousands and increase every day. Those of you whose names are not in this book are in my thoughts, if not my prayers.

CANDIDATE
WITHOUT
A PRAYER

CHAPTER 1

IN THE BEGINNING

"South Carolina is too small for a republic and too large for an insane asylum," observed Congressman James L. Petigru, shortly after South Carolina seceded from the Union in 1860 and declared itself a republic. Had television existed, no doubt many of its politicians at that time would have been fodder for late-night comedians. I've lived in South Carolina since 1976, and stories that make our local politicians famous no longer surprise me. The comedy group Capitol Steps takes its name from the escapade involving former congressman John Jenrette, who had sex with his wife on the steps of the U.S. Capitol in the late 1970s. More recently, our former governor Mark Sanford had sex with his "soul mate" in Argentina, which he mistook for the Appalachian Trail. Come to think of it, South Carolina may not be "too large for an insane asylum."

Some might argue that I'm also a candidate for this asylum. As a liberal, Yankee, Jewish atheist with four strikes against me, I decided in 1990 to run for governor of the great state of South Carolina. It wasn't through blind ambition or unrealistic expectations, and certainly the devil didn't make me do it. There really was a method to my madness. But first, let's start at the beginning. My beginning.

I was born in Philadelphia in 1942, the first and only child of Fannie and Sam. Before their marriage, Fannie Deutsch and Sam Silverman lived with their parents across the street from each other on a treeless Poplar Street in Philadelphia. Sam was shy and Fannie wasn't. As legend has it, twenty-three-year-old Fannie told twenty-seven-year-old Sam they should get married and they did. Everything I saw in their relationship points to the truth of this story.

Sam dropped out of school at fifteen to work for his first and only employer, Beresin and Loeb Concessions, a Jewish-run business that my family said was the only local organization in the 1920s to hire un-skilled Jews. He put Hershey bars and other sweets into boxes shipped to subway stations. Sam packed candy bars for fifty years and retired in 1974 when he turned sixty-five. He was proud of the gold watch his company gave him at his retirement party, which was apparently the seventies equivalent of a 401(k).

After getting married, Sam crossed the street to move in with Fan-nie's parents, Anna and Meyer, who lived in the back of a shoe repair shop where Meyer worked. They spoke broken English and were func-tionally illiterate in English, though they read Yiddish. Sam's parents had come from Poland and Fannie's from Hungary around the turn of the twentieth century. I can't be more specific because nobody in the family talked about the "old country." Sam's parents, Bessie and Her-man, had six children. Herman supported his family on his meager salary as cantor at a small Orthodox synagogue.

When I was born six years later, my parents moved with me to an apartment around the corner. Herman died a couple of years before I was born, and the Jewish custom was to name a child after a recently deceased relative. My mother didn't like the name Herman, so "Her-bert" became her first-syllable compromise.

I could not have had a more patriotic beginning. I was born on Flag Day in 1942, during World War II, at Liberty Hospital in Phila-delphia, birthplace of the nation and the flag purportedly designed by Betsy Ross. I wanted to believe family members who told me that flags were hung in honor of my birthday. My first public speech was at a fourth grade Flag Day ceremony. I was chosen to read my essay, "What the American Flag Means to Me." I wrote about looking at the flag when "The Star-Spangled Banner" was sung at major league baseball games, hoping I would one day be a player on that field. I'm pretty sure my essay was picked because I happened to mention Flag Day was my birthday. Or maybe the other essays were even worse.

About the same time I delivered my award-winning Flag Day essay, I joined the Cub Scouts. This was my mother's idea because she wanted me to make some friends. I was a shy kid and my mother's strategy worked for a while. I even enjoyed wearing my uniform. Then one

My brief career as a nudist in 1943

day our Scout leader, a former army officer, told us to do something that seemed stupid to me. I don't remember what it was, but I asked him why we had to do it. He just repeated his order, and I again asked why. He said, "Herbert, with an attitude like that, you will never be successful in the military." I said, "OK, so I won't join the military." He responded, "Frankly, I don't think you are good Cub Scout material either." I became the only one in my troop to be "dishonorably discharged" from the Cub Scouts. Thus ended my "military" career.

I felt both sad and puzzled by my dismissal. I wasn't trying to be obnoxious, as my Scout leader must have thought. I almost certainly would have done as I was told had I been given a reason. I also wondered why other troop members didn't have the same question, and I thought some of them might have been secretly relieved that they hadn't unintentionally stepped out of line as I had. They probably remained friends with one another, but there was no way for a shunned former trooper like me to know.

This Scout leader was the first to question my patriotism, because I allegedly showed disrespect for the military. My views on patriotism in general and Flag Day in particular changed considerably over the years. Suffice it to say that the anniversary of my birth has become a day when opportunistic politicians regularly attempt to take away freedoms for which our flag is supposed to stand. On my twelfth birthday, President Dwight D. Eisenhower signed into law the addition of "under God" to the Pledge of Allegiance, turning a secular pledge into a religious one. This melding of God and Country resulted in my feeling less patriotic when I no longer believed we were under any god—or gods.

Early Judaism

My extended family lived in a Jewish ghetto in Philadelphia, around Girard Avenue and Sixth Street. The only outside sounds I heard from our small, drab, third-floor apartment came from passing trolley cars. Decades later I learned that I had lived several blocks from Bill Cosby, who described his neighborhood in a comedy routine. Those Philadelphia blocks may as well have been miles apart, because a Philadelphia address then and now is a strong indicator of a person's race, religion, and economic status. Bill Cosby and I also overlapped at Temple University, though we never met.

My parents were mainly cultural Jews, whose concept of Judaism was to associate only with other Jews and things Jewish. They deferred to my Orthodox grandparents on religious matters. I attended an Orthodox synagogue, where we thought members of a nearby Reform temple were almost as bad as *goyim* (Gentiles). The Orthodox say "synagogue" because they believe a "temple" can only exist in a particular place in Jerusalem. If it is ever rebuilt, some Orthodox expect to resume the tradition there of animal sacrifice. Reform Jews reject such practices.

My grandmother usually began a conversation with me by asking what I had learned in school, and she seemed delighted by whatever I reported. One exception occurred before Christmas, when I answered her question by singing "Silent Night." I didn't know what a "virgin" or a "holy infant" was, but I noticed an unexpected frown on my grandmother's face. Since my family didn't want to appear "un-American," they wouldn't think of complaining about Christianity being promoted in school. But they were especially upset when I learned "Silent

Night" in German. After the Holocaust, all things German instilled fear in our family.

All I knew about the Holocaust was that it brought new people to my neighborhood in 1947. They had come from Europe and were known as "DPs" (displaced persons). I remember only one, and for a good (actually, bad) reason. Like many five-year-olds, I enjoyed shooting my cap gun at friend, foe, and stranger. To my amazement, one DP boy ran away crying whenever I pointed my gun at him. I was used to being the intimidated, not the intimidator, so I took particular delight in my ability to scare an older boy of seven. Several years later, I learned about concentration camps and that the boy had been liberated from one. I knew at the time that I was probably doing something wrong, but I had no idea of its magnitude or severity. I can only hope that the displaced boy later understood I acted more out of ignorance than malevolence.

Dependency Forever

My mother was a control freak. Had she been born two generations later, she likely would have had a satisfying career. Unfortunately, she was a homemaker without much of a home or appreciation and praise from those inside it. With little to control outside the family, she made the most of every inside opportunity. My mother's idea of raising her only child was to make all possible decisions for and about me.

My mother, father, and I slept in the same bedroom until I was ten, when we moved out of our small apartment. I was rarely away from my mother until I started kindergarten, and then she'd walk the three blocks to school with me. My cousin Rosalie, one year younger, sometimes came over after school to watch me drink milk. I didn't understand why, until after a hospital visit for surgery when I was six years old.

Tonsillectomies are no longer routinely performed, and my symptoms likely wouldn't warrant the procedure today. However, this operation was a life-changing experience for the better, and it had little to do with tonsils.

It started with ether. The doctor told me to count backward from ten and I would be asleep before I got to one. When I awoke, the doctor told me I was the only patient who had ever counted fast enough to reach "one." Easily the greatest accomplishment in my six years, I felt that I must be mathematically gifted. I can't say for sure that my professional career was decided on that day, but I can't say it wasn't.

Then there was the battle of the bottle. Hydration is important after a tonsillectomy. When the nurse gave me a glass of milk, my mother took the glass from me and began pouring the milk into my baby bottle. The nurse told my mother I would drink the milk from a glass. My mother argued that I had never done that before, and I wasn't about to start then. Other health professionals intervened in support of the nurse. To my amazement, my mother lost the battle. Glass milk unfiltered through a rubber nipple tasted great. Never again would I hit the bottle. I also learned there were people who could stand up to my mother, and win. I wanted to become one of those people.

Another positive by-product was the postoperative need for cold stuff like ice cream, which became my primary health food for a couple of weeks. Since then, I've craved my Vitamin I almost to the point of addiction. One of my favorite movie scenes is in Woody Allen's *Sleeper*. The hero is revived two hundred years after a surgery gone wrong, and he learns of the hitherto unknown health benefits of hot fudge sundaes. That, for me, would be a much better heaven than a Muslim's seventy-two virgins.

I don't doubt that my mother wanted the best for me, though she always took it on herself to be the decider. It was never easy to get my own way, but my mother and I eventually reached an unspoken agreement. She got her way most of the time, but I argued at length when I really wanted something, and usually won. This is in contrast to my father, who never prevailed. I don't even recall many times that he tried.

I often struggled with the conflicting desires to be independent and to have chores done for me. I knew I could always opt for the latter, and usually did. Each night my mother put clothes on a chair for me to wear the following day. She even put one sock in each shoe, presumably so I wouldn't make the mistake of wearing both socks on the same foot. This must have worked, because I never did. That practice lasted through college.

I don't remember ever taking pride in what I wore, caring only about comfort, which meant that clothes arguments were reserved for "dressy" occasions like bar mitzvahs, graduations, funerals, and weddings. I learned years later from an aunt that one of my mother's unappreciated nightly chores was to wash and iron my shoelaces. Had they given a perfect shoelace award in school, I would certainly have won.

I mentally partitioned my clothes into two categories: the kind my mother bought without me, and the kind I had to accompany her to the store to buy. Fortunately, I was rarely needed. But on such occasions, I'd try on my mother's requested item. The salesman would typically ask me, "How do you like it?" My mother would respond, "He likes it fine," or "He thinks it's too big." After several such "conversations," the salesman would become aware of the absence of my presence. He'd turn to my mother and ask, "Does he like this color?" or "Does he feel comfortable in this?" I actually enjoyed playing the third-person game, occasionally chiming in with, "How much longer does he have to be here?" or "He's becoming very impatient."

Low Finance

We certainly weren't rich, but we lived much poorer than we were. My father's low pay had some financial perks, or at least my mother made it so. Here's an example of how it worked. Our family doctor said I needed orthopedic shoes for my flat feet, so my mother took me to the shoe store. After hearing the cost, she pulled out my father's pay stub (which I think she carried whenever she went shopping), and asked the shoe salesman how he had the audacity to charge us so much. After several minutes of haggling, my mother got the orthopedic shoes for the same price as regular shoes.

Sometimes, if initially unsuccessful, my mother would demand to see the store manager. To my amazement, she almost always wound up paying less than the list price. Inflation was not a winning argument for the store, either, because she would counter that my father's paycheck was no larger. I expect our victories had less to do with my mother's financial arguments than with the manager's desire to get her out of the store as quickly as possible. I viewed such exchanges with equal parts embarrassment and pride.

My mother did her grocery shopping at Penn Fruit, our only local supermarket. Later, when several others opened, she made shopping lists based largely on clipped coupons, and matched each item on her list with the supermarket that sold it for the lowest price. Grocery shopping usually took the whole day, traipsing from one store to another to compare prices. Time was not a particularly valuable commodity. Saving money was.

Penn Fruit turned me into an "A" and "B" expert, probably the only one in the world with such a specialty. As an enticement to shop there, customers earned free volumes of an obscure encyclopedia. Since we only managed to buy enough for volumes A and B before Penn Fruit discontinued the perk, I tried to fit school assignments into topics that started with the letter A or B. For example, when we had to write about our favorite president, most of my classmates chose Washington, Lincoln, or a Roosevelt. I was the only one who picked John Adams. Were it not for the Adams family, it would have been considerably more difficult to justify why my favorite president was Chester A. Arthur or James Buchanan.

During my childhood, money (or lack thereof) was a legitimate everyday concern. But in later years when more money was available from savings or from me, it never brought less worry for my mother. Though she could have been financially comfortable, she denied herself "luxuries" like a color TV because her old black and white set still worked. Whenever I told her she could afford to treat herself better, she dismissed my argument with one sentence: "You don't know what the Depression was like."

Early Travels

Following the custom of the time, neither Fannie nor her only sibling, Eleanor, ever worked outside the home. They both graduated from high school, though their husbands hadn't. Eleanor married Norman Roth in 1948 when I was six. Norman grew up in the same neighborhood as my family. Eleanor and Norman followed my parents' lead by moving into the same apartment building, one floor below us.

What I liked best about Norman was that he had a car. Every year, the five of us took a sixty-mile, four-day trip in Norman's car from Philadelphia to Atlantic City. We went in August, but my mother began planning for our big adventure in April. Mostly, I think, she checked for the cheapest hotels and other ways to save money. In their entire lives, neither of my parents ever traveled more than those sixty miles from where they were born. I didn't break my own sixty-mile travel barrier until I went off to graduate school.

Aside from Atlantic City vacations, we rarely left the neighborhood, except for a weekly two-mile trolley ride to a Horn & Hardart Automat for Sunday dinner. I was thrilled by the responsibility of fetching my own food. Through glass windows, I could see my desired prey. I'd pop a few nickels my mother gave me into a slot, and watch food magically pop back out. That was the closest I came to preparing my own food until I left home for graduate school at the age of twenty-one.

Television

I really thought Eleanor had married especially well when in 1950 Norman bought a TV set I could watch. My favorite show was *Howdy Doody*, a puppet that for some reason I trusted implicitly. When Howdy told us kids to try a "delicious" drink called Ovaltine. I nagged my mother until she bought it for me. It tasted terrible, and I learned a valuable life lesson about specialized abilities. Howdy may have been a talented puppet with an engaging sense of humor, but he had a lousy sense of taste. (Incidentally, one of my favorite radio shows at the time starred Edger Bergen and Charlie McCarthy. Several years later, when I saw the duo on TV, I wondered even as a kid why a ventriloquist had been on the radio. That still remains one of life's mysteries for me.)

Howdy Doody, actors, and athletes may be superb in their chosen professions, but the public grants them an inordinate amount of respect in areas unrelated to the fields in which they achieved. At least Howdy's personal life was impeccable, if somewhat wooden.

Good or Bad for the Jews?

As with many Jews in the 1940s and early 50s, my parents were trying to fit in as second-generation Americans. Though they were born in America to immigrant parents, their Judaism still made them feel like outsiders. A common question about any happening was, "Is it good or bad for the Jews?" I was too young to understand that the question might sometimes be meaningful when it related to geopolitical issues. I usually only heard it asked when a comedian or (much less frequently) an athlete was identified as Jewish.

One notable exception for me in 1953 was a horrible incident my family regarded as good for Jews—the execution of American Communists Julius and Ethel Rosenberg, convicted for conspiracy to commit espionage. I was only eleven and don't remember a discussion about whether the Rosenbergs were actually guilty, nor did it seem relevant. The family deemed them guilty of being bad for Jews and hoped their executions would make life easier for Jews. I had become increasingly uncomfortable with generalizing about and stereotyping any class of people, but it was especially problematic for me to hear Jews stereotyping Jews. Anti-Semites would think nothing of referring to "the Jews" in what they viewed as a meaningful and definitive way, but it seemed odd to hear Jews doing likewise. I didn't appreciate this commonality between Semite and anti-Semite.

Family Racism

Baseball was my boyhood love, and my parents occasionally took me to Philadelphia Phillies games. However, we skipped the games I most wanted to see—those that featured Jackie Robinson and the Brooklyn Dodgers. My family considered themselves liberal about race because they believed Jackie Robinson should be allowed to play major league baseball. This actually was a progressive position in the early 1950s. Some Brooklyn Dodger players, led by Dixie Walker, had even circulated a petition in 1947 requesting that Robinson not play for the team. When that failed, Walker asked to be traded. He was, and ended his career with the Pittsburgh Pirates.

My family had nothing bad to say about Robinson, a superb athlete, but my mother "protected" me from the kind of undesirable people (blacks) who came to watch Robinson play. My beloved Phillies didn't have a black ballplayer until 1957, ten years after Jackie Robinson integrated baseball. Not coincidentally, the Phillies were a mediocre team while the Dodgers won several pennants. My family admired some successful blacks in sports or entertainment, but they were seen as exceptions that proved some rule I never understood.

Uncle Norman was an "installment collector." First he picked up *shmatahs* from a distributor. (*Shmatahs* is the Yiddish word for "rag," which my family generalized to mean any undesirable item.) He then sold the *shmatahs* on installment to blacks (which my family called *shvartzahs*, essentially the Yiddish equivalent of "niggers").

Norman's customers could afford only small payments, which he tried to collect weekly. He would brag about collecting from some customers long after their items had been paid for. He felt no guilt over this deception, since other customers simply took his wares and were never seen again. Norman's rationalization fit conveniently into the family approach of not distinguishing one *shvartzah* from another. Since Norman dealt directly with them, he had unquestioned family credentials to stereotype them. Even as a child I knew what Norman did was wrong, but I remained silent.

Norman claimed his real job satisfaction came from being viewed by his customers as a very important person. Most were on relief (now called welfare). He knew when relief checks would be coming and stopped by to collect on that day. When customers complained to Norman about not having received their checks, he'd say, "Don't worry. I have friends in government. I'll make sure you get your check tomorrow." The checks almost always arrived the following day, and Norman happily wore the VIP mantle his grateful customers allegedly bestowed on him. He also knew birthdays of their children and would sometimes give them inexpensive presents. Norman was probably the friendliest white person that many of his customers ever encountered, a sad situation that unfortunately would still be true in many American communities today.

Sam and Norman were the only close adult males in my early life, though they were by no means my role models. I did admire Norman for how comfortably he could talk to anyone, since I could comfortably talk to no one. I admired my father for not being my Uncle Norman. I never heard my father say an unkind word about anyone. Then again, he rarely said much. Neither did I. I had a lot to say, but not to those around me. So I generally exercised my right to remain silent. I preferred thinking to speaking.

The Depression and Holocaust were the two seminal events my family never got over. They maintained a lifelong distrust, if not outright hostility, toward *goyim*. Just like the myth of no atheists in foxholes, they believed that even the nicest *goy* was a closet anti-Semite. These two life-shaping events collided more than once when my family worried about whether they had enough money to move to a different Jewish neighborhood. Whenever they could afford to move, it seemed the complexion of the new place would soon change for the worse (in both race and ethnicity). Though it was sometimes necessary to deal with *goyim*, the goal would be to minimize such encounters. So when one of my father's brothers voluntarily began consorting with the enemy, it puzzled and disturbed the rest of the family.

Intermarriage, a Crime Against (Jewish) Humanity

I had two cousins about my age, Rosalie (daughter of my father's sister, Ethel) and Allen (son of my father's brother, Max). Both lived a block away. I was allowed to visit Rosalie's house frequently, but rarely Allen's. Even though I preferred Allen, there was a major impediment because Max had had the audacity to marry a *shiksa* (a female *goy*). It wasn't until I reached high school that I learned *shiksa* wasn't a synonym for "whore." Max's wife, Steffi the *shiksa*, was the favorite topic of family gossip, though as far as I could tell, there was no truth to any of the wild stories about her. The family acted coolly toward Steffi, but tolerated her for Max's sake. Max was not religious, but Steffi had agreed to bring Allen and his brother Bob up Jewish for the sake of family harmony.

Max had always been sickly. Over the course of their marriage he had four heart attacks, which the family blamed on the grief Steffi must have caused him. Max essentially become an invalid, barely able to walk up stairs.

The Jewish shit hit the *shiksa* fan in 1958 when Max died from his fifth heart attack at age forty-seven. My father's sister, Anne, concluded that Steffi had murdered Max. Her evidence: the ambulance *might* have been called too late because Steffi wanted to be relieved of caring for Max. The family quickly found Steffi guilty as charged, and sentenced her, in absentia, to life in the court of gossip. Presumably, they didn't report the murder to authorities because Steffi would have hired a clever lawyer to bamboozle the jury into believing that the *shiksa* argument didn't constitute evidence beyond reasonable doubt.

This would merely have been a small-minded, innocuous, gossip tale had it only involved Steffi, who learned years earlier to ignore what the rest of the family might say about her. But then came Max's funeral, followed by the Jewish custom of "sitting *shiva*," which took place at the home of my father's brother Jake. *Shiva* lasts for eight days as family and friends gather to offer condolences and comfort to the bereaved. Not this time. At Max's funeral, I heard relatives whisper about Steffi's presumed hypocrisy, the way she carried on with what they deemed to be crocodile tears. When Steffi also began to cry at the *shiva*, Aunt Anne had had quite enough. All present heard her refer to Steffi as more of a murderer than a grieving widow.

Allen and I were both sixteen, and he said what I was thinking: "You're all a bunch of bastards!" He then turned to his mother and older brother Bob and demanded, "Let's get the hell out of here." Steffi and Bob followed Allen out the door. Good for cousin Allen, whose take-charge walkout I silently admired. Had I had the courage, I would have walked out with them.

Then came the unanimous family verdict about the *shiva* exchange by the self-appointed family jury.

Juror #1: "Did you hear the kind of disgraceful language Allen used?"
Juror #2: "Yes, especially with young children around."
Juror #3: "He probably learned that kind of talk from his mother."

I said nothing out loud during the "trial," but I recall saying to myself, "Maybe I was adopted." However, there was no more evidence for my adoption than for Steffi's murdering Max. The next seven days of *shiva* were sat without Max's widow and sons.

In elementary school, I read the short story, "The Man Without a Country," about a man who renounces his country and is sentenced to spend the rest of his days at sea without ever receiving news about the United States. Deprived of a homeland, the man misses it more than he could have imagined. Had I gotten my occasional wish to become the boy without a family, I expect I, too, would have become like the man in the story.

Following Max's death, Steffi became a cashier at Penn Fruit grocery store. She was the only "working woman" in the family, which somehow reflected poorly on her motherly duties. Steffi was never again invited to family affairs, though numerous sightings continued to fuel Steffi gossip. When seen entering a bar with a man, less than a year after her husband had died, she was branded a tramp and an alcoholic. These family labels lasted the rest of Steffi's life, even into her eighties when she developed Alzheimer's.

Of my seven first cousins, three went beyond high school. Betsy, three years my junior, graduated from nursing school. Steffi's children, Bob and Allen, both became lawyers. My mother's sister, Eleanor, who had the same hairdresser as Steffi, started the new family spin. According to Eleanor, the hairdresser mentioned that Steffi bragged constantly about how she put her boys through law school. The family concluded that Steffi denigrated her sons by taking all the credit for their accomplishments. Steffi deserved a lot of credit, and I regret never having had the opportunity to tell her so.

Nonetheless, a Good Upbringing

Though I certainly saw failings in my parents, I didn't recognize how fortunate I had been. My family could not have been more stable, and I had no idea how instability could affect children. I didn't like that my father never took my side when I argued with my mother, but the flip side was that I never heard them argue. While some arguing may be good, many childhoods (and subsequent adulthoods) have been traumatized by frequent parental disputes. My mother cared deeply for me, to a fault. But better to care too much than too little. I always felt someone would be there for me, even when that someone would only be myself. That was, and still is, a comforting way to go through life.

My father was a hard worker and provider who never complained. My mother fixed his breakfast at 6 a.m. each weekday morning, and went back to bed until it was time to wake me for breakfast and get me ready for school. My father was home from work at 5:30 p.m. and my mother had dinner on the table for the three of us at 5:45 p.m. After dinner, she did the dishes while he went to the living room to watch TV. My mother joined my father when the dishes were done. He would fall asleep on the couch until she woke him when it was time for them to go to bed.

My nightly routine at twelve was only slightly more varied than that of my parents. I'd either watch TV or go to my room and do homework before going to bed. I didn't know what I wanted in life, but I knew I wanted more than what I saw. My parents, too, wanted more for me than what they had.

If love is measured by worry and concern, then my mother's love for me was deep and strong. But love was not much mentioned. We were not a family of huggers. Physical contact between a parent and me, or even between my parents, seemed out of place. When I was about fifteen, my mother told me I should kiss her goodnight before going to bed. I expect she learned about the importance of such rituals from an article in *Reader's Digest*, the one magazine she read religiously. I began giving her bedtime cheek pecks, but more often than not, only when reminded. We eventually reached an unstated compromise: I'd kiss my mother goodnight when we had company.

The Hustler

Though less than ideal, I had a suitable family upbringing. It was neither so dysfunctional that I would almost certainly fail, nor so functional and prosperous that I would almost certainly succeed. I would not be going into my father's business. We had a derogatory expression for those who got ahead through family connections. They had "pull." I had no pull, or almost none. A little pull did get me a part-time job at fifteen, which lasted until I was twenty-one.

Beresin and Loeb Concessions, for whom my father diligently packed Hershey bars in boxes, also supplied refreshments at sporting events. My father's "pull" gave me entry into selling items at basketball, baseball, and football games. The hustlers, as we were called, earned 15 percent of sales. On a good night, I made close to $10.

The real "pull" came in my being hired illegally. The union at Convention Hall, where the Philadelphia Warriors played basketball, required a minimum working age of sixteen, but the company trusted that my father and I would keep my age a secret when I first started working there. I told people about my job as a "hustler," until someone pointed out that the word was a synonym for "prostitute." Several years later, I learned yet another meaning when I saw the movie with that name starring Paul Newman and Jackie Gleason as pool sharks. Of the three professions, mine was the most legal and least profitable.

When I turned sixteen, I was told to join the union. Once a month, management (the person who gave us supplies and took our money) was required to meet with union workers. He began with, "Any questions?" After about ten seconds of silence he'd say, "Good. Let's get to work."

Several months later, a slightly longer union meeting changed my relationship with my family forever. A 4 percent state sales tax on beverages had just been instituted, which meant we needed to collect twenty-six cents for a twenty-five-cent drink. Aside from having to deal with frequent customer complaints, as if we were to blame, it took a lot more time to give seventy-four cents change than three quarters.

Before the boss could end another ten-second union meeting, I responded to "any questions?" with, "Why doesn't management pay the extra penny because it's so time consuming for us to collect it?" The boss said I could just eat the penny (absorb the loss) if I liked. As a budding young mathematician, I responded, "A penny might not seem like much to you, but we make less than four cents per sale. So a penny loss per drink is a pay cut for us of more than 25 percent." When the other workers also began to grumble, the boss abruptly ended the union meeting and said it was time to get to work.

Hustlers who had ignored me now sought my advice. I explained their union rights and that we could take our grievance to others if we didn't get satisfaction. They called me courageous for speaking out, since they worried about such insolence costing them their livelihood. One hustler asked how we could lose 25 percent when we were making only 15 percent, my first attempt at teaching remedial mathematics. I would never question the value of college after seeing how few options many unskilled workers had. When I left that evening, the boss just glared at me. I said to him, "You know I'm right, don't you, and so do the others." That was my most satisfying day on the job.

Chip Off the Old Block?

The next day, my father came home looking upset, and whispered something to my mother. She then stormed over to me sounding angrier than I had ever heard her before.

"How could you hurt your father that way? He's been working there for over 30 years without anyone ever complaining about him. He stuck his neck out getting you this job, and this is what you do? Just who do you think you are?"

To which I responded, "I think I'm someone who sticks up for his rights, not someone who allows people to walk all over him." My implication was far from subtle.

To which she responded, "You're not half the man your father is, and never will be. You may be smart in book learning, but you don't have an ounce of common sense."

This negative correlation between education and common sense was a refrain I heard frequently. With each new academic degree or award, my mother would be proud and at the same time disappointed that I wasn't also becoming more of a *mensch* (an admirable person). I was surprised by my mother's anger, since I often saw her argue vociferously on financial matters. At some level, I expect she admired what I had said to my boss. But hurting my father, and not even being aware of it, trumped any positives. (Fortunately, but not surprisingly, my father's employer took no action against him and he continued to do what he had always done until he retired at sixty-five.)

What seemed surreal was that my mother and I were talking about my father in his presence, but neither of us looked at him. I've been in similar positions, where I listened quietly to adults talking about me as if I hadn't been there, like when my mother and clothes salesmen would discuss whether I liked what I had just been told to try on.

I never felt particularly close to my mother, but we did periodically engage prior to this union incident. When it became clear how worlds apart we were, I mostly stopped talking to her. I'd answer her questions monosyllabically and never volunteer information. I wasn't giving her the silent treatment, but it was close enough for all practical purposes. I knew my indifference hurt my mother, but I felt she had brought it on herself.

Years later, I realized I had been too arrogant and selfish to notice that my mother had a point. I grew up not thinking about my father's feelings. I assumed his role was to work hard so I could have a better life than he did and that I owed him nothing in return. He worked for decades at a job he didn't like, and only when it was too late did I understand that showing a little kindness and appreciation for his efforts would have gone a long way.

Aside from the union episode, my mother's angriest moments came when I referred to my father as "your husband." I think she was especially upset that the label fit on a couple of levels. My father didn't know how to communicate with me, and my mother didn't encourage him to try. Sometimes she would get tired of arguing with me and say to my father, "Tell him to do blah, blah, blah." My father then dutifully turned to me and said, "Do blah, blah, blah." My mother was at least partially responsible for my thinking of him more as her husband than as my father.

My mother was right when she said everybody liked my father, or at least nobody disliked him. For instance, people in our circle didn't normally bring gifts when invited to family or neighborhood gatherings, but my father was an exception. He would always bring a couple of Hershey bars or similar chocolate that he took home from work. The kids in the neighborhood called him "Sam, the candy man," which pleased him.

Promotion

I continued to work as a hustler for Beresin and Loeb with a nice change a couple of weeks after the union meeting in which I spoke up. We returned to selling soft drinks for twenty-five cents, with the company eating the penny sales tax. No reason was given, and nobody asked for one. A few months later, I was offered a "promotion" to join the management team at selected events. Instead of hustling refreshments, I collected money from hustlers and handed them their wares. The job was easier and paid better. I probably got the job because managers thought I was more honest and reliable than hustlers who had been working there before I was born. My mother was pleased, but I wondered how she felt about my father's never moving into a more responsible position. Perhaps they had conversations about Sam's dead-end job, but none that I ever heard.

My work for Beresin and Loeb included Philadelphia's professional sports teams, the "Big 5" college basketball teams, and many other events where concessions were sold. At one Mummer's Day parade, an annual New Year's tradition, a clown said to me, "It's fuckin' freezing. Gimme one of those fuckin' hot chocolates." I had difficulty integrating his big painted-on smile with his word choice, especially when I had never heard adults in my neighborhood use that kind of language in front of a teenager like me. I liked that the clown treated me as a grown up.

My least favorite selling jobs were at wrestling matches and automobile races, sports I neither enjoyed nor appreciated. I couldn't see why people thought wrestling, with its fake villains and heroes, was legitimate. Once I saw a wrestler writhing in pain as his foot was being twisted. He continued to writhe when his opponent accidentally found himself holding an empty shoe. I later understood that many, I hope almost all, viewed professional wrestling primarily as entertainment. I also came close to becoming a wrestling casualty. As I was walking near the ring selling my Cokes, I saw the 601-pound Haystack Calhoun hurtling down toward me. The Graham brothers, each of whom weighed 350 pounds, had tossed him from the ring. I stepped aside just in time.

Except for the money, I disliked everything about Hatfield speedway, just outside of Philadelphia, and home to midget and stock car races. The noise and air pollution were offensive. Other hustlers looked forward to what I dreaded most—car crashes. With bad accidents, usually in midget car races, fans had nothing much to do but buy our junk food during the long breaks to clean up the mess. And if one of the drivers died, we were assured a full house the following Saturday night. I wanted to earn money, but not that badly and not in that way. I was literally making blood money.

My Life in Crime

Many hustlers "earned" extra money by short-changing customers. It was low-risk thievery, since a hustler could easily claim he had just made a mistake. I wasn't dishonest, at least not in that way. My chosen criminal activity involved bribery, and occurred in 1959 when I worked as an usher at Philadelphia Eagles football games. It was an easy job that paid only two dollars per game, plus tips. I did more than just show people to their seats; I wiped their seats with a rag. After a few wiped seats, the rag became dirtier than the seats. But the wipes served the purpose, my purpose, of getting more tips. I became bolder with some who didn't tip, saying, "Will that be all, sir?" My behavior was certainly obnoxious, but not illegal.

Then one day, at the beginning of the second quarter, a man handed me a dollar and asked if he could move down to the better seats. This, to me, looked like a win-win situation. Almost nobody arrives after the first quarter. He got a better seat, and I got an extra dollar. Professional football was not the national religion in 1959 that it is today, and the stadium was often less than half full.

At the end of the first quarter of the next game, I announced to those in the cheaper seats that for a dollar they could move to a better seat. These alternative "tips" added $20 to my take, more than I had ever made before. Some season ticket holders learned my new tradition and would ask after the first quarter, "Is it time to move?" Only once did someone come late with a ticket for a seat I had "sold." No problem; I provided him with an even better seat, for which I received an unsolicited tip. Nobody ever complained, and I was never caught collaborating in these victimless crimes.

Would I do something like that today? No, but not because of a claim to moral superiority over my seventeen-year-old self. I simply needed extra money then, which I don't now. During my career with Beresin and Loeb, I was either saving money for college or working my way through college. Without those jobs and a government loan, I might not have been able to pay my college tuition. All things being equal, I have more sympathy for those who commit petty crimes because they need money than for those who just want more money.

Hero Worship (of Me)

I graduated from Temple University in 1963, and retired from my "career" with Beresin and Loeb when I left for graduate school at Syracuse

University. But I came out of retirement for one special day, September 2, 1964. I timed a visit home to coincide with the Beatles concert at Philadelphia's Convention Hall. Despite a packed house, I made very little money that night. The audience didn't eat much, or, as it turned out, hear much of the Beatles. Fans were screaming so loud that they drowned out the performance. However, they were excited and thrilled to attend this memorable event. The major excitement for me occurred long before the Beatles went on stage.

Hustlers arrive at least an hour before scheduled events because people are more likely to buy if nothing else is going on. When I got to the entrance, I saw hundreds of people hoping somehow to get a ticket to this sold-out concert. I showed my pass, which enabled me to walk through the ropes that kept away throngs of people. One person shouted, "He knows the Beatles," and suddenly others yelled for me to come closer. I did, briefly enjoying the undeserved adulation. My joy quickly turned to fear when Beatles fans started grabbing at my clothes and pulling my hair, hoping for a souvenir.

My only other short-lived hero worship from "fans" had come after Philadelphia Phillies baseball games. Hustlers and players left by the same exit, where autograph seekers waited (for the players, not the hustlers). Most players refused to sign, but if one did, then fans would swarm around him. I was old enough at twenty, if not talented enough, to be a major league baseball player. Occasionally, some kid would see me exit and ask for my autograph. I happily obliged, and others rushed over. Then some spoilsport inevitably asked, "Who the hell is Herb Silverman?" My admirers would quickly leave me alone with my poised pen. On the other hand, it was a lot less dangerous being a Philly than a Beatle.

CHAPTER 2

GOD THOUGHTS

My parents never talked to me about God or sex, but my mother told me how happy I would make her if I one day married a nice Jewish girl. That seemed to be the primary religious lesson my mother wanted to impart. I thought at the time that nice Jewish girls, by definition, didn't have sex. Since my most stimulating conversations had been with myself, it seemed natural to carry this over into my sex life. Perhaps, I thought, my secret talent would help make my life with some nice Jewish wife more tolerable.

Three of the ten students in my advanced Hebrew school class were girls. We were permitted to converse only in Hebrew. I'm not sure if our teacher occasionally asked us personal questions because he was bored, because the students seemed bored, or because of more nefarious reasons. After I answered a particularly difficult question, he smiled and asked each girl whether she liked me. The first said, "*Lo!*" the Hebrew word for no. Somehow being rejected in Hebrew sounded a little better than being rejected in English. The next squirmed a bit and said the Hebrew equivalent of "kinda." I kinda think she felt sorry for me and didn't want me to hear another "*lo.*" The third, to my surprise, and probably the surprise of the other two girls, gave a bold and unqualified "*kane,*" meaning yes.

I immediately began having erotic fantasies about this girl Rifka, instead of imaginary girls. I even spoke to her, though never about anything personal. One day, our teacher told us her father had passed away. I was relieved that at least he died without knowing about my sordid fantasy relationship with his daughter. When Rifka returned the following week, I said to her, "Sorry about your father," which turned out to be the last time we spoke. I never again had carnal thoughts about Rifka. I'm not sure what Sigmund Freud or Woody Allen would have said, but for me sex and death just didn't mix.

I enjoyed studying Torah, and Talmud was even more fun. The Torah (Hebrew Bible) is the foundation for religious Jews. The Talmud is a collection of writings by rabbinical scholars who attempted to clarify scriptural passages and biblical law. I found it fascinating to read clever commentaries in which different sages made good arguments to justify their points of view, even though they came to opposite conclusions. Perhaps such Talmudic study might explain why so many Jews grow up to be lawyers.

Something very few people know about me is that I was once a practicing lawyer, and I was only six years old at the time. As Paul Harvey used to say, "Now, for the rest of the story."

My maternal grandfather died when I was six. One night my parents went to the movies, and left me with my grandmother. Since she couldn't write in English, she asked me to write (actually, all I had learned to do at that time was print) her will. She wanted to leave her furniture and mementos to her two daughters, Fannie and Eleanor. Mostly, I think, my grandmother was proud of my first-grade education and wanted to see me make use of it. She lived another thirty years and gave her remaining trinkets to her daughters before entering what we euphemistically called "The Home." Though my grandmother's will was useless and lost, I can at least imagine some frustrated executor trying to decipher a child's scrawl, while relatives and their attorneys squabble over the estate.

My first paying job, at twelve, was teaching Hebrew. When a member of our congregation asked the rabbi to recommend a tutor for his eleven-year-old son, the rabbi recommended me. I enjoyed tutoring, and earned fifty cents an hour. However, I eventually had to quit when the job became too violent. The father listened to the lessons and got angry when his son made mistakes. He'd hurry over and hit his son on the side of the head. I wanted to tell the father that his "spare the rod and spoil the child" approach was a bad teaching method, but I remained silent. His son and I were both frightened by him.

At the Hebrew school, I had some good teachers who encouraged questions. However, my rabbi refused to answer, "Who created God?"

He said my question was inappropriate, but I thought he just didn't know the answer to this decidedly un-Talmudic inquiry.

One of my best teachers asked, "Why does the Torah say 'God of Abraham, God of Isaac, God of Jacob,' instead of the more concise 'God of Abraham, Isaac, and Jacob'?" His Talmudic explanation was that each had a different god, and we must search for and find our own god. I took his statement very seriously and applied Talmudic reasoning to draw my own conclusion, rather than rely on the wisdom of ancient scholars. My search beginning at age twelve eventually led me to a god who wasn't there. I was thrilled and a little bit frightened. I didn't believe there was a god and I didn't know if anyone else thought as I did.

In Talmudic speak, you might say that God led me to mathematics and turned me into an atheist. My cerebral interests as a youngster were theology and mathematics. I was fascinated by the idea of an infinite God with infinite power who lived an infinite time. I began to feel that studying "infinity" would be a way to understand God. I became enthralled with Zeno's Paradox of 300 BCE, an updated version of Aesop's Tortoise and Hare fable of 600 BCE. A descendant of the rabbit asks a descendant of the turtle for a rematch. The turtle agrees, provided he is given a hundred-yard head start. The turtle reasons, "When the rabbit gets to where I just was, I will have gone farther. If I keep doing this, the rabbit will never catch me and I will surely win." Of course the rabbit easily avenged the humiliation of his ancestor, leaving the turtle and lots of Greeks befuddled.

When I heard that this paradox as well as many other puzzles of the infinite could be resolved mathematically through the study of limits in calculus, I became a devotee of mathematics. I continued to equate the mysteries of "infinity" and "god." I learned that infinity is not sensible (known through the senses) and that there are multiple infinities. Are there also many gods?

The most important lesson I learned was that infinity is a theoretical construct created by humans, and that a number "infinity" does not exist in reality. If finite man created infinity, perhaps finite man created God and gave him infinite attributes. Infinity is a useful concept to help solve math problems. Was God merely a useful concept to help solve human problems?

I also read about Giordano Bruno, who taught that the universe was infinite with an infinite number of worlds like ours. It was considered heretical in the sixteenth century for finite man to discover the nature of the infinite, which was so clearly allied with the nature of God. Bruno was burned at the stake, courtesy of the Roman Inquisition.

I didn't understand why a so-called infinite god who created such an imperfect world could be called perfect, whatever that means. I did learn what "perfect" means in mathematics. A number is "perfect" if it is the sum of its proper divisors. For instance, 6 (1 + 2 + 3) is perfect, as is 28 (1 + 2 + 4 + 7 + 14). The next two perfect numbers are 496 and 8,128. It is still unknown whether there are infinitely many perfect numbers. Of course, mathematicians could just as easily have called these numbers "wonderful" instead of "perfect." However we define such numbers, at least we know they exist.

Despite my doubts about God's existence, I continued my Hebrew studies. At bar mitzvahs, thirteen-year-old boys typically read only a "haftorah," a portion from the Prophets. The whole Torah is read publicly, over the course of the year, with one major portion read each week at the Saturday morning service. I was one of the few bar mitzvah boys who read in Hebrew the entire Torah portion for the week, which I was praised for doing flawlessly. My grandmother said it was the proudest day of her life and the Orthodox wing of my family told me how happy they were with my performance. My mother was thrilled that I was able to please such a normally tough audience.

Following my bar mitzvah, the rabbi offered me a scholarship to continue my studies for another year, which I did. The congregation then offered to pay my way to a high-school yeshiva, which could lead toward a rabbinical path. I was flattered by their faith in me. It was nice to hear external validation about my being really good at something, but I didn't think I wanted that kind of career. While I enjoyed the praise and attention, something didn't feel right. Maybe it was the God thing.

The prayers all sounded fine to me in Hebrew. My Hebrew singing was even aesthetically pleasing to my young ears. But somewhere around age fourteen, I began translating what I read into English and thinking carefully about the meaning of the words. After Pat Buchanan's combative "culture-war speech" at the 1992 Republican Convention, columnist

*Fannie and Sam Silverman, my proud parents at
my bar mitzvah in 1955*

Molly Ivins quipped that the speech "probably sounded better in the original German," implicitly comparing Buchanan to Hitler. Somehow, for me, the Torah sounded better in the original Hebrew. In English, I was praising God's holocaust of humanity minus eight (Noah, his three sons, the four wives) and the holocausts described in Deuteronomy of the Hittites, Amorites, Canaanites, and all other peaceful inhabitants that stood in the way of Israel's brutal conquest of the promised land.

Two thoughts came to mind: either the God of the Bible didn't exist, or he could be as bad as and more powerful than Adolph Hitler. I preferred the former, which seemed more humane and more likely. I had been a mindlessly observant Jew following rules and rituals because they were, well, rules and rituals to be followed. I then made a decision to follow only those that made sense.

I had been fasting on Yom Kippur, the holiest day of the year, since I was eight. At fifteen, I ate. If God existed, I didn't believe he would determine on that day (as tradition has it) who shall live and who shall die in the coming year. My parents, Aunt Eleanor, and Uncle Norman were the only ones who knew I had stopped fasting. They were upset, even though they also hadn't been fasting. When I pointed this out to Eleanor, she said, "Yes, but I didn't have all your education."

One component of Judaism that made sense to me was its emphasis on mitzvahs (good deeds), though mitzvahs certainly aren't unique to Judaism or religion. I wrestled with whether hypocrisy and dishonesty could be a mitzvah and decided it could. So as my mother requested, I again went to synagogue with my grandmother on Yom Kippur. Only this time I just pretended to be fasting. I felt good about pleasing my grandmother and bad about living a lie. I wondered if that was what people meant by "maturity."

I hadn't heard the word "atheist" and knew no nonbelievers. More accurately, I didn't know anyone who acknowledged nonbelief. I, too, became an unacknowledged nonbeliever. I had some vague notion of Communists being so evil that they rejected God, but I was certainly not a Communist (whatever that was). I had the usual teenage insecurities, wanting to be liked and to fit in. But something always seemed to get in the way. I didn't want to live a lie, so I mostly kept to myself.

I felt better about myself after reading Bertrand Russell's "Why I Am Not a Christian" when I was sixteen. Russell was more than not a Christian. He was as many "nots" as me, and brave enough to say so. I still kept to myself, but at least I knew I wasn't alone.

I had trouble understanding why religion was still more important to me than to most of my acquaintances, even though I had no god beliefs. Perhaps others were at peace with their apathy. I periodically went through an exercise of weighing advantages and disadvantages to being a believer. When I realized I had no choice because I couldn't delude myself, I became comfortable with my godlessness. Honesty was the best policy, I concluded, even though it was at that time only a silent honesty.

I also didn't know why so many people were comforted by what I viewed to be an unreasonable faith. I was more comforted by logic and reason, which undoubtedly played a role in choosing a career in mathematics. Mark Twain succinctly captured my thoughts on the matter: "Faith is believing what you know ain't so." Some can have such faith. I can't, and wouldn't want to if I could.

A Different High School

I didn't go to the yeshiva, but my mother was still pleased that I was accepted into Philadelphia's Central High School because over 80 percent of its students were Jewish. Admission was based on grades and a test (probably IQ). It was an all-academic, all-male school, still the only high school in the country with authority to confer academic degrees, by an act of the Pennsylvania General Assembly in 1849. Central was considered one of the top public schools in the nation. Famous alumni include Noam Chomsky, Daniel Guggenheim, Alexander Woollcott, and Larry Fine (of *The Three Stooges* fame). Andrew Weil and Jeremiah Wright were students when I was there.

Dr. Gerald Hamm, my senior-year English teacher and class advisor, had a major impact on my life. He told members of our graduating class to wear ties every Friday as a demonstration of school spirit. When I came to school tieless as usual the next Friday, he asked me to sit in the back of the room and write an essay explaining my behavior. I incorporated in my essay some unsolicited advice from another student. I began, "This jerk sitting next to me just told me to say I forgot my tie. Well, I didn't." I then explained how "school spirit," if it was important, which I didn't think it was, could not be forced. The following Friday, I again came without a tie and Dr. Hamm said nothing. He didn't admit I was right, but the Friday tie seemed to have changed from a requirement to a request. This incident must have been significant to me, since I still remember it, but I will describe a far more important conversation I had with Dr. Hamm. (I still don't wear ties except for extremely important occasions, such as when my wife insists.)

Dr. Hamm later made a more reasonable request of seniors, to write short essays from which he'd choose three to be read at graduation. When he announced the winners, it was no surprise to me that I wasn't one of the chosen. As I was leaving class, Dr. Hamm told me to stop by his office after school. I assumed he would tell me how furious he was about what I had written.

When I walked into Dr. Hamm's office, he closed the door and said, "I wish I had the courage to choose your essay. You see, I'm in a responsible position, and you're not. I hope someday, when you are in a responsible position, that you'll have the courage to do the kinds of things I don't do."

My teacher's remarks both angered and elated me. My first thought was about his being a coward. My second thought was about his liking my essay. My third thought, which should have been my first, was that I was talking to a special teacher. He was the first who had been honest enough with me to admit his foibles and regrets. He was also confident that I would someday be in a responsible position, something I had doubted about myself. I made up my mind that whenever future conflicts arose for me between self-respect and respectability, I'd opt for the former. I would take risks even when in a responsible position. I didn't realize until years later that this wonderful teacher had taken a risk by confiding in me the way he did.

When graduation day arrived, my one memory was of exchanging smiles with Dr. Hamm while a fellow student droned on about the joys of John Keats. I felt for the first time in my life that I was on the same wavelength as one of my teachers, and that we were looking at each other as equals.

I hoped that one distant day in the future I would be important enough to be invited as a graduation speaker. My address would be titled "Fulfilling Your Dreams." I would first describe the incident above, and then deliver my belated essay. I pictured it as being one of the few speeches graduates would actually remember. Alas, I have not yet received such a speaking invitation.

So what was my rejected essay? It would not be nearly as shocking or as original today as it would have been in 1959, but it would likely still be rejected at most graduation ceremonies. As best as I can remember, it went something like this:

Words are neither clean nor dirty. I still believe one of the sayings I learned in kindergarten, "Sticks and stones may break my bones, but words will never hurt me." Morality should be based on how we treat one another, not on our choice of words. What is so wrong with saying the word "fuck" in public? For those who don't know its meaning, there can be no harm. For those who know that "fuck" is a synonym for "sexual intercourse," why is one term acceptable and the other not? Why are we not allowed to see people fuck (or, if you prefer, have sexual intercourse) on television or in the movies? Are we afraid this will inspire others to do likewise? On the other hand, we can see plenty of violence and killing on television and in the movies. For my part, when children grow up I would rather they fuck than kill.

This essay, written two years before I'd hear about Lenny Bruce, was something I could not then have imagined anyone's saying in polite company. Had I been allowed to deliver my essay, I undoubtedly would have shamed and disgraced my entire family. Frankly, that wouldn't have bothered me. But I know now that I benefited more from a rejection than from an honor. I wrote about this event in 2009 for *The Humanist* magazine. Afterward, a representative from the Central High School Alumni Association got in touch with me and asked if I would like to nominate Dr. Hamm for the Central High School teacher honor roll. I did, and he is now so honored.

Though I never had an opportunity to offer my essay at a graduation, I did get to deliver it at another ceremony. A party was thrown for me in May 2009 when I retired as a Distinguished Professor at the College of Charleston in South Carolina. I announced that I would give a speech I had been waiting for decades to deliver. I read the essay at the party to faculty, students, deans, and the provost. Afterward, many of those present told me they were relieved by my "mild" speech. They had been worried I would disclose embarrassing moments from their pasts. Times have changed, and so have movies.

CHAPTER 3

AN EASY COLLEGE CHOICE

Choosing my college couldn't have been easier, since I felt I had no choice. I couldn't afford an out-of-town school, so I'd be going to one in Philadelphia. My only interaction with college students consisted of selling refreshments at "Big 5" basketball games, but basketball would not be a criterion. Three city schools were Catholic institutions (La Salle, St. Joseph's, and Villanova), which left me with the University of Pennsylvania and Temple University. Penn was for rich Jews and Temple for poor Jews. I had no worries about being accepted by Temple, the only college to which I applied. I'd been told that no Central High School graduate had ever been denied admission. If not literally true, it was probably close enough.

Philadelphia students started elementary school in September or January, depending on birth date. Since I started in January, I graduated from Central in January 1960 and began classes at Temple that same month. (I also took classes my first summer at Temple so I could graduate in the spring of 1963.) The school had a large proportion of commuter and first-generation college students like me, serving well the needs of those without much money. A government loan paid for half my tuition and I worked to pay the other half. I have no complaints about the education I received, but if I had a do-over I'd have applied for a larger loan to go to a non-Philadelphia school. Leaving home four years earlier would have served more as a maturity loan than an academic loan.

I took what turned out to be suitable courses in my first year at

Temple, but only because two wrongs made a right. In my senior year of high school, my mother took me for a free (naturally) aptitude test at a local Jewish agency. I scored highest in mathematics, a subject I always enjoyed, and so the counselor advised me to become an accountant. I had no idea at the time how dissatisfied I would have been in such a career. I became a theoretical mathematician, which is closer to philosophy than accounting. I suppose the "number-loving nerd" stereotype is why some people view accountants and mathematicians as interchangeable. I might have become the first accountant who had never balanced a checkbook (and I still haven't). In chapter 15, I include a nontechnical explanation about what mathematicians do.

Fortunately, I didn't have an advisor in my first year at Temple to help me decide on a course schedule for accounting. I took liberal arts courses that I thought I'd enjoy rather than business courses. By the time I found out I wasn't on track for accounting, I had also learned enough to know what I wouldn't want to be.

Carpooling

My parents never learned to drive, but I wanted to and took a driver-education course at Central. After some arguing, my mother said she'd buy a used car if she acquired a driver's license. Insurance would be considerably cheaper were she the principal driver.

Aunt Eleanor's husband Norman agreed to teach my mother to drive. He would have preferred teaching my less-hyper father, but my father thought he was too old at fifty to learn. Those several months were probably the most frustrating in Norman's life, but my mother finally passed her driving test. We bought a used car for $400 from Norman's friend. The car was probably worth the money, but again Norman regretted his involvement. My mother complained to Norman whenever we had car problems.

I took the subway to Temple University my first week. When I saw ads at the university from students willing to pay for rides, I convinced my mother to let me drive her car to school. After attending an all-male high school, where I almost never came into contact with girls, I knew my college transition would be more socially difficult. Since the would-be passengers were mostly girls, I thought my driving service would be a good opportunity to meet them. It was, but they were not the kind I had hoped to meet.

All three of my Temple carpool passengers were friends with one another. It quickly became clear that I was more of a cab driver than a potential boyfriend for these sophomores, all elementary education majors who almost never mentioned courses or academic careers. Mostly they talked about boys, who were divided into creeps or dolls. If they talked about me at all when I wasn't around, I knew the category I'd be in. Unfortunately, boy talk was their most elevated conversation. Temple was (and still is) located in a depressed neighborhood, with many boarded-up windows. My passengers delighted in making fun of the residents. They'd sometimes refer to the "baboons" hanging out of windows. When we saw an African-American man getting out of his beaten-up car, one of my passengers pointed to him and laughed, "Look! He's coming out of his house." I began to question whether I wanted the money enough to keep these passengers.

A couple of weeks later, I got a call from a nervous-sounding boy, who also wanted a ride. I assumed he was lazy because he made sure I'd give him door-to-door service. He sounded on the phone like someone my other passengers would classify as a creep like me. I hoped he'd be black, mainly to upset the others, but I knew from his address it was unlikely. The next day I drove to his house first. His mother answered the door and told me how grateful she was for my taking "Freddie" to school. She invited me inside and said Freddie would be ready in a minute. I sat uncomfortably with Mrs. Coe, thinking Freddie must be quite the mamma's boy.

Finally, I heard a noise from the other room, as if something had fallen. Then I recognized the sound of clicks with every step. Suddenly I was blinded by the sunlight shining on a metal object; just as suddenly I could see again. What I saw, I wished I hadn't. The sight of Freddie frightened me. He was shaking uncontrollably. His head was moving as if he had water in his ears and was trying to get it out. His crutches slid back and forth as if he were on ice. Nothing about him looked normal.

We exchanged hellos, and I put my hands in my pockets as a reminder not to extend for a handshake Fred would be incapable of giving. After several uncomfortable minutes, Fred made it to my open car door. I asked Fred what year he was in, avoiding the obvious question.

When he said he was a junior, I thought it ironic that he was the right age for my passengers. When Fred asked who else would be coming, I said, "Three girls." I didn't respond to his next question, "Are the broads cute?"

When we picked up Belle, I introduced her to Fred. She said "Hello," and remained silent as I asked Fred about his major, high school, and teachers. The other girls were also quiet. I did more car talk that day than the previous two weeks combined. It was Belle, Evy, and Josie in the back, with Fred, his crutches, and me up front. I tried not to look at Fred. He never stopped shaking. From head to toe, he never stopped shaking.

I soon ran out of meaningless questions, so I became silent. The three girls started talking, but they weren't listening to one another. Each was watching the back of Fred's head shudder. I wanted to tell Fred that I once broke my ankle and had it in a cast for six weeks, but that seemed inappropriate.

When we neared the campus, there were no comments about the dilapidated neighborhood. The girls quietly got out. I too got out and opened the car door for Fred. Students crossing the street glanced at him and continued their conversations. I felt as if the whole world was watching Fred struggle with his crutches, but he appeared not to notice. When Fred freed himself from the car, crutches in hand and knapsack with books on his back, he said, "Thanks, Herb. I can manage from here." I felt a bit queasy, so Fred must have been managing better than I was. The scenario was new to me, but not to him.

The next day, Fred's mother said, "I'm sorry. Freddie's not going to school today." When I asked why, she said, "It looks like rain. Freddie isn't allowed out on rainy days." Mrs. Coe asked if Fred had told me what was wrong, and I said he hadn't. She said, "It's multiple sclerosis. He got it when he was up at the University of Wisconsin." I told her I didn't know he had gone to Wisconsin.

Fred's mother dropped her eyes and asked if I had a minute. She then invited me into the living room.

"When Freddie was in high school, he was the star of the football team," she continued. "He was offered nineteen scholarships. He chose Wisconsin because it had such a beautiful campus. He was up there when this happened."

"How old is he?" I asked.

"He was all that any mother could ask for," she said, ignoring my question. "He was good in school. He was runner up to Mr. Philadelphia; girls were chasing him. And he was engaged to the prettiest girl you would ever want to meet, up in Wisconsin."

"Is he sensitive about it?"

"No. You can say what's on your mind. He likes to pretend nothing is wrong."

"How old is he now, Mrs. Coe?" I asked again.

"He's twenty-three, dear. The rehabilitation center is paying his way at Temple. We can't afford it. His drugs are so expensive. You think his girl would visit him? She never even called, and he still talks about her."

"He seems so happy," I remarked.

"Oh, you'll never see him angry. He was always like that. When Freddie could no longer remain in Wisconsin, he told me about the disease he had contracted, and that he would be coming home for a 'visit' on the next plane. I met him at the airport, expecting the worst. But it was much worse than I could ever imagine. I had no idea. When I saw him, dear God... my boy... my baby... looking like he did. And he wasn't nearly as bad then as he is now. And that smile... he was smiling... and telling me that it was all right... that he would be scoring touchdowns again in a few months."

All I could do was tell Mrs. Coe how sorry I was, a gross understatement, and leave to pick up my other passengers. When they asked where Fred was, I told them he couldn't come on rainy days. They asked no more, and I volunteered no more. I couldn't tell if they didn't want to know about his condition or if they just didn't want to talk to me. I didn't particularly want to talk to them either. Their car talk was somewhat more subdued than pre-Fred conversations, but with the same general themes.

After class, I looked up "multiple sclerosis" in the library. I learned it was a progressive disease with no known cause or cure. Freddie would get worse, and die from it. I felt numb. I had never known anyone personally who would die so young.

The next day was clear, so I picked up Fred and the others. When Belle, Evy, and Josie were in, I proudly announced, "Fred used to go to Wisconsin," believing this comment sufficient to start a pleasant conversation.

"How was it there?" Josie asked, thinking herself obliged to say something. Fred said, "Oh, man. It was nice. I'm going back there after graduation to get my master's degree. You can't get anywhere with just a bachelor's degree, you know."

The girls didn't say another word, so I asked Fred, "Which do you like better, Wisconsin or Temple?"

"I hate to disappoint you, son, but Wisconsin has it all over Temple. Out there, the broads are really swinging." Fred grasped at my shoulder, and whispered loud enough for everyone to hear, "At Temple, the broads are frigid."

Fred came with us the rest of the year, except when it rained. Sometimes we talked about his disease, but usually Fred made small talk. The girls talked to one another and rarely to Fred or me. The four of us were obviously uncomfortable. Only Fred seemed at ease, though I could never be sure.

The following year, Fred did not come. He was placed in a home for incurables. When I visited him, he retained his smile and optimism, talking about the cute broad on the third floor, or returning to Temple soon. The girls stayed in my carpool. When they asked if Fred was coming, I told them no. They asked no more; I volunteered no more. The three girls continued to sit in the back seat. Everything else was the same: engagements, dolls, and creeps. I no longer minded. I was getting paid for my service. After all, it was only a business proposition. I was alone up front.

With each succeeding visit to Fred, I saw further deterioration. His speech became increasingly difficult to understand and he was wasting away. One day, he told me he was happy because he had found Jesus. He had never before mentioned religion. I thought about the cliché of there being no atheists in foxholes. I also thought for the first time that Fred was no longer pretending he would recover. Two weeks later, Mrs. Coe called to tell me Freddie was dead, and thanked me for what I had done for him.

I didn't deserve Mrs. Coe's thanks. I visited Fred in the hospital mainly because I would have felt worse had I not done so. I remembered Fred's mother talking about his former fiancée who never contacted him, and I didn't want to be like her. Fred was so different from anyone I had ever known that I didn't understand my reaction to his death. On the one hand, I mostly felt a sense of relief. I'm not sure if my relief was more for Fred finally being out of his misery or for my being spared future visits. My conversations with him had always seemed unreal. The sicker he got, the more difficult it was to pretend with him that he would soon get better.

On the other hand, just knowing Fred became one of the most moving experiences in my life. I don't think I could ever be so cheerful about disability, assuming Fred was as content as he seemed. I also thought about whether a happy delusion trumps truth. Oddly to me, the desperate way Fred found Jesus at the end of his life made me believe more strongly than ever that no god existed. Such a foxhole belief is not a reality-based belief.

I had been well prepared academically for my first year at Temple, but woefully unprepared for either coeds or handicaps, as they were then called.

Writing Revenge

My carpool experience has an addendum. Though I was majoring in mathematics, I took an advanced composition course in my sophomore year because I liked to write. Mr. Berkowitz, our professor, usually read one or two of our essays, and he chose my carpool story to read and discuss with the class. The following day I got an angry call from a former carpool girl, who heard about the essay from a girlfriend and threatened to sue me. Not only had I included her racist comments, I also used her real name. The gossipers didn't like to be gossiped about, especially when the gossip was true. Having such shallow pockets, I wasn't worried about being sued. I said I'd love the opportunity to read my essay in court, for all to hear. I never heard back from her. I'm not a vengeful person, but occasionally revenge can be sweet.

I also wrote about my religious beliefs for the first time in this course. Mr. Berkowitz didn't read that story in class, though I hoped he would. As a math major who understood what a proof was, I called myself an agnostic because I could neither prove nor disprove the existence of God. I mentioned how sad it was that people were afraid to openly admit nonbelief, and closed my essay with, "We have freedom *of* religion in this country, but I hope someday we will also be able to say we have freedom *from* religion."

Mr. Berkowitz allowed us to write comments or questions at the end of our essays. I wrote, "What are your religious beliefs? If you don't answer, why don't you?" He responded, "I don't mind answering, but I detest questionnaires. If you ask me decently, I'll tell you."

After class Mr. Berkowitz invited me to his office and said, "I'm an atheist, and agnostics are just gutless atheists." We discussed religion, and I agreed with him that jury evidence would favor God's nonexistence "beyond reasonable doubt." So Mr. Berkowitz "converted" me from agnosticism to atheism. It really wasn't much of a conversion. My beliefs didn't change, just my nomenclature because of how my teacher framed the distinction. I still couldn't prove God's nonexistence, but I was comfortable with my new "beyond reasonable doubt" criterion for nonbelief. Same with the Tooth Fairy, whose nonexistence I also couldn't prove mathematically.

I was fascinated at the time with differences between atheists and agnostics, but I later felt that people with the same worldviews wasted too much time arguing about labels, a distinction without much of a practical difference. I asked Mr. Berkowitz if he knew other faculty who were atheists. He claimed that all thinking faculty probably were, but they didn't talk to him about it.

Years later, I learned a closet could be something for gays to come out of, and how "coming out" could end a stereotype. I thought of Mr. Berkowitz and how atheists might achieve the same kind of success as gays by coming out of their closet of undisclosed disbelief. Many faculty members today are open atheists, and they don't have to wait for an obnoxious student to ask them about it.

Time for a Relationship

However satisfying my triumph over the carpool girls, I had not yet developed a real relationship with any girl. A couple of years later, I became close to someone I thought might be my first true love. Marlene was one of the few female math majors, and the only attractive one. She was smart and friendly. Most of the other math majors also had a crush on Marlene, but I was especially privileged because she felt comfortable enough to talk about her feelings with me. Unfortunately, her feelings were usually about boys she was dating. I tried to appear understanding, but I would also try subtly to undermine her relationships with boys whose math backgrounds were far beneath ours. I was hoping she'd realize I was the one for her. She didn't, nor did I tell her I wanted to become more than a confidante.

Being the virgin Herb was not particularly problematic, since most of my friends (mainly other math nerds) were similarly encumbered. At a typical school lunch with Marlene and several boys, someone would inevitably set her up with a "racy" joke like, "What do virgins eat for breakfast?" Raucous laughter would accompany Marlene's answer, "I don't know." We eventually had to move on to different questions that elicited other double entendres when Marlene changed her answer to "cereal."

We knew Marlene was a virgin, and I would have thought less of her had she not been. I was even shocked when she told me, "I hope my future husband is not a virgin because *someone* has to know what to do." This gave me added incentive to lose my virginity. Philosophically, I was convinced there was nothing wrong with a girl losing hers, but something about it just didn't seem quite right to me at the time.

Forty years later, while on a sabbatical leave at the University of California at Davis, an article about me appeared in a Sacramento newspaper. A student came to my Davis office and asked, "Are you the same Herb Silverman who graduated from Temple University?" She then said, "I'm Marlene's daughter, and she'd like to invite you to our home for dinner and to meet the family." At dinner I revealed to the family the crush I once had on Marlene, and she responded, "Don't you think I knew that?" I didn't, but I responded, "I'm finally over it."

Even though Marlene's husband wasn't a mathematician, I had no interest in undermining her relationship with him. Marlene's daughter had a big laugh about her mother's and my former views on virginity. What a difference a few decades make. Marlene's daughter looked more like Marlene used to look than how Marlene looks now. On the other hand, I still look just as I did in college—at least in my own mind.

My First Presidency

I wasn't exactly the fraternity type, but I joined Pi Mu Epsilon Honorary Mathematics Fraternity at Temple University, and became its president in my senior year. This was my first responsible position, and I was sometimes innovative, sometimes irresponsible, and sometimes both. At member meetings, we usually either discussed mathematics or listened to math talks from our teachers.

I made two changes: I asked math majors to give talks, which usually benefited the speakers more than the students listening; and I invited outside speakers, usually potential employers. Since I had passed the first two exams required to become an actuary (eight were needed), I invited a local actuary, William F. Sutton III, to speak to our Pi Mu Epsilon group. My "clever" introduction of him went something like this:

> What's in a name? When bank robber Willie Sutton was breaking into the Corn Exchange Bank in Philadelphia, our Willie Sutton was getting a degree from the University of Pennsylvania. When the other Willie was robbing a Broadway jewelry store, our Willie was studying for his actuarial exams. When the other Willie was sent to Attica State Prison, our Willie was hired as an actuary. When the other Willie said he robbed banks because that's where the money is, our Willie said he became an actuary because that's where the money is.

At that point, everybody was laughing. Well, everybody except for one person. Turns out Mr. Sutton III was rather stuffy and had no sense of humor, or at least had no appreciation for mine. He simply glared at me and fumbled through a talk about what he did as an actuary. Every so often you could hear giggles from students still thinking about my outrageous introduction. I subsequently learned that nobody even called him "William," let alone "Willie." It was always, "Mr. Sutton." I realized then that Mr. Sutton's organization would never hire me.

Just as well. He gave me the willies.

I did have an actuary interview for a summer job, though not with Sutton III's firm. The interview didn't go well. I kept asking what an actuary did, and the interviewer kept telling me how much money I could make. He said becoming an actuary was as difficult as getting a PhD in mathematics. I had never heard anyone say that getting a PhD in mathematics was as difficult as becoming an actuary, so I began leaning much more toward graduate school. When I talked to my math professor Albert Schild about becoming an actuary, he told me that the industry could be anti-Semitic (Schild was also a Jew). Shortly thereafter, I received a rejection letter from the firm with which I had interviewed. It was probably less due to anti-Semitism than to a bad interview, but I couldn't be sure.

Nevertheless, I had decided on graduate school even before receiving my actuarial rejection. One major advantage to graduate school for me would be no tie and jacket requirement.

CHAPTER 4

LEAVING HOME, AT LAST

Even without applying, Temple awarded me a teaching assistantship in 1963 for its graduate program. I was pleased, but preferred a different institution for two reasons. First and foremost, I wanted to leave Philadelphia and finally run away from home. Also, Temple at the time offered only a master's degree in mathematics and I wanted a PhD. I was thrilled when I received a teaching assistantship from Syracuse University. I applied when I noticed, as president of the local chapter of Pi Mu Epsilon Honorary Mathematics Fraternity, that the first chapter was established at Syracuse. Not a particularly sound reason, but Syracuse was a good school that was away though not too far away. I'd be teaching two math courses per semester, with a stipend of $2,000 per year, plus tuition.

I was excited and nervous about finally being on my own. I flew there to find accommodations. I had never been on an airplane, and the three hundred–mile trip was five times longer than my Atlantic City excursions. When I called for a plane reservation, the agent told me the price was something like $150 for first class and $80 for coach. I asked, "What's the difference?" She said, "$70." I chose coach, and let her think I was mathematically ignorant rather than travel ignorant.

The math department secretary suggested I put my name on their bulletin board to find an apartment roommate. I did, but knew I wouldn't be capable of handling my fair share of apartment chores. Since I didn't know how to cook, clean, shop, or do whatever people normally do in a dwelling, I looked for the simplest possible arrangement. I found a house where the landlady rented furnished rooms. I could take a room, eat meals out, and keep things in a common refrigerator. The landlady told me she'd save a room for me as soon as I gave a deposit. Since two rooms were available, there was no rush.

Back in Philadelphia, I got a call from Bill Nathan, another incoming math graduate student, who had seen my name on the bulletin board and wanted to know if I'd be interested in sharing the furnished apartment he had rented. My mother answered the phone, found out what he wanted, and said to him, "Are you Jewish?" When Bill said he was, my mother handed me the phone. I explained to Bill that I had lived at home my whole life and didn't know how to cook. He told me he'd had an apartment as an undergraduate and could cook. I reiterated my general incompetence, but he said he would teach me whatever I needed to know. Bill was in for quite a surprise.

Incompetence 101

Bill had rented a sparsely furnished one-bedroom apartment for $85 per month, including utilities. A few days before classes, I met Bill to sign the lease. Based on my mother's question, Bill asked if I was religious. He was relieved to learn I was a Jewish atheist like he was. We bought inexpensive food that Bill could cook. When he asked me to boil water, I gave my first of many "how?" responses. Bill thought I was making a Polish joke when I answered his request to change a light bulb with "how?" Initially he found my incompetence hilarious, but later became increasingly irritated.

I hadn't realized how unusual my helplessness was. I partly blame my mother for not encouraging me to learn the rudiments of taking care of myself. However, I mostly blame myself for not being assertive or interested enough. I began trying as best I could to do things for myself. I followed Bill's lead the first time we went to the Laundromat. I thought I was doing quite well until Bill said, "Don't you think you should put your clothes in the washer before putting them in the dryer?"

Despite my past dependence on others (my mother) for everyday tasks, I thought of myself as an independent person. That's because I mostly lived in my mind, where I engaged in independent thought. I was prepared for the intellectual rigors of graduate school, but not for ordinary tasks that others took for granted. I had rebelled against my mother by hardly speaking to her, but not by doing things for myself.

Bill and I developed a close relationship with another first-year math graduate student, Tony Geramita. He and Bill were from New York, known to many in Syracuse as "the city." The first time I heard that expression, I asked, "What city?" Apparently, there is only one. Eventually I began telling people I was from a suburb of "the city" called Philadelphia. Bill and Tony had the city in common, while Bill and I had Jewish atheism in common. Tony was a believing Catholic, but rational about most other things. The three of us had interesting theological conversations and good times together.

At first I didn't talk much to Bill and Tony about my mother, but they learned plenty when she did the talking. I let them listen to her weekly calls, on the condition that they not laugh. My mother would go on automatic pilot with instructions on how to live my life, while I occasionally chimed in with an "uh huh." She would yammer about how to dress for different kinds of weather, what and when to eat, and how to comb my hair.

Bill and Tony would occasionally violate the "no laugh" pledge, which I understood was not always within their control. One such violation occurred when my mother wanted to give me a phone number. She carefully instructed me to put the phone in my left hand and hold it up to my left ear so that my right hand would be free to write the phone number with a pencil using my right hand. Bill and Tony were still (barely) under control, but lost it when my mother added, "You're right-handed, you know." I used to respond to such comments with something like, "Oh. And all these years I thought I was left-handed." But my sarcasm never worked, so I stopped.

I had mixed feelings about creating a situation for Bill and Tony to laugh about my mother. I justified it because she didn't know and wouldn't be hurt. Overall, this was a liberating experience for me. I had never talked to others about my relationship with my mother, largely because I found it both embarrassing and difficult to describe. With Bill and Tony, I let my mother paint a more accurate portrait of our relationship than I ever could have. It was cheaper than going to a psychiatrist, and also more fun.

When Bill learned that Tony and I were virgins (Tony by choice, as a practicing Catholic), Bill tried to advise me on how to lose my virginity. We both tried to convince Tony it would be okay for him to do the same before marriage. Alas, neither project was brought to fruition during our first academic year. On the contrary, sophisticated Bill became virginlike. He began dating a graduate student, whom he eventually married. Bill's claim that they weren't having sex surprised me because of his many past conquests, which required more than the fingers on one hand to count. I believed Bill's return to abstinence then, but in retrospect I expect his girlfriend mandated this pretense.

Tony and I got closer as we became more distant from Bill. Tony and I questioned and challenged each other respectfully, but Bill enjoyed ridiculing me for my inability to deal with simple things in life, and ridiculing Tony for his belief in an afterlife. Tony showed an honesty and vulnerability I had never before seen, and I was happy to reciprocate. We talked about religion, family, sex, and issues I had rarely discussed with anyone. It felt liberating to say what was on my mind. Tony taught me what it meant to have and be a friend and confidante. He was the first with whom I was able to express my feelings, and my relationship with him helped me establish good future relationships.

And there was an added bonus. I had rejected the family view that goyim couldn't be trusted and we should stick to our own kind. But it was a theoretical rejection. I never before had any Gentile friends, for at least two reasons: I didn't know many Gentiles and I didn't have many friends. It was exhilarating to put a face on a theory, and I was looking forward to more such faces in the future.

Assuming I'm mature now (though some doubt it), that first year away from home at twenty-one started me on the road to maturity. When asked where I grew up, I sometimes answer, "Syracuse."

Fraternity Life?

Tony lived in a furnished room, as I almost had. He started eating with Bill and me, and sharing grocery expenses. My undergraduate math fraternity was not representative of fraternity life in general, but I picked up at least one fraternity habit in graduate school—drinking. A number of math graduate students would go to The Orange, a local bar near campus. We met there around midnight, after studying. Tony taught me how to drink, or at least what to order.

The only alcohol I had previously consumed was Manischewitz wine, and just at Passover Seders. It tasted like grape juice, only sweeter. When I took a sip at religiously appropriate times, my mother would mumble a dire prediction about my becoming an alcoholic. I think Manischewitz deserves some credit for the low percentage of Jewish alcoholics. When Tony asked what I liked to drink, I said "orange juice." So he advised me to order a screwdriver (orange juice and vodka). I managed to handle one or two per night, without ever getting drunk.

My drinking wasn't exactly fraternity-level quality, but Bill, Tony and I periodically deployed a fraternity-worthy prank. One day I came home, walked through the apartment door, and was suddenly soaking wet. Bill and Tony had put water in an empty milk carton, tied it with a string above the door, and rigged it to come down when someone opened the door. All three of us thought my getting soaked was funny, especially the other two. The next time I was home alone, I set the carton and it again worked perfectly when Bill came through the door. This tradition continued, though we all developed the habit of kicking the door open before entering.

Once the three of us came home and saw the wet evidence that someone had been inside. It wasn't difficult to figure out the culprit. Our landlord periodically lowered our thermostat in the cold Syracuse winter. He wasn't supposed to enter without permission, so he couldn't complain about the trap he must have assumed we had set for him.

One of Bill's students lived in our apartment building and would come over unannounced for math help, though Bill repeatedly told him to come only to his office hours on campus. Once we saw him coming to the apartment, and set the water trap. We had a good laugh at his expense, so Bill helped him with his math. As the student was about to leave, he told us how immaturely we had acted. We apologized profusely, but couldn't contain our laughter when he opened the door to leave and once again received the water treatment. The student never came to our apartment again.

As a child, I had wanted a dog. My mother compromised on a less-expensive and more-manageable species. We purchased three goldfish for a quarter. I fed them, and learned quickly that too much or too little food became a death sentence. We bought three more, but they also expired within two weeks. I'm not sure if it was the way I fed them or the quality of the fish we bought. After the first death, I became responsible for goldfish burial honors—flushing them down the toilet.

My roommates and I got a dog. We named him Feces, after his accident on the drive back from the pound. Unfortunately, he stayed true to his name. We'd put paper on the floor, and he'd take this as a challenge to perform where the paper wasn't. Feces learned a more interesting trick, which friends would come over to watch. One day he started rubbing against a towel I was holding. His movements became more rapid, until he relaxed and walked away. I can't take credit for teaching Feces to masturbate, but my roommates and I regularly provided him with his favorite sex toy. Years later, when watching David Letterman's "stupid pet tricks" segment, I thought of Feces.

Kennedy Assassination

Members of my generation know exactly where they were on the afternoon of November 22, 1963. I was teaching calculus when someone in the hall shouted, "President Kennedy's been shot." It was my third month of teaching and I didn't know what to do, so I continued to teach. Gradually, students left my class. Since the remaining handful weren't paying attention, I finally told them they could leave. Minutes later, all classes were cancelled.

President Kennedy's assassination wasn't on my mind the following summer, but should have been. My roommates had returned to New York, while I stayed to take a graduate math course and teach summer school so I'd have enough money to buy a used car. I lived in a dormitory and spent a lot of time in the math library. I was there alone on Sunday evening, August 2, 1964, when a man came in and told me to leave. I explained that I was a graduate student and showed him my key to the library, but he again told me to leave. I asked why, and he again told me to leave. I noticed the man didn't look or dress like a student or faculty member, so I asked him what he was doing there. Again, he told me to leave, looking more annoyed. Then it hit me. He was probably some sort of security for the upcoming August 5 visit of President

Lyndon Johnson. I asked him if he was, and, of course, he responded by telling me to leave.

Three years later, this conversation came to mind when I heard the Paul Newman line in the movie *Cool Hand Luke*: "What we've got here is a failure to communicate."

I've often tried to reason with people who either couldn't or wouldn't reason with me. I knew I had gone too far after saying, "Look, President Johnson won't be speaking for another three days. Why should I leave now?" I then pointed out the window, and added, "Johnson's speech will be a couple blocks away, and, even if I wanted to, I couldn't possibly harm him from here." All true, but not exactly a politic response.

This time the man didn't tell me to leave. He whispered into a talking device, and a minute later two other men rushed in. They didn't take out guns, but their jackets were unbuttoned in a way that I could see bulges that were probably loaded. I finally said what I should have said earlier. "I'm leaving now," and I held up my hands so nobody would think I was about to draw. And I quietly left the building.

President Johnson's Important Speech

I attended President Johnson's August 5 speech. I didn't think about it at the time, but the library incident probably triggered a secret service alert to watch me. I made no news that day, but Johnson's speech may well have been the most important one he ever gave. He was invited to dedicate a new campus building named after its chief benefactor, publisher S.I. Newhouse. It was billed as the largest, most sophisticated center for the study of public communications in the world. We expected the speech to be largely about Newhouse, but Johnson barely mentioned either Newhouse or the center.

Johnson's speech was almost entirely on foreign policy. He cited an incident on the previous day in a place I had never heard of, the Gulf of Tonkin. I had no idea I was watching history being made, and very bad history. Nobody I knew was talking about Vietnam. That changed two days later when Congress approved the Gulf of Tonkin Resolution, authorizing force against Communists in Southeast Asia. Not only was the Vietnam War to become a disaster, but also the Tonkin incident had been manufactured.

I now think President Johnson should have been impeached for ly-ing us into a war. At the time, I was a strong supporter for the courage he had shown in passing the landmark Civil Rights Act the previous month. It outlawed racial segregation in schools, workplaces, and all public accommodations. It also banned unequal application of voter registration requirements. After Johnson signed that bill, he purport-edly said to an aide, "We have lost the South for a generation." Unfor-tunately, it's been considerably more than a generation.

Johnson, more than any president in my lifetime, was responsible for a mixed bag of both great and awful accomplishments.

Sex and Social Politics

In that summer of 1964, I lost my virginity with no one special. The only thing memorable was my relief in losing it. So my second year of graduate school was my first year as a man, if you don't count my bar mitzvah at age thirteen. However, my newly acquired status didn't turn me into the chick magnet I anticipated becoming. I at least began to feel better about my lack of sexual success, attributing it as much to my being particular as to my inherent social deficiencies. One date was insulted when I asked why she wore lipstick; others didn't like my not opening car doors for them. I thought of myself as an early feminist, while they thought I was just being a jerk. We were probably both right.

Tony and I became roommates in our second year, along with a third roommate, Gary. He was a virgin like Tony, though not by choice. As a virgin once removed, I was the most "experienced." Gary was also a graduate student in math, with a considerably better math vocabulary than English vocabulary. He once came home very early from a date and asked me what "erudite" meant. When I told him, he said, "Oh, that explains it." His date had asked him to say something erudite and he thought it meant "dirty." So he said, "Do you want to fuck?" Her response was, "Please take me home, right now!" I said to Gary, "Either your date thought you were too crude or too vocabulary-challenged."

Sociable Tony suggested that he, Gary, and I host a Christmas party for math graduate students and faculty in December 1964. Gary was willing, but I felt it would be too much trouble. I finally consented, with one condition. Since our apartment was small, I'd write an appropriate invitation. When Tony and Gary read my "invitation," they reluctantly agreed. My letter, signed by the three of us, went something like this:

> You are invited to apply for a partyship. Your application should include why you would be an interesting guest, and what topics you would like to discuss. Since there may be more qualified applicants than we have room for, some of you may receive an "alternate partyship," which means you might get a late invitation should some of our preferred guests cancel. We will also offer "time partyships," which will allow you to stay for a limited time but require you to leave when other guests arrive.

A little background is in order. Before I received my teaching assistantship from Syracuse, I got a letter saying I was an alternate and would be awarded one if enough recipients turned theirs down. I immediately wrote to Dr. Kibbey, the mathematics department chair, and explained why I would be a worthy recipient. I also described the innovative mathematics I was working on. Sometime during the first year, I asked Dr. Kibbey if my letter had helped. He said it did, but added, "I thought the math was bullshit, but your initiative put you at the top of the alternate list."

Tony and I watched faculty and graduate students take invitations from their mailboxes, and we enjoyed the looks on their faces as they read them. Most of the graduate students took it in good humor, and many wrote funny "applications." However, no faculty member had yet applied. So I went to Dr. Kibbey and said I hoped he would be able to attend the party. He said he had another engagement that evening, but he would be happy to attend for a little while. I then offered him an appropriate "time partyship." When we let it be known that Dr. Kibbey would be at our party, several other faculty members decided to attend.

Math faculty members had never before attended a party arranged by students. The highlight for me was when Dr. Kibbey told me he had to leave. I shouted for all present to hear, "I'm sorry Dr. Kibbey, but your time partyship is up. You'll have to leave now." Kibbey was a gruff and sometimes intimidating man, but he played along beautifully and feigned disappointment that he was required to leave.

Kibbey's sense of humor was soon on display again. I filled out a form for a fledgling computer dating system at the university, and I was matched with a senior undergraduate. I asked her to meet me in the math department, and said we would go to lunch from there. Other graduate students gathered to see what the computer had found for me. When there were around fifteen of us milling about, Dr. Kibbey came out of his office to see what was happening. I told him, and he joined the group. When my computer date arrived, she wondered aloud who the real "Herb Silverman" was. Finally, Dr. Kibbey, a fat, bald man in his mid-fifties, moved to the front. When the laughter subsided, I stepped forward. The actual date was anticlimactic. I think she preferred me to Kibbey, but not by much. I was hoping for someone who could appreciate a joke, and she was hoping for someone who didn't act like a jerk. We were both disappointed.

Jew Dating

An unexpected source for dates came from Milton Elefant, Orthodox rabbi and head of Hillel (a national organization that promotes Jewish life on campus). Teaching assistants worked at registration to match students with classes. Because of room constraints, some were on Saturday morning. Regardless of race, color, creed, or national origin, nobody wanted Saturday classes. I volunteered to decide acceptable excuses. Jewish students had previously been automatically excused because Saturday was the Jewish Sabbath. Not anymore. When they told me they couldn't take Saturday classes for religious reasons, I said, "*Haeem atah midabare Evreet*? (Do you speak Hebrew?) I then assigned Saturday classes to the many students who responded, "Huh?" Even letters from the rabbi weren't good enough for those who failed my religious test.

Shortly afterward, Rabbi Elefant invited me to discuss my reported anti-Semitism. I told him that atheist Jews like me deserved no special dispensation and that he had signed excuses for students who were no more observant than I was, and considerably more ignorant of Judaism. I said I'd excuse students if he produced evidence they were not using electricity on *Shabbas* (Saturday). The rabbi laughed and said I had chutzpah, but that he couldn't disagree with my reasoning.

I was not used to an Orthodox rabbi acknowledging another point of view, and I wound up liking him. He invited me to participate in weekly brunches for Jewish graduate students, with speakers and discussions. In addition to the discussions, where I quickly earned a reputation for being a Jewish gadfly and the spokesperson for nonbelievers, I found a ready supply of female graduate students for whom being a math nerd was actually a positive attribute.

One day Rabbi Elefant presented me with an interesting dilemma. A major contributor to the Hillel program was upset that his daughter was dating a Gentile. He assumed it was because she couldn't find a nice Jewish boy, and the father secretly asked for the rabbi's help. Rabbi Elefant asked the girl if she liked any boys at the brunch, and she mentioned me. The rabbi asked me if I'd be willing to date her. I said I was flattered, but it would be unethical for me to take advantage of her under the circumstances, since I wouldn't otherwise date her. Rabbi Elefant agreed, but he could at least tell her father that he had tried.

During Christmas breaks, I visited New York City and stayed with my roommate and best friend, Tony. I liked his parents, who became my surrogate parents. A Hillel girl from the city invited me to meet her parents. A couple of days later, I invited her to meet my surrogate parents. Afterward, I asked them what they thought of her. Tony's mother said she was nice, but his father felt I could do better. I was elated that my surrogate dad thought an average girl wasn't good enough for me. His reasons, primarily that she didn't have enough of a sense of humor, were sound. Shortly thereafter, we broke up. The following Christmas, I brought someone who met the enthusiastic approval of "Dad."

Mature Dating

I met "Esther" when she was in her last year of medical school in Syracuse and I was in my next-to-last year of graduate school. She was bright, funny, and attractive. Though I was no longer a virgin, Esther was more experienced. She had recently ended a passionate relationship because he wasn't Jewish. I didn't feel comfortable knowing that my major advantage over him occurred at birth. On the other hand, what Esther learned from her Gentile probably made her a better lover, and she helped me along.

There was one day in the 1960s, I can't say exactly which day, when the culture (or at least the culture in which I lived) made a 180-degree shame turn for unmarried women: from shame for not being a virgin to shame for being one. I think, for the most part, this was a shame change for the better.

Esther had joked about how medical students on specialized rounds often developed symptoms of the patients in the specialty (medical students' disease, she called it). While doing OB/GYN rounds, Esther developed pregnancy symptoms. I accompanied her to the lab so she could test herself. When she came out, she said, "Hello, Papa."

Neither of us was ready for children, especially me. But this was about Esther, not me. I was scared, and so was she. I had stopped using condoms when she started taking birth control pills, which she had been somewhat casual about doing. Esther was willing to have an abortion, which was illegal in the United States in 1967. She knew a doctor who knew a doctor in New York City who performed abortions. However, the day before we were scheduled to drive there, the illegal clinic was shut down.

Esther, who had been reasonably calm, began to sob. She suggested we go to an amusement park, but neither the roller coaster nor the bumper cars induced the hoped-for spontaneous abortion. Esther began talking about knitting needles. I couldn't tell if she was serious, but I said, "Rather than resort to that, I'd marry you." What I thought was a gallant remark made Esther cry uncontrollably. She said, "Who the fuck needs you? I don't want to marry you, with or without a shotgun."

I stood beside Esther, feeling numb, and waited for her to calm down. I felt terrible, but I knew she felt much worse. I wanted somehow to help her. I didn't know what to say or do, so I said and did nothing. Looking back, probably the best thing would have been for me just to hug her.

A couple of days later, Esther's medical connections helped her arrange for an abortion in Puerto Rico. We pooled our money, but it wasn't quite enough. I asked my roommate Tony if I could borrow some. He asked why, and I said, "Please don't ask." He was opposed to abortion then, but I'm grateful he gave me the money with no questions asked.

The abortion was successful, despite traumatic experiences for Esther leading up to it. Several doctors and fellow students wondered about Esther's absence and other "suspicious" behavior, and Esther worried about being kicked out of medical school. A cab driver picked her up at the San Juan airport and took her to a private house instead of her requested hospital. The driver knew about the hospital and said, "My friend can do it cheaper." Esther then screamed for him to take her to the right place, and he relented. I had favored abortion rights before, but much more so after this experience.

Esther and I continued to see each other, but she never again talked about the abortion. I wanted to, but I respected her right to remain silent. When Esther graduated from medical school, she took her internship at Montefiore Hospital in New York City. We occasionally met for weekends in Albany, halfway between Syracuse and New York. She had hoped I'd find a faculty position in New York City, but we decided to stop dating when I accepted a position in Massachusetts. Esther suggested that we get married in ten years if we were both still single. "Sounds reasonable," I said, making no commitment.

Two years later, I received an invitation for Esther's wedding to another doctor. I phoned her and asked if she really would like me to come, and she said she would. The wedding was in Syracuse, so I took the opportunity to attend and also visit some old friends. Esther seemed perfectly comfortable with my presence, as did her husband. Some of Esther's relatives, whom I had met before, were less comfortable. After Esther danced with her new husband and then with her father, she looked at me and I came over for the third dance. Mainly we talked about the looks on her relatives' faces. Afterward, one relative apparently wanted to console me and said, "I'm sure you'll find another girl better than Esther." I said, trying to look sad, "There will never be another Esther." Esther overheard and laughed, which was the sense of humor I would miss most in her.

CHAPTER 5

Teaching and Protesting

My PhD advisor was well respected in his field, which helped me receive numerous job offers when I completed my dissertation in 1968. I wanted a small PhD granting university near a big city, so I chose Clark University in Worcester, Massachusetts, which is forty miles from Boston. I had been a student since I was four and it felt strange at age twenty-six to have a full-time job as an assistant professor.

I taught a graduate course in my specialty, complex variables, an area I liked because it dealt with infinite processes and abstract reasoning. I still felt more comfortable hanging out with graduate students, who were closer to my age than most faculty members, so I struggled with a sometimes-thin line between being a friend and authority figure. I didn't like the textbook and some graduate students suggested I convert my class notes into a book. I rejected a colleague's advice to focus solely on my research and write textbooks only in the twilight of my career. I spent a couple years working on my complex variables book, subsequently published by Houghton-Mifflin.

On Thanksgiving morning, 1968, I did not shave. Just about everyone I knew in Worcester had gone home for the holidays. I also didn't shave on Friday, Saturday, Sunday—or ever again (though I'd continue to visit a barber who would cut some facial and head hair). When my stubble turned into a full-fledged beard, a number of people asked why I was growing a beard. I replied, "I'm *not* growing a beard. It's growing all by itself." I then asked them why they wasted time shaving. The question I asked myself was why I had ever started. After thinking about it, the act made no more sense to me than making a bed in the morning (which I never did), only to unmake it at night.

Back to Family

My mother literally screamed when she saw the beard during my annual December visit, and I refused her order to shave. Several months later she told me that Uncle Jake, my father's oldest brother, had died two weeks earlier. My mother hadn't told me at the time because she didn't want me to come to the funeral where others would see my beard.

I didn't mind missing Jake's funeral, though he had been the relative with whom I most identified. His wife Estelle used to prepare Thanksgiving family meals. Much to her dismay, Jake would eat quickly and then sit alone on the porch. I often got tired of family chatter and sat on the porch, too. Jake would say hello and I'd answer his hello with a hello, followed by nothing more. We both preferred this one-word outside conversation to the multiword inside conversations. Had I attended Jake's funeral when family members said their "goodbyes" to him, I might have whispered a more fitting "hello."

When I was growing up, my parents socialized almost exclusively with Fannie's sister Eleanor and her husband Norman. Until I left Philadelphia at twenty-one, the five of us lived in the same building. They rented adjacent apartments until I was nine, and then bought a duplex house, where my parents and I lived on the floor above Eleanor and Norman.

The bond between Fannie and Eleanor seemed closer than the one between the wives and their husbands. My mother became quite upset in 1965 when Eleanor and Norman inexplicably moved into a highrise apartment building in a different neighborhood. My mother had spent most of her time with Eleanor during the day, doing I don't know what. After the move, they phoned each other about a dozen times a day. My maternal grandmother moved into the vacated first floor of the duplex, so my mother spent a lot of time with her.

In 1975, my grandmother went to a retirement home for elderly Jews who couldn't properly take care of themselves. Since my grandmother had no money, she was admitted for free. This facility was just three blocks from where she had been living below us, so my mother continued to see her daily. My father had retired the year before, with nothing much to do, so my mother arranged for him to volunteer at my grandmother's new dwelling. He wound up counting pills and putting them into bottles, not unlike his former job packing Hershey bars. I also think my mother bargained for extra perks for my grandmother because of my father's service.

Eleanor and Norman rented the downstairs part of the duplex to strangers when my grandmother moved out. My mother was furious at Norman for not giving her veto power over potential renters. I'm not sure why she didn't like the new tenants, perhaps because they weren't relatives or because she didn't get to choose them. When my grandmother died in 1978 at the age of ninety-three, my mother agreed to sell the duplex. Norman wanted to sell it sooner but needed Fannie's permission. My parents couldn't afford Eleanor and Norman's upscale apartment building, so they found one about three miles from them.

Norman died in 1980 at age sixty-five. I was thirty-eight years old and living in Charleston, South Carolina. I returned to Philadelphia for the *shiva*, where friends and relatives swapped stories about him. Norman had been gregarious and enjoyed his harmonica. He was the only one in my extended family who played an instrument, not counting my elementary school triangle career. When asked to say something about Norman, I mentioned how happy I had been when we rode in his car to Atlantic City. I also said I liked watching his television, and added, "Uncle Norman used to get really excited and involved watching Friday night prize fights on television." I was about twelve at that time, with no interest in the fights. I couldn't understand why he shouted at the fighters and even threw punches in the direction of the TV set. Fortunately, he never made contact with the television set or me. I had thought of telling him that his living-room punches weren't affecting the outcome, but I didn't want to dampen his enthusiasm.

At one point during the *shiva*, I was alone with Eleanor and she surprised me by saying, "Do you know why we moved out of the duplex? Uncle Norman couldn't stand your mother asking him whenever he went out, 'Where are you going? What will you do? What time will you be back?' " I said, "I know how Uncle Norman felt." Eleanor smiled and said, "I know you do." I felt this was Eleanor's way of telling me she knew my mother had been too protective and smothering. I had never before heard Eleanor say something critical about Fannie.

It seemed then that Eleanor and I might someday establish a real relationship. This exchange was a start, but Eleanor was more Fannie's sister than my aunt. I was cautious about getting close to Eleanor for the same reason I hadn't wanted to get close to my mother. I didn't value their opinions on most issues and didn't like being told by my mother what to do. Distancing myself was my way of showing independence from her when I was young, a pattern that continued into my adult life.

When I started teaching at Clark University, my mother would phone me weekly and I would visit for three days in December and on special occasions like funerals. She would offer advice I ignored, ask questions I answered monosyllabically, and gossip about family members who didn't much interest me. This went on for twenty-five years. When my mother became old and frail and I became less immature, I cautiously reestablished some kind of relationship with her and other family members, as I will describe in chapter 19.

Yoga

I learned to play racquetball at Clark University, but would get frequent aches and pains. When someone suggested yoga for flexibility, I took a class in 1970. Our teacher told us about an upcoming yoga weekend retreat, with other interesting activities. That turned out to be quite an understatement. New Age practitioners, before "New Age" had been defined, led the "interesting activities." One leader regressed several participants to their past lives. Most had impressive backgrounds as former kings, queens, and warriors.

When the professional regressor told us we all had many past lives, I asked him how that could be when more people are born each year than die. He was unfazed, saying matter-of-factly, "You didn't take into account life on other planets." He was right, I hadn't. I think a better explanation would have been, "You didn't take into account other species. Some of you were once mosquitoes or cockroaches." At least we know there are other life forms on this planet, but those at the retreat likely preferred thinking of themselves as former royalty than as former garden pests.

After the session, I talked to a couple of the regressed, trying to discover if they had been plants (in the ringer sense, not in the past-life sense). They believed their past life experiences were real. Otherwise, they seemed normal, which made me question the meaning of "normal." More than forty years later, I'm still questioning "normal."

Another teacher was an aura specialist, a clairvoyant who drew inferences about a person's emotional state based on his or her supposed aura color. She would put a person on stage and say something like, "He has a blue aura. Can you see it?" After several such demonstrations, many participants became confident about their aura-reading abilities. Then I said to the clairvoyant, "To test how good we've become, why don't we write down the aura color we see *before* you tell us what you see?" The clairvoyant must not have been psychic, because she didn't see my question coming and felt insulted by it. Some of the others were also upset with my "test" for the professional clairvoyant.

Years later, I had a similar experience in South Carolina at a group reading organized by "internationally renowned channeler" Darlen-De, an intermediary for a dead guy who answered questions about the future. The deceased was like your typical fortuneteller, only dead. Darlen-De went around the room soliciting questions. She would repeat each question, be silent for a minute, and then answer in a funny voice (presumably the voice of the dead guy). People seemed happy with the answers.

When my turn came, I said, "I've been worried about Calvin. He doesn't apply himself. Will he go to college?" The dead guy answered, "Don't worry. He'll go to college, but perhaps not the school you like." I then asked, "Do you know what college my cat Calvin will go to?" This time Darlen-De didn't ask the dead guy, though I expect "obedience school" would have been an appropriate answer. Again the wrath of the participants was directed toward the exposer rather than the exposed. Apparently, people enjoy being gullible as long as their gullibility isn't pointed out to them so blatantly.

I once had an epiphany at a revival meeting that a fellow graduate student at Syracuse persuaded me to attend (for fun). The reverend gave us postcards so he could take our prayer requests up "Prayer Mountain," where presumably he would be closer to the recipient of our requests. I wrote on my postcard to the mountain climber, "Pray for my PhD." About two weeks later, I got a major breakthrough on my thesis. No,

I don't think these two events were connected in any way, but I did receive a letter from the reverend requesting a "love offering." My handwriting not being the finest, the letter was addressed to Hub Silverman. For the next couple of years, I received numerous "Hub" donation requests from a variety of organizations. My epiphany was that providing an address to hucksters significantly increases your junk mail.

My weekend yoga retreat gave me some unexpected long-term benefits. I had been a meat-and-potatoes guy all my life, but only vegetarian food was available at the retreat. I liked it a lot, learned more about its health benefits, and to this day remain mostly a vegetarian. I did go overboard around that time, taking unnecessary supplements and megadoses of vitamins. I was following the advice of Nobel Prize winner Linus Pauling, which shows that even Nobel Prize winners aren't always right.

Vietnam

Vietnam War protests in 1970 were raging at universities throughout the country, and Clark was no exception. I was jailed briefly in a large mass arrest. More than a hundred students and some faculty sat down and blocked the entrance to the Worcester draft board. We prevented draftees from registering for several hours as police officers carried us out and took us to jail. Some of the more optimistic students thought we would stop the war. I just wanted to do something instead of nothing. The police put me in a cell for a couple of hours with three Clark students, one of whom was in my class and took the opportunity to ask me math questions. Just as my student was finishing his homework, we were released. So my first stint in jail turned out to be a bit like holding office hours.

My second arrest came a month later. At a small gathering of antiwar faculty, I pointed out that the mayor would be presenting a military leader the key to our city at a public banquet. The other faculty drafted me to attend and protest. So as the mayor rose to speak from the podium, I rose from my table to give a short counterspeech: "As a concerned citizen of Worcester, I think the key to our city should be reserved for those dedicated to protecting the peace, not destroying it." I was dragged back to jail for another few hours.

At my trial, the judge told me I was charged with disturbing the peace and asked how I pled. "Not guilty," I responded. "I'm trying to protect the peace. Our military leaders are disturbing the peace." After a puzzled look on the judge's face, I thought I detected a faint smile when he understood my pun. But the judge must not have liked puns very much, because he didn't agree that I was not guilty. He did let me go free on a continuance, and told me the case would be dropped if I didn't get into any more trouble in the next three months. I didn't. The day after my trial, I heard radio callers discussing my protest. One referred to me as a "commie atheist." He was half right.

Someone would invariably pass around a joint at peace-meeting strategy sessions. Since we were trying to bond, I'd take a puff like everyone else. I might be the only one in the country who believed Bill Clinton when he said he had smoked marijuana, but didn't inhale. I don't know about Clinton, but that was true for me. I had never smoked tobacco and didn't know to inhale, so I just blew into the joint. I felt nothing and eventually began passing it on without inhaling or blowing.

During the height of protests, students and faculty would gather to discuss "strategy" to end the war. One moment of levity amid a horrible tragedy occurred on May 4, 1970, when members of the Ohio National Guard shot and killed four unarmed students at Kent State University. During heated discussions about the most effective way to show support for our allies at that institution, one student proposed that we change the name of Clark University to Clark Kent University.

A student accused me of favoring the Vietnam War because I refused to change his F grade, which he said would end his draft deferment. I announced to all my classes on the first day of the next semester, "If I pass you undeservedly, then some other poor bastard will have to serve." That year, my male students studied harder than usual.

Since we hadn't ended the war by 1972, many activists put their hopes in presidential candidate George McGovern's promise to do so if elected. Despite my strong support for McGovern, I was ever the realist. I won several bets that McGovern wouldn't carry more than five states against incumbent Richard Nixon. Massachusetts, unfortunately, was the only state that voted for McGovern (he also won in Washington, DC). The following year, after the Watergate scandal became headline news, I used my winning proceeds to purchase and give away bumper stickers that said, "Don't blame me, I'm from Massachusetts."

I learned an unintended political and organizing strategy from a graduate student who enjoyed playing bridge in the math lounge. He would regularly ask people to be a fourth for bridge (the required number to play) until he found three others to agree. "It's easier to recruit a fourth than a second" became for me a guiding principle that I still employ in a variety of contexts. People are more likely to join a cause if they can be convinced they are needed, and you can't find a fourth for any cause, no matter how important, before first finding a second.

Massachusetts Dating

In 1968 I began dating Celia, a math professor at Quinsigamond Community College, a few miles from Clark University. After several months, Celia said she loved me. She was the first woman to tell me that, and I was taken aback. I reciprocated by telling her I liked her but didn't love her. When she said she hoped we would one day marry, I said it might be better if we stopped seeing each other. We did.

Meanwhile, a local radio talk-show host informed his friend, the wife of one of my math colleagues, that he was planning a show on the joys of bachelorhood, and asked if she knew a single faculty member from the university who would be willing to be a guest. She arranged for me to be on the show.

Before the show began, the host told me I'd be free to speak my mind, but I couldn't use certain words on the air. When I playfully asked, "What words?" he said, "You know, like the four-letter word that rhymes with fire truck."

I repeated his warning on air, adding, "As far as I'm concerned, the four-letter word that has caused the most harm, the word that has been the source of the most hypocrisy, is the word *love*." The host shouted, "That's the most awful, disgusting thing I've ever heard. You should be ashamed of yourself, making fun of such a beautiful word. We better take a commercial break now and come back for phone calls."

During the break, he said matter-of-factly, "I agree with you. I think the show is going quite well, don't you?" My first radio interview taught me that you couldn't necessarily expect hosts to believe what they spout.

The following year, I had a near-marital experience. An ultra-Orthodox (Hasidic) faculty colleague, Joseph, knew my religious views, but invited me anyway to his house for a Passover Seder. Most of the guests were from the same cult as Joseph, including one of his elderly aunts, who said, "I have a lovely niece in Toronto. Would you like to meet her?" When I said "Okay," she looked remarkably happy.

Joseph had been listening with a big grin on his face. He later explained, "If you like the niece, you'll be expected to marry her." Joseph and I agreed that we should find an excuse to cancel my "date." I had my chance when the aunt approached me with a confession, "I must tell you that my niece is kosher, but not *glatt* kosher." (Hasidim go beyond ordinary Orthodox Jews by requiring special rabbis to inspect the food according to a more stringent standard of Jewish dietary law.) My response to the aunt was, "Well, in that case, I'm not interested." When the aunt said her niece would be willing to become *glatt* kosher, I said that still wasn't good enough. Joseph could hardly contain his laughter.

I neither arrived at nor left the Seder alone. Joseph had told me that two female Orthodox students needed to walk the mile and a half to his house, and he asked if I'd accompany them. I agreed, knowing that Orthodox Jews don't ride on holy days. While walking home with them, I asked how long they had been Orthodox. They said they weren't, but that their teacher (Joseph) said I was, and he asked them to keep me company on the walk. Joseph sure told a lot of lies on one of his holiest days of the year.

The next summer, I got a call from an old Temple classmate. Sheldon was teaching mathematics at the University of Hartford and suggested we go to Europe together. He had found an inexpensive two-week group tour of London, Paris, and Amsterdam. It would be the first overseas trip for both of us.

We were the only unmarried pair, and the tour leader periodically called roll to make sure we were all there. It went something like, "Mr. and Mrs. Jones, Mr. and Mrs. Smith, . . . Dr. Eisenberg and Mr. Silverman." Sheldon and I both had PhDs in math, but Sheldon flaunted the title. He claimed that "Dr." often got him better service. I expect many of the couples thought we were gay, but nobody mentioned it to us.

Had Sheldon and I been more open with our tour compatriots in Paris, we could have dispelled any gay gossip. Paris being Paris, Sheldon and I decided to visit a whorehouse. We got to pick from about a dozen prostitutes staring at us. I chose the only one not smoking. Sheldon chose the least attractive because he felt sorry for her and thought she would be appreciative.

My new amour was businesslike, getting me ready as quickly as she could. It didn't take long for me to have an orgasm, after which she whispered in my ear those three romantic words, "You are finished?" I was, and went downstairs to wait for Sheldon, but he was already there waiting for me and grinning. This might have been the day Sheldon lost his virginity, but he never said one way or the other. That was my first and last whorehouse experience, but I've reminisced to friends who know better than to always take me seriously, "I wonder if my old Paris girlfriend still thinks about me."

Dissertation Students

I had two students who wrote PhD dissertations under my supervision. An interesting incident occurred with the first, Evelyn Silvia, after she passed her qualifying exams in 1972. To celebrate, I took her to a local bar. The bartender came over and said the bar was for men only. Worcester was a reasonably progressive city, so I thought he was kidding, but he wasn't, and we left. The following day I returned with another graduate student, this time a black female. I understood the dilemma of a bartender who would rather be called a sexist than a racist. After the bartender had a brief conference with the manager, they let us sit down and buy drinks. The next day I brought Evelyn back for a second visit, and this time the bartender served us. Many books have been written about the history of civil rights in America, but this is the first (and no doubt last) book to mention my Worcester bar contribution.

Evelyn and I had, of mathematical necessity, been seeing a lot of each other, which led to a sexual relationship. Though not considered completely proper, it was not as unacceptable then as now. I tried to separate our private and professional relationships, but one can never be certain. When Evelyn completed her PhD thesis and took a professorial position at the University of California at Davis, we began a long and fruitful mathematical collaboration on numerous research papers. I would visit and stay with Evelyn in the summer, unless she or I were dating others. Eventually, Evelyn married a colleague in her department. I had mixed emotions, but overall I was happy for her.

Once I heard Evelyn close a phone conversation with her husband, "And I love you, too." Strangely, this cliché sign-off bothered me more than when she told me she was getting married. Another cliché came to mind: "Better to have loved and lost than never to have loved at all." I knew I'd lost, but had I ever loved? I concluded that my philosophical avoidance of the word, even though I must have had stronger feelings than others who used it, was pretty stupid. I resolved to someday say the L-word.

In the fall of 1973, my research sabbatical for the following year was approved. Since Don Telage, my second PhD student, would be coming with me, I chose the University of Delaware over the University of California at Davis. I could do research with colleagues at either institution, but Don would more easily be able to travel back to see his wife, a school librarian in Massachusetts.

After receiving his PhD in 1976, Don took a three-year position as visiting professor at the University of Kentucky. However, he left academe in 1978 to pursue his interest in computers, a new field that I thought was a fad. Don knew of my Luddite tendencies and wisely ignored my views on the future of computers. He prospered financially beyond the dreams of any college professor. Don became a senior vice president for Network Solutions, which had the lucrative domain-name registration market cornered. He subsequently left to become a venture capitalist, making huge profits in a variety of deals. Don remains as down-to-earth and unpretentious as when he was a graduate student. He had thought about asking me to invest in Network Solutions, but wasn't as confident then as now of his ability to forecast success. After talking with Don in 2009 about his latest venture, On-Ramp Wireless, Inc., I invested in this start-up company. I trust Don about its prospects for long-term success, but I didn't put in more than I can afford to lose.

Tenure Problem

In the spring of 1974 at Clark, I got disappointing news. Typically, successful faculty members are granted tenure and promotion to associate professor in the sixth year. I received an early promotion to associate professor in my fifth year and assumed my tenure would be automatic. Though faculty committees recommended me for tenure, the president of the university turned me down. He brought up financial problems, saying the university was thinking of ending its PhD program in mathematics and would be cutting back on faculty. The only other department member who came up for tenure that year was also denied, as was the one faculty member who came up the following year. A faculty member denied tenure is allowed one additional year at the institution. In my case, my sabbatical year also became my terminal year with Clark University. Nevertheless, I had a good research year at the University of Delaware.

I began to look for a permanent position, but the job market was not as good in the mid-1970s as it had been in 1968 when I first got my position. I applied to all the universities that had previously made me offers, but none had openings. It also didn't help that I was now an associate professor while most institutions were hiring only at the assistant professor level. When my sabbatical year ended, the University of Delaware offered me a visiting position for the 1975–76 year, which I accepted. Strangely, I wasn't "qualified" to teach their graduate course in complex variables even though my newly published textbook was being used for the course. Only permanent faculty, who would be available to supervise PhD students, taught graduate courses.

In Mel Brooks' 1968 movie, *The Producers*, a character played by Gene Wilder concocts a scheme to massively oversell shares in a Broadway production called *Springtime for Hitler*. He expects it to be a horrific flop, which would justify avoiding payouts to investors. Unfortunately, it becomes a smashing success and the schemers go to jail. Aside from my modest textbook royalties, I made additional money with the same scheme. I sold 100 percent of the movie rights for *Complex Variables* to five different graduate students, for $1 each. They knew they would not be collecting from this business venture, but they enjoyed showing to others my handwritten movie contract.

I could have remained a visiting faculty member at the University of Delaware for several more years, but I wanted a permanent position. So in 1976, I widened the kinds of schools I would apply to, not restricting myself to PhD-granting universities. This led to my first southern exposure, to which I am still exposed: the College of Charleston in Charleston, South Carolina.

CHAPTER 6

SOUTHERN EXPOSURE

Culture Shocks

My interview at the College of Charleston in South Carolina was my first trip below the Mason-Dixon Line, and like many in the North, I had stereotypes about life in the South. I was open to changing my mind and hoped I would. Charleston is a lovely city, known for its gracious living. I've never been known as a gracious liver.

My mathematics interview talk went well. I was especially pleased when I overheard one professor say to another, "That was a really nice talk." People typically say something like that to the speaker, but a behind-the-back compliment is more meaningful. In addition to meeting the department, I had interviews with the top two administrators.

Ted Stern, the president, talked about the College "family" and the importance of community service. The only questions he asked were whether I liked to teach and whether I liked students. I wanted to ask him if any prospective candidate had ever said "no," but I thought better of it. Stern became an Episcopalian when he applied for the presidency at the College. I subsequently developed a friendship with Ted's brother, Bob, a fellow atheist, who told me Ted had assured the family he was still a Jew and not to worry about the "conversion."

Jack Bevan, the academic vice president, wanted to make the small college more research oriented, and hoped I would help to do so. Bevan had a PhD in psychology and was an academic before coming to the College; Stern had been an officer in the navy and was hired with only a bachelor's degree. In my eyes, Stern and Bevan represented a difference between Old and New South. I wanted to assist in transforming Old to New.

Academics are usually expected to do research (new and creative publishable work) as well as teach. The media promote discoveries in areas like history and science, but rarely in mathematics. Math findings are generally too difficult to explain and not of much interest or practical value to those without math backgrounds. I'll have more to say about this in chapter 15 (which you can skip to if you can't wait). Suffice it to say for now that mathematicians consider mathematical research important.

Hugh Haynsworth, the math department chair, wasn't engaged in research, nor were most in the department, but he was comfortable with Bevan's research-oriented philosophy. Hugh showed me around the city, including a visit to the Battery, a posh residential area at the tip of the peninsula, where he said the "War of Northern Aggression" began. Hugh was a southerner, but could laugh at this Charleston euphemism for the Civil War. Some also referred to it as the "War for Southern Independence" or the "Late Unpleasantness." I knew Charleston would be an interesting place to live.

In a surprising conversation, Hugh asked, "With a name like that, are you Jewish?" I answered, "Yes," wondering about the follow-up question. Hugh said, "A Jewish person applied last year, but he told me all the days he would miss because of Jewish holidays, so we didn't hire him. Would you miss all those classes?" I responded, "I'm Jewish, but not religious. If I'm religious about anything, it's mathematics."

I accepted the College of Charleston's offer as associate professor of mathematics. The three academic levels are assistant, associate, and full professor. Because of my prior experience, I had more seniority than most in my new department.

After receiving the offer from Hugh, he became alarmed when I told him I could have sued for religious discrimination. Though Hugh had a legitimate point about potential teaching problems in hiring the Orthodox Jew, I thought it strange to hear about this at an interview. I would not have sued had they hired a different candidate, but I know people who would have. Perhaps that was one difference between North and South.

I came to Charleston a couple of weeks before classes began. If I believed in hell, I'd describe Charleston in August as "hot as hell," only prettier. Another cliché that came close to ringing true was, "It's not the heat, it's the humidity." For me it was definitely both, though the humidity was considerably worse. One amusing Charleston controversy at the time was whether horses drawing carriages should be required to wear diapers. I'm generally a naturalist, but I was aromatically pleased when the diaper faction won.

Charleston periodically wins "most polite city in America" awards. Initially when I was out on the street, I became perplexed about whether I knew passersby. Most would smile warmly and say "Hi," the kind of exchange I'd had in New England only with close friends. I learned to accept such gestures as typically polite Charleston greetings, without reading anything more meaningful into them.

The compact College of Charleston, founded in 1770, lies in the heart of historic downtown Charleston. With its lush trees, flowers, and fountains, the campus has a rural look in an urban setting. Randolph Hall, built in 1828, is the oldest functioning college classroom building in the nation, and it still shows damage from cannon fire during the Civil War, when the College provided barracks for Confederate soldiers.

The most intriguing site for me is a gravestone outside my office building with the inscription, "Near this spot is buried Elizabeth Jackson, mother of President Andrew Jackson. She gave her life cheerfully for the independence of her country." I've since learned that Elizabeth died in 1781 and was buried in an unmarked grave in or near Charleston. A more official marker was erected about a mile from campus, behind City Hall, by a chapter of the Daughters of the American Revolution. Andrew Jackson was the only American president born in South Carolina.

When I asked who placed the Elizabeth Jackson gravestone on campus, I heard many interesting but undocumented accounts. Charlestonians are famous for not letting cold, hard facts interfere with a good story. Some of its most popular attractions today are "ghost tours" around our graveyards, dungeons, and jails.

During my first week in Charleston, I noticed a sign for duplicate bridge at the Christian Family Y. I didn't have a partner, but they found a pleasant woman for me. After we finished playing I said, "I'm from the North, where they have YMCAs. Is that the same as the 'Christian Family Y' down here?" She looked at me for a minute, and responded, "Oh, you must mean the *black* Y." When the local white YMCA had refused to integrate, it was kicked out of the national organization. The local group reopened as the Christian Family Y, while a smaller YMCA remained, the so-called black Y, with no bridge games. That ended my Charleston bridge career.

I began dating Day, a professor of Spanish at the College. What we liked most about each other was how different we were from anyone we had ever dated before. She was born and bred in Charleston, the daughter of a former diplomat, and had never dated a Yankee. Day jokingly said to me, "You're the first Jew I ever had sex with." Had I met Day several years earlier, shortly after my Paris experience, I could have responded: "You're the first Gentile I didn't have to pay for sex." (Perhaps I'm stereotyping, but my Paris friend didn't *look* Jewish.)

When Day invited me to her family's Thanksgiving dinner, she tried to warn me what to expect. At the table, Day's father told me I didn't have to say grace with the Christians if I didn't want to. I didn't. But the highlight for me came when I was alone with Day's aunt and neither of us had anything to say. Finally, the aunt declared, "So, you're a Jew!" I responded, "Yes," and that ended our conversation. I'm sorry I didn't add, "I'm not just a Jew. I'm also an atheist." I feel that Woody Allen's "spirit" must have been in the room. The following year he had a similar dinner scene in his movie *Annie Hall*, which I made a point to see a second time with Day.

I lived in a one-bedroom apartment, one of two faculty carriage houses behind a main college building. History professor Jack Censer lived in the other. We were both politically progressive atheist Jews and became lifelong friends, even though Jack left the following year to take a position at George Mason University, where he is now Dean of the College of Humanities and Social Sciences. Our carriage houses were former slave quarters, behind the old master's house. The main difference was that we each lived alone in our respective carriage houses, instead of sharing with what might have been a dozen others. Also, nobody whipped us.

I joined the hiring committee in my first year, hoping to bring on more researchers. Males in the math department had PhDs, but females had only master's degrees. I thought it important to hire a woman with a PhD. When we invited one to Charleston for an interview, I was embarrassed by what transpired. A couple of faculty members brought their wives to dinner with the candidate, and the wives offered to take her shopping the next day. The candidate later told me she couldn't accept an offer from such a school. I understood and insisted that this never happen again.

The following year we hired Kathy Alligood, our first woman PhD. A few weeks into the semester, Hugh Haynsworth was talking to a student as Kathy and I passed by. Hugh introduced us to the student as Dr. Silverman and Kathy Alligood. A minute later, I left and said, "Goodbye Dr. Alligood, goodbye Hugh." Hugh got the message.

Fortunately, Kathy had a wonderful sense of humor. We were on a faculty committee with an elderly southern gentleman who rose whenever Kathy entered the room and didn't sit down until she did. I suggested to Kathy that she sit, but then get up immediately. She did, and so did he. I wanted Kathy to prolong the procedure, but she had more sense than I did. Kathy, who was single at the time, declined an invitation to join the "Faculty Wives Club," now thankfully defunct.

Hugh Haynsworth was a nice guy, but I couldn't resist playing little jokes on him. The College had just hired Ralph Melnick, who had a PhD in Jewish Studies. Hugh saw me talking to Ralph and asked me what field he was in. I told Hugh that Ralph was a "kike-ologist." When Hugh said, "What's that?" I suggested he ask Ralph, which he did. It's easier to get away with religious slurs when you're a member of the tribe.

I sat next to Ralph at his first graduation ceremony and timed my phony question perfectly. "Did you hear about the wave of anti-Semitism at the College?" As he said "No," the alma mater began, to the tune of the song with the familiar refrain "*Deutschland, Deutschland über alles.*" The alma mater melody had long preceded its association with Nazi Germany, but it took Ralph aback.

College Involvement

I was on the College Faculty Research Committee in my first year and elected its chair the following year. After spending many hours deciding how best to award the funds set aside for summer research grants, I received a call from President Stern. He told me he was cutting our research budget in half and wanted me not to tell grant applicants. As chair of the committee, I felt it my duty to be honest with the applicants and faculty, and I explained to them why some deserving recipients would not be receiving grants.

The faculty appreciated what I said, but President Stern definitely did not. I didn't have to wait long to find out the extent of his displeasure. Two faculty awards were given annually, one for distinguished teaching and the other for distinguished research, and faculty committees recommended recipients to the president. When a committee recommended me for the distinguished research award, President Stern asked them for two names from which he would choose. The committee said I was the most deserving, and they recommended only me. At graduation, President Stern reluctantly presented me with the award, along with the $500 that went with it.

As it turned out, I was fortunate that the amount in 1978 was only $500, instead of the $1,000 it became a couple of years later. Academic Vice President Jack Bevan discussed faculty raises with department chairs and made recommendations to President Stern, who almost always went along. Except not in my case. Bevan told me that Stern had cut my recommended salary raise by $500 because I had received $500 for my research award (he didn't similarly cut the teaching awardee). Fortunately, Stern retired in 1978. I received tenure and promotion to full professor in 1979. My $500 research award was a one-time occurrence, but I lost that additional $500 per year for the next 30 years, along with percentage raises based on it. So my award cost me over $25,000.

Getting Political

The College of Charleston was undergoing changes in 1980, but not quickly enough for me. There was an "old guard" faculty, mostly southern gentlemen, who had been around for many years. And there were "young Turks" like me who wanted this small southern school to become more national. With encouragement from the other "Turks," I ran for Speaker of the Faculty, elected annually by the faculty. The speaker conducted faculty meetings and met with the president, staff, and Board of Trustees.

The speaker at the time of my challenge was Professor Thomas Palmer, a distinguished gentleman who took pride in the traditions of the

College and was well liked by the Board of Trustees. He didn't seem particularly interested in working for change and got along well with the president. Palmer was elected in 1978, reelected in 1979, and expected to be reelected in 1980 when I was nominated as his opponent. Campaigning had never been done and was perhaps thought to be ungentlemanly. I surprised many by circulating a campaign speech. I stated six issues I'd work on if elected and steps I'd take to achieve those goals. One was a faculty newsletter to improve communication among faculty, and between faculty and administration.

The campaign promise that received the most buzz was, "If elected, my first act will be to appoint an ad hoc committee to help me purchase a suit for meetings with the Board of Trustees and other appropriate gatherings." As at other institutions, I wore shorts and sandals daily until it got too cold. In Charleston it almost never did, so shorts and sandals became my year-round attire. I also wore T-shirts from races, my primary form of exercise. My favorite said, "I ran through Hell," from a race in Hell, Michigan.

To Palmer's surprise, I was overwhelmingly elected Speaker of the Faculty. There were three somewhat overlapping groups who supported me: the young Turks; those who appreciated my taking the time to write a campaign letter; and those who wanted to see me in a suit. I kept my campaign promises of both suit and faculty newsletter.

In the second issue of my monthly newsletter, a faculty member wrote a letter to the editor (me) saying how disappointed he was that I continued to wear T-shirts, shorts, and sandals while presiding at faculty meetings. He said the faculty deserved the same respect and dignity as the Board of Trustees. I responded, "I respect the faculty more than I do the Board of Trustees, which is why I assume the faculty will judge me on what I do and not on how I dress. As promised, I have worn my suit to Board of Trustees meetings as well as to a gathering with parents of incoming students. I didn't want those constituencies to be distracted from what I had to say because of my attire."

I added that if twenty faculty members were to sign a petition for me to preside at faculty meetings in more dignified apparel, I'd honor that request. The next newsletter contained a letter signed by considerably more than twenty faculty members, requesting that I preside at faculty meetings in my birthday suit. I managed to resist that temptation.

Now that I owned a suit, I established a suit-wearing tradition: I wore it to class once a year, on Halloween. When shocked students asked why, I told them, "I'm dressing up as a professor for Halloween." Over the years, first in the math department and later in other departments, faculty ties and jackets became a rarity. Nevertheless, my attire remained the most casual. My favorite comment in a student evaluation was, "Give this professor a big raise, so he can afford to buy some decent clothes!"

Attire aside, I addressed some important issues as Speaker of the Faculty. To save money, a state legislator proposed merging the College of Charleston and the Medical University of South Carolina (MUSC) into a comprehensive university. The College was about a mile from MUSC and both were state supported. One trustee worried that a merger could turn us into another Berkeley. This just showed the ignorance of some politically appointed board members. A merger of two mediocre institutions would not create a great institution like Berkeley. One faculty member succinctly expressed his fears about our small college merging with a large institution like MUSC: "How do you merge a goldfish with a shark?"

After a study showed that the merger would actually increase costs, the proposal was dropped. Some good did come out of discussing the pros and cons of a merger, since the College and MUSC developed a closer working relationship. Students at one institution began to get credit for taking courses at the other, and faculty at both schools started to collaborate more on research projects.

I became concerned about our public college's occasional disregard for separation of church and state, including its annual "Spiritual Enrichment Day." All presentations in the year I monitored were from a fundamentalist Christian perspective. When I asked the organizer about the imbalance, she told me that most students were Christian and the program suited their needs. Though it was supposed to be voluntary, some teachers gave extra credit for attending and others required their students to attend. I spoke with administration officials, and the following year they had more inclusive events. However, Spiritual Enrichment Day continued to upset various factions and eventually the College wisely dropped it altogether.

Then there was a problem in the Counseling Center, where one counselor's "specialty" was Christian counseling. When a student informed me that the counselor told him he could overcome his difficulties by giving his life to Jesus, I spoke to the counselor. She didn't deny the accusation. In fact, she named two students and asked if it was one of them who lodged the complaint. It wasn't. Her response was so inappropriate at so many levels that I went directly to the president of the College and told him about our exchange. The counselor was quietly let go and we haven't since hired that specialty.

College Racism and Sexism

The College of Charleston hadn't integrated until 1967, but it was trying to change its well-deserved racist reputation. I brought a resolution to the Board of Trustees, passed overwhelmingly by the faculty, to name the new College Education Center after Septima Clark.

Septima Clark was a long-time educator and nationally known civil rights activist from Charleston. President Jimmy Carter had presented her with a Living Legacy Award in 1979. Clark's autobiography, *Ready from Within: Septima Clark and the Civil Rights Movement*, won the American Book Award. I presented to the board much evidence of her accomplishments, and explained how we could improve race relations significantly by naming the building to honor her. The chairman of the board, F. Mitchell Johnson, said they would take up the faculty resolution in executive session, which meant I had to leave the room. He told me they would announce their decision the following month.

The Board decided, instead, to name the building after Thaddeus Street, a chairman of the Board of Trustees from the time when the College was still segregated. The primary argument for choosing Street over Clark was that he was a graduate of the College (as well as captain of the golf team), and she was not. The board failed to consider that Septima Clark's skin color would have prevented her from being admitted.

At least the faculty was considerably more progressive than the board, and I was hoping that future board replacements would bring about needed changes. A few years later, a room in the Thaddeus Street Education Center was named after Septima Clark.

I thought I had been productive in my year as Speaker of the Faculty,

and decided to run again. One of my political fantasies had been to require an incumbent to deliver the same campaign speech for reelection
as he or she gave for election. So I reran my original campaign speech.
I had accomplished just about all I had set out to do, and I easily won
a second term.

I had another interesting exchange with the chairman of the
Board of Trustees in my second year, and a better outcome. I was
on the search committee for the newly created position of provost,
who would be chief academic officer and the person to whom all vice
presidents report. Our committee decided on five candidates to invite
for an interview. Several of us thought the most qualified candidate
appeared to be the one woman, Jacqueline Mattfeld, former president of Barnard College. We were concerned that the Trustees would
not appoint a woman. I argued successfully to also bring in our sixth
candidate, a black man who was not as experienced as the others, but
whom I thought was well qualified for the position and could be a
fine provost.

The chairman of the Board of Trustees had breakfast with the first
five candidates, but did not have breakfast with or even meet the black
candidate. The chairman approved Jacqueline Mattfeld for the job.
Perhaps he was relieved by our recommendation of a qualified white
woman instead of a qualified black man, Herman Blake, who went
on to an illustrious academic career. In 2007 he joined the Medical
University of South Carolina, where he serves as Humanities Scholar
in Residence.

Provost Mattfeld encountered problems at the College. Some vice
presidents, all of whom were male, openly complained about their
discomfort in reporting to a woman. An alumnus and influential politician was upset that Mattfeld ordered furniture for the College from
New York, rather than from the local furniture store that the College
had been patronizing. It didn't seem to matter that Mattfeld saved
money on the out-of-state purchase. Mattfeld's stay at the college was
marked by such controversies, and she eventually left in 1983. I'm
pleased that we've since had other women provosts and administrators. So the South does change, but not always as quickly as I would
like.

I think I played a tiny role in gradually transforming the College of

Charleston from a small southern school into a more national and diverse institution. The College has hired and retained some outstanding researchers, and eventually about the same number of women and men on the math department faculty.

Jimmy Carter and Me

I spent the summer of 1988 doing research at the University of Michigan. Steve Kahn, a friend in the math department at Wayne State University in Detroit, showed me a notice for volunteers at a Habitat for Humanity project in Atlanta, where former president Jimmy Carter would participate. Fortunately it said no experience was necessary, because neither Steve nor I knew the first thing about building houses. I admired what Jimmy Carter was doing and liked the idea of working with him, so Steve and I signed up.

Quite a few of the two hundred volunteers were experienced house builders. Each of us in the project worked on one of twenty houses. After checking our skills, the leader assigned Steve and me to hammer nails. Others were amused that we had to learn to hammer without too much finger damage. When we became marginally competent, Steve and I competed over who could hammer more nails per minute.

I was pleased to see that Jimmy and Rosalynn Carter were there to work, not for photo ops, and they were good workers. Some volunteers had worked with Jimmy on other Habitat projects and treated him like any other worker. Steve and I eventually stopped gawking and we tried to pretend that Jimmy was just one of the guys.

I knew that Habitat for Humanity was a Christian organization, but I didn't know how Christian. There were prayers to Jesus before breakfast, lunch, and dinner, along with inspirational sermons. Habitat founder Millard Fuller was a tremendous and forceful speaker. After one of his sermons, he asked Jimmy Carter to say a few words. Jimmy said that Millard was a tough act to follow, and Jimmy was right. Had Carter been as inspiring and skilled at communicating as Fuller, he might have been reelected president.

I told Millard Fuller that he could attract more volunteers if his inspirational messages were more inclusive. I had talked to other Jews (all atheists) working on the project and they too were uncomfortable.

My brief career as an inept manual laborer in 1988 at a Habitat for Humanity project in Atlanta, led by former president Jimmy Carter. I am just behind Carter's right shoulder.

"After all," I said, "we're all here to build houses for poor people." I was shocked by Fuller's response: "Not me. I'm here to build houses for Jesus." He even went so far as to tell me he would stop building houses if he believed Jesus didn't care.

I preferred Jimmy Carter's brand of Christianity to Millard Fuller's. Whatever his views on Jesus, Jimmy made it clear that he was there to help give poor people the opportunity to help themselves. When Jimmy asked where I was from, and I said "Philadelphia," he told me he had worked in poverty-stricken communities around the world, but the worst one was in Philadelphia. The community he described was a few blocks from Temple University, my alma mater.

A reporter from a Jewish newspaper in Atlanta interviewed me about what it was like for a Jew to work with a Christian organization. She learned I wasn't a religious Jew, nor was she, but that didn't matter. As she was asking me a question, Jimmy Carter passed and said, "Hi Herb." The reporter stopped mid-question and said, "Wasn't that

Jimmy Carter?" It then became clear that she lost all interest in interviewing me, though she dutifully continued.

Workers for Habitat ate lunches and dinners at different black churches in the region. Our meals always included fried chicken. I thought at the time that nutrition projects, as well as housing projects, were needed. Once I walked with Jimmy into a church auditorium for dinner, and all the church members stood and applauded enthusiastically. I whispered to Jimmy, "I hope you don't mind. This happens to me wherever I go." My little joke didn't even elicit a smile from him. I still think Jimmy Carter is a wonderful human being, even though he didn't laugh at my joke.

Strangest Place on Earth

Easily the most interesting country I ever visited was Papua New Guinea (PNG). Professor O.P. Ahuja, the math department chair at the University of Papua New Guinea, invited me to be a visiting professor for one semester in 1987. We had never met, but he and I had published a couple of joint papers. Ahuja thought we could be more productive mathematically if we spent time together, and I was intrigued by the idea of visiting such an exotic place.

I flew from Charleston to Australia, with a side trip to New Zealand, before arriving in Port Moresby. I left Charleston on June 13 and landed in Australia on June 15, passing the International Date Line. (Since the lost day happened to be my birthday, perhaps I can claim to be a year younger.) Ahuja met me at the airport and commented about the nice, cool day. I thought he was kidding, but he wasn't. I arrived in the very hot PNG June winter, and left in the unbearably hot PNG December summer.

I hadn't realized the prestige that went with my position as professor. At UPNG, there can be at most one full professor per department. The department chair, an associate professor, and I were the only ones who didn't have to share an office. The best perk for me was the only air conditioned office in the department. I felt uncomfortable when other faculty addressed me as "Professor Silverman," while they called each other by their first names. With effort, I got some of the more senior faculty to call me Herb.

Over eight hundred languages are spoken in PNG, reflecting the isolation of its many tribes. Fortunately for me, English was the official university language. PNG gained its independence from Australia in 1975. Headhunting and cannibalism once occurred in many parts, but this no longer happens. About one third of the population lived in extreme poverty on less than $1.25 per day. In the late 1920s and early 1930s, Australian explorers discovered the highlands of PNG, home to roughly one million people who had never before encountered Europeans. In a video I saw of this "first contact," one PNG woman said they thought white people were gods, but changed their minds after having sex with them.

Not only were most students at UPNG the first in their families to go to college, they were the first to leave their village tribes. Part of our mission was to persuade students not to continue their ongoing tribal disputes at the university. The "payback" system in PNG condoned the use of physical harm by a family member whose relative had been harmed. A tribal member explained to me how it worked. If a member from Tribe A killed a member from Tribe B, a designated member from Tribe B could legally kill any member from Tribe A. If he killed more than one member, "payback" would again kick in. UPNG was supposed to be a payback-free zone.

Professor Ahuja helped me buy a used car when I arrived and helped me sell it for essentially the same price when I left. When I got my PNG driver's license, I learned some rather strange driving customs. If I were in a serious accident, I should *not* stop at the scene. Instead, I should drive directly to jail, where the police would protect me. The tribal "payback" system also allowed a relative of someone harmed in an accident to legally take revenge on the driver. At least PNG drivers could save on car insurance, lawyers, and court costs. Fortunately, I never had a driving accident.

I was assigned one of the largest faculty houses, which was one of the few with air conditioning. Guards were posted outside the house twenty-four hours a day. The previous tenant had done something considered worthy of payback and he immediately left the country. It wouldn't have helped to put up a "new tenant" sign because hardly any tribal members could read. I was one of the few Caucasians in Port Moresby and got stares wherever I went. Though there was quite a lot of crime, I remained safe the entire time.

Women were treated so poorly that PNG was the only country I knew where men outlived women. Village men typically resided in a house, while women and pigs (yes, pigs!) lived in a shack behind the house. Both women and pigs were sold or used for barter, the woman/pig ratio depending on the quality of both the woman and the pigs. Further, wife beating was legal and common.

Missionaries of all kinds visited Port Moresby. I could always spot Mormon missionaries from a distance. They, along with the U.S. ambassador, were the only ones I saw with ties and jackets in that hot weather. One PNG resident asked me which Christian club I belonged to. When I looked puzzled, he told me he had joined the Catholic club because they gave him free food. That was the depth of his theology and, I expect, of many converts there.

The Catholic missionaries deplored the "ungodly" sight of bare-breasted women. When I asked one why he focused more on bare breasts than on wife beating, he said they couldn't change everything and breasts were a good place to start. I attended a university beauty pageant with five participants, four bare-breasted. When I saw that the primary judge was a Catholic priest, I confidently predicted the winner to my colleagues (resisting the temptation to place huge bets). After the breast-covered woman won, my colleagues showed me an undeserved respect for my ability to judge beauty.

I'm not used to being one of the better-dressed people, which I was at UPNG. I continued to wear T-shirts, shorts, and sandals, but most students also wore T-shirts and shorts, while going barefoot.

Ahuja and I published several joint math papers, so he was pleased with my visit. He, like many faculty members there, was looking for a position elsewhere. Ahuja asked me for a letter of recommendation to teach at the Saudi Arabia School of Mines, a position that paid extremely well. Their math department recommended him for the position in 1988, but the administration rejected him. Ahuja was later told informally that he was rejected because of my letter, but not from anything I said. It was my name, which indicated to them that I was a Jew. Ironically, Ahuja didn't even know I was Jewish.

Several faculty members at UPNG asked if I could get them a position at the College of Charleston. There was one, Dinesh Sarvate, who I thought would be a good fit. The College hired him in 1988, and he continues to be an outstanding colleague.

Before Dinesh arrived in Charleston, he asked me to find housing for him and his family. His primary criterion was that it be in a location where his young daughter could attend a decent public school, not such an easy task in the Charleston area. I found an apartment in a neighborhood that had a good school, but the landlady wanted more information when I told her it was for a colleague. When she found out that Dinesh had been born in India, she asked, "How dark is he?" I became visibly annoyed and told her he was a fine mathematics colleague and a nice person with a nice family. She said she personally didn't care about skin color, but that her neighbors did, and then repeated her question. So I squirmed a bit and said, "Not too dark," resisting the temptation to give a more appropriate three-word reply.

The landlady said it would probably be OK, but she'd decide when she met him. Dinesh's family had stopped at Disney World in Florida before arriving in Charleston, and ten-year-old daughter Sawali was wearing a Mickey Mouse hat. When we got to the apartment, Dinesh told Sawali to take off her hat. I quickly said, "No! Keep it on." The landlady smiled when she saw the hat on Sawali, and told her what a lovely little girl she was. Dinesh got the apartment.

The following year I was on a sabbatical leave in California and Dinesh rented my place in Charleston. One day, I got a phone call from him and he was so excited and happy. He said, "Herb, you just won a million dollars! You have a letter from someone named Ed McMahon telling all about it." I told Dinesh, "I've got plenty of money, so you can keep my million dollars." He had a lot to learn about American culture.

Life was good in 1989, when I was forty-seven. I enjoyed my role as professor of mathematics and was making contributions in teaching, research, and service to the academic community. All my friends were in academe and I rarely communicated with people in the outside world. I thought of the question in a Gershwin song, "Who could ask for anything more?" At the same time, I couldn't quite get out of my mind the question posed in Peggy Lee's haunting song, "Is That All There Is?"

This song is both pessimistic and optimistic. It suggests there is not much to what we think are the good things, like circuses and love, or ultimately life itself. Perhaps even academe? It also suggests moving on after bad things, like a fire. The song ends on a more humanistic note, that we should keep on dancing and enjoy life while we can.

I had always been realistic about my mathematical research. I liked doing it and had a small following among those in my narrow area, but I knew my contributions to mathematics would not change our culture or even the broader field of mathematics. I know I've made a difference to some students, but not nearly as many as I had hoped. Since a year of mathematics was required for graduation at the College of Charleston, most of the mathematics courses faculty members taught were to freshmen who merely wanted to satisfy their degree requirement.

So is that all there is? Some have discovered more to life through finding God. I knew I wouldn't be one of those people. Ironically, I would soon discover more to life through not finding God. Little did I know that a casual conversation with a colleague at a faculty meeting was about to dramatically change my life.

CHAPTER 7

THE CANDIDATE WITHOUT
A PRAYER

Constitutional Problem

At a faculty meeting in the spring of 1989, I sat next to Hugh Wilder, a professor of philosophy and close friend. We are both atheists and we chatted quietly before the meeting. Hugh said, "Did you know the South Carolina Constitution prohibits atheists from becoming governor?" At first I thought he was kidding, but the next day he showed me Article 4, Section 2 from the state constitution: "No person shall be eligible for the office of governor who denies the existence of the Supreme Being." Not only were atheists ineligible, but also agnostics, Buddhists, and anyone else who didn't believe in *the* Supreme Being of South Carolina.

While I'm no constitutional scholar, I knew this violated Article 6 of the U.S. Constitution, which prohibits religious tests as qualification for any public office. I stopped by the office of Charleston attorney Edmund Robinson, since I knew he had handled some cases for the American Civil Liberties Union (ACLU). "How," I asked, "can this clearly unconstitutional provision be removed?" Robinson said, "The best way is for an open atheist to became a candidate." He added, smiling, "In fact, the very best candidate would be you—in a 1990 race for governor of South Carolina."

After giving this surprising suggestion much thought, I agreed to run. I assumed, in my political naïveté, the state attorney general would then simply consent to bring South Carolina into compliance with federal law. Edmund knew better. He told me I would have to conduct some sort of campaign so he could file a lawsuit against the state and establish in court that I was a legitimate candidate. I told him I'd soon be leaving for a year's sabbatical at the University of California at Davis, but I could return in August 1990 to campaign. Edmund said my temporary absence would not hurt my standing as long as I maintained my South Carolina residency.

I went to Davis at the end of May and told some colleagues there about my coming "campaign." One mentioned it to Elisabeth Sherwin, a reporter for the *Davis Enterprise*. Like many outside the South, she was fascinated by the Bible Belt mentality and wanted to know more. She asked if I had campaign literature, which I hadn't, and she suggested I furnish her with a platform so she could write a story about my candidacy.

Aside from merely challenging the religious test clause, I came up with issues I thought might be of interest in South Carolina. I said I supported a strong national defense, which could be achieved primarily through education and grounding students in critical thinking, not a reliance on pledges and prayers. I said that our country's strength must be maintained by killing illiteracy and innumeracy. I also described myself as being both prochoice and prolife because I supported a woman's right to choose and opposed capital punishment. I added that the most effective way to reduce the number of abortions would be to promote sex education in schools, prenatal health care, day-care programs, and other support systems for women wishing to give birth.

I said I wanted to raise South Carolina's cigarette taxes (lowest in the nation) and use the additional revenue for drug prevention programs and tobacco farmers who wished to convert their crops from life-destroying to life-enhancing products. I also said I wanted to decrease violence by legalizing all drugs, since the war on drugs was as much a failure as the war on alcohol during Prohibition. I wanted a state lottery with the proceeds going to education. Finally, I wanted to remove the Confederate flag from atop the state capitol because it has long been a symbol of intolerance and racial bigotry.

On March 13, 1990, I received my first (and only) editorial endorsement. It began, "The *Davis Enterprise* usually doesn't editorialize in favor of candidates in out-of-state elections, but in this case we'd like to make an exception." The paper printed my positions on the issues and ended, "We find it hard to disagree with Silverman's platform. We endorse this candidate for governor of the great state of South Carolina."

About a week later I got a call from Richard Winger, publisher of *Ballot Access* News in San Francisco. He helped political parties and individuals attain ballot status. He had read about my case in the *Davis Enterprise*, and told me about minor parties in South Carolina that might consider backing me. I decided the best fit would be the United Citizens Party (UCP), a black-led civil rights group formed in the 1960s and relatively inactive at the time.

I spoke with UCP leaders, but they were deeply religious and said they'd feel uncomfortable nominating an atheist. The national UCP presidential candidate in 1988 had been Lenora Fulani, who in 1990 was running against Mario Cuomo for governor of New York under the banner of the New Alliance Party. I phoned her and she became enthusiastic about the possibility of my revitalizing the floundering UCP in South Carolina with a constitutional victory. She also told me she was an atheist. When Fulani intervened on my behalf, local UCP leaders agreed to nominate me. I filled out the paperwork and became the nominee of the UCP party, placing me on the ballot.

The Associated Press picked up the story, along with *USA Today* and several other newspapers. Rush Limbaugh even mentioned my candidacy on his radio show, though not in a supportive way. I began to realize that "atheist" was a very sexy word. I assumed this would be my Andy Warhol fifteen minutes of fame.

Soon after, I got a call from a very distressed woman in Philadelphia—my mother! She read about my candidacy in the *Philadelphia Inquirer*. I had to admit this was not the best way to find out that her only child was a gubernatorial candidate, and an atheist. She worried that my candidacy would sully my reputation and hurt Jews. I had thought that the lack of publicity for my campaign would spare her such grief.

Meanwhile, a reporter asked South Carolina governor Carroll Campbell what he thought of my candidacy and constitutional challenge. Campbell said, "The South Carolina Constitution is fine just as it is because this country was founded on Godly principles." Clearly, I had a lot more support in California than in South Carolina.

I thought I might even run into some controversy in Davis when I was invited to appear on the Don Dudley radio show, along with a Catholic nun. But Sister Mary didn't fit my nun stereotype. She supported all forms of birth control and sex education, and was prochoice. She agreed with all my political positions and said she wished she could vote for me. When the show ended, the three of us went for a drink.

I was delighted to receive a call from the Unitarian Church of Charleston, inviting me to speak at its forum on May 6, 1990. I returned to Charleston a few days ahead of the talk and gave a number of interviews. I told one reporter that I knew of no acknowledged atheists in public office, but I expected there were "closet atheists" all around the country, including South Carolina.

A May 3 Associated Press story in the Charleston *Post and Courier* printed reactions from South Carolina legislators. Rep. Lenoir Sturkie called my statement "political maneuvering and a bunch of hogwash." He added that he knew of no atheists in the state legislature. Rep. Larry Martin assured citizens that more than 90 percent of the legislators were "very active in their local churches above and beyond their belief in God." Martin also offered to pray for me.

I was even called a McCarthyite on a radio show for my remark about there probably being atheists in the legislature. I had hoped to foster tolerance for other points of view, rather than generate controversy. I was beginning to identify with the opening sentence in George Orwell's wonderful 1937 essay "Shooting an Elephant": "In Moulmein, in Lower Burma, I was hated by large numbers of people—the only time in my life that I have been important enough for this to happen to me." Orwell was a conflicted officer in charge of stemming the tide of anti-European feelings even though he didn't support the imperialism his government represented. I was more perplexed than conflicted. I didn't doubt that my cause was just; I did have doubts about whether my approach was best, and even more doubts about whether I was the best spokesperson for it.

My ACLU lawyer suggested I add a couple of voters to our lawsuit because their right to vote for the candidate of their choice would be denied if I were ineligible. Voters, he said, are usually given more standing in these matters than candidates. I gave Edmund two names from the College of Charleston, but he said I should have at least one outsider. My life was so confined to academe that I couldn't think of anyone else. I told Edmund I'd look for another voter when I spoke at the Unitarian Church.

The audience at the Unitarian Church was remarkably supportive. After my talk, an enthusiastic woman, Sharon Fratepietro, came over and introduced herself. She had read about my candidacy, liked what I said at the forum, and offered to help in my campaign. When I got back to Davis, I phoned Sharon, who was a technical writer for a software company. She was well spoken and she accepted my invitation to become the second voter in my pending lawsuit. David Cohen, head of the College of Charleston Library, was the first.

Meanwhile, the South Carolina Election Commission suggested there might be "irregularities" in the way I had obtained the nomination of the United Citizens Party. On May 15, it voted 3–2 to recommend that the State Law Enforcement Division (SLED) investigate. The following day, the Charleston *Post and Courier* ran an uncomplimentary editorial about my alleged misdeeds under the headline, "Panel Wants Silverman Inquiry." Neither the election commission nor the newspaper offered me an opportunity to defend myself against any charges, although I had informed SLED of my willingness to cooperate and provide them with appropriate documentation.

After hearing nothing for eight weeks, I called SLED. They told me their investigation was nearly complete and that my input wouldn't be needed. A few days later, the election commission announced that SLED had found irregularities and I wouldn't be allowed on the ballot. It turned out that SLED investigators had badgered Reverend Fred Dawson, head of the United Citizens Party, about his support for an atheist. Eventually, Dawson said he hadn't understood the document he signed that gave me the party nomination. I had witnesses who could have proved otherwise. My ACLU lawyer said I had a legitimate grievance, but that my case would not be jeopardized if I campaigned as a write-in candidate.

My Campaign Groupie

I was in California while all this was going on, but in phone contact with Sharon Fratepietro, the second voter in my lawsuit. She offered to get bumper stickers that could further establish my legitimacy: silver and red, to associate with my name and the devil. I liked her sense of humor. At first we spoke only about the campaign, but gradually conversations became personal. We exchanged long letters (real letters, since e-mail was not yet common.) I began to like Sharon more and more. It would be ironic, I fantasized, to have as a girlfriend someone I had met in church. I looked forward to spending time with Sharon when I returned to Charleston in late August.

On July 24, 1990, I flew to Madras (now Chennai), India, to speak at a math conference and several universities around the country. After that, I planned to give talks in Israel. Since India didn't have diplomatic relations with Israel at the time, I couldn't fly there directly. So I was scheduled to fly from India to Kuwait and then to Egypt, where I would spend a couple of days with a math colleague before flying to Israel.

As I waited at the New Delhi airport for my morning flight to Kuwait on August 2, news broke that Iraq had invaded Kuwait and its airport was closed. After many hours in the Delhi airport, I was rerouted to Dubai, a place I'd never heard of. After many more hours in the Dubai airport, I finally got to Egypt the following morning. My patient colleague, Muhammad, picked me up and took me to his home. When we arrived, his wife and her mother ran from the room because their faces were uncovered.

Muhammad was reasonably secular, but his wife was not. When he suggested we go sightseeing, I asked if his wife would join us. Muhammad feared that someone might throw rocks at her if she were seen with two men. (And Egypt was known to be one of the more secular Middle Eastern countries). Had my (nonexistent) wife been with me, it would have been acceptable.

When I finally got to Israel, I met with math colleagues and gave talks at the University of Haifa and Bar-Ilan University. I then took a few days to sightsee. My most memorable experience was at the Jordan River, where John the Baptist allegedly baptized Jesus. A young man approached me and asked if I'd be willing to baptize him. He said he chose me because I looked so spiritual and I reminded him of Jesus. So this atheist made a young man happy by going through baptismal motions. I wished him well and told him to go in peace. For a brief period, I became "Herb the Baptist." I've been told before that I look like Jesus because of my beard and sandals. A friend even gave me a WWJW button (What Would Jesus Wear?).

When I returned to Charleston, I visited Sharon and our relationship quickly grew beyond friendship. This added an extra dimension to the campaign. Neither of us was married, so there was no risk of political scandal. In an irrational moment, Sharon said, "I hope you won't be too disappointed if you lose the election." I laughed, and said, " I'll only be disappointed if our relationship doesn't last a lot longer than my candidacy." Regardless of what would happen on Election Day, Sharon and I were having a great time campaigning, and were beginning to think of staying together forever. I had never thought about anyone that way before.

Back to Teaching

I didn't talk about the campaign in my math classes, but I invited students who asked about it to see me afterward. Students who spoke with me were supportive; those who communicated anonymously were not. I found notes pinned to my office door calling me the Antichrist, a Satanist, and an "atheist shithead." Most of the letters I received were neither profane nor profound. They contained Bible verses like, "I am the Way, the Truth, and the Light." I wondered if such writers expected me to slap my forehead and say to myself, "Gee, I never knew that. Now I'm a believer."

The media often referred to me with what they viewed as an appropriate adjective, like "self-described atheist," or "so-called atheist," and even "admitted atheist." I wondered how other candidates would react if they were described as "so-called Methodists" or "admitted Baptists." On radio shows, Christian conservative callers often asked if I worshipped Satan, since "I had to believe in something." However, the oddest comments came from those who thought my not believing in a judging God meant I must feel free to rape, murder, and commit any atrocity I can get away with. I'd respond, "With an attitude like that, I hope you continue to believe in God." I was beginning to think that changing hearts and minds of some of my fellow South Carolinians was more important than changing the South Carolina Constitution.

I expected the courts to eventually do the right thing; I wasn't as confident about those who held unquestioned, Bible-based beliefs.

As a math professor, I had been more used to talking to students than to the media and the public. But after several talk show interviews and reactions by callers, I got to know the kinds of questions people would ask. Here is a sample, along with my answers.

Q: What do you think are your chances of winning the election?

A: I'm an atheist, not a fool. (Since I wasn't going to win, I felt free to be honest.)

Q: What would be the first thing you would do if elected?

A: Demand a recount! (I had been asked many times why atheists were so angry. I wanted to show we could have a sense of humor.)

Q: What would make you believe in God?

A: Perhaps if I won the election. It would take that kind of miracle.

Q: What will happen to you when you die?

A: I know exactly what will happen. I'm going to medical school, just like my Jewish mother always wanted me to do. I want to use my body parts to their fullest while I'm alive, but I hope others will be able to make good use of them when I die.

Q: If the law were changed, do you think an atheist would be elected in South Carolina?

A: No. But fifty years ago, no woman or African American could get elected. Fortunately that has changed, and I'm hoping for the day when we will judge candidates on their positions and integrity, not on their professed religious beliefs.

Q: When was belief in the Supreme Being made a requirement?

A: At the Constitutional Convention of 1868. According to transcripts, one delegate worried that a candidate might just pretend to believe in order to hold public office. Another delegate responded, "This law is intended for a man so depraved as to come out boldly and deny a belief in the Supreme Being. Such a man has lost his reason and is unfit for any office." The head of the Election Commission said essentially the same thing about me when he indicated I wouldn't have been questioned about my religious beliefs had I kept quiet about them. In other words, I should have lied and deliberately violated our state constitution. We have enough ethical problems with our political leaders without formally sanctioning such hypocrisy. I think some of our politicians would profess belief in the Tooth Fairy if they thought it would help them get elected.

Q: Why are you wasting so much time on something so frivolous?

A: I find it appalling to be ineligible for an office because of my lack of religious beliefs. And to challenge a law that gives credibility to such religious intolerance and bigotry is not frivolous.

Gubernatorial Debates

I was invited to participate in a "Meet the Candidates" night in Spartanburg in the northwest part of the state, near fundamentalist Bob Jones University. Sharon and I made the four-hour drive from Charleston, excited about my first opportunity to meet candidates for many other state offices.

Each candidate had three minutes to speak. I learned a lot about southern politics that evening. One candidate told his wife and children to stand while he spoke, I assume to show good family values. A spokesperson for a woman congressional candidate assured the audience that she shopped at the local supermarket, "just like you." I'm not sure what her political opponent did for groceries. Another candidate accused his opponent of attending the wrong church—that is, a church outside his district.

The gubernatorial candidates spoke last. Theo Mitchell, the Democrat, was an attorney serving in the state Senate. John Peeples represented the American Party, the old George Wallace Party. John was living in an abandoned airplane in the woods near the Charleston airport. Incumbent Republican governor Carroll Campbell was expecting an easy victory, so he didn't bother to show up.

Mitchell spoke first, blasting Campbell for being absent. Peeples next railed against "violent nationalism," and warned that raising taxes was a conspiracy similar to what the Nazis did by feeding people rutabagas and potatoes instead of meat. He closed by condemning the government for confiscating comic books from someone named Joey Rorie. Sharon and I didn't dare look at each other for fear we would break out laughing. I spoke last, about why it was unconstitutional and undemocratic to require a religious test for public office. It was obvious that the three of us gubernatorial candidates were operating on different wavelengths. John Peeples sounded like he was from a different planet.

After the speeches, the audience had an opportunity to talk to the candidates over refreshments. They kept their distance from Sharon and me until almost everyone had left. A man then hurried over and whispered that he was a high school principal, and that he wanted to let me know how brave I was to say what I did. Before I had a chance to reply, he rushed away. Following that reception in the upstate, Sharon and I were happy to return to "liberal" Charleston.

Several people offered me campaign contributions. I refused to accept any and told them to donate instead to causes they wanted me to work on if elected. One student jokingly handed in his math exam and asked if he could contribute to my campaign. I laughed, and pointed out to others that campaign contributions are generally not quite so blatant, but tit for tat is often expected.

My day in court came on October 5, about a month before the election. Presiding judge David Norton had recently been appointed to the U.S. District Court on recommendation by U.S. senator Strom Thurmond. My attorney argued against the state's three lawyers and was not optimistic of victory, even though privately the state's lawyers acknowledged we were legally correct. It was discouraging to hear that the law isn't always the primary criterion in deciding cases.

My gubernatorial candidate costume in 1990,
which I still wear on special occasions

As Election Day approached, I prepared for a live, one-hour gubernatorial candidates' debate on South Carolina public television. The
debate occurred on November 6, with all four gubernatorial candidates
invited. As usual, Governor Campbell declined. Theo Mitchell, John
Peeples, and I were again on different wavelengths. We agreed on one
topic—that Campbell should have been there. At least I assume this
was Peeple's reason for calling Campbell "a yellow dog political party
animal."

Senator Mitchell closed with, "May God bless each and every one
of you." I followed and remarked, "I don't think God will bless me." I
ended with a quote from Eugene V. Debs, "It is better to vote for what
you want and not get it, than to vote for what you don't want and get
it."

Overall, I was satisfied with my performance. My friends thought I had won, but I expect friends of the other candidates thought they had won. A year later, there was one objective measure for determining the winner. Of the three candidates in the debate, I was the *only* one not in prison. John Peeples, the American Party candidate, was in prison for driving without a license and refusing to get one. He was a militia type who opposed any government requirements. Theo Mitchell, the Democratic candidate, was in prison for more traditional reasons—tax evasion.

A few days before the election, Judge Norton dismissed my case on the grounds that it was not ripe, meaning it would be premature for him to rule on the merits of the case unless I won the election. To the surprise of no one, I lost.

Notary Public

So with politics now in my blood, where could I go from there? I decided to try and fulfill my lifelong dream of becoming a notary public. Actually, I discovered that South Carolina's Constitution prohibited atheists from holding *any* public office. My lawyer told me I could challenge this by applying for a notary commission. The U.S. Supreme Court in *Torcaso v. Watkins* had struck down an identical provision of the Maryland Constitution in 1961. If South Carolina were to grant me a notary public license, it would be an admission by the state that religious tests could no longer be a qualification for public office.

My attorney expected this notary campaign to be successful and shorter than my gubernatorial campaign. Shorter, it was not! South Carolina is normally one of the easiest states in which to become a notary. The governor's office routinely approves all applications. So I paid my $25 fee in October 1991, but crossed out "so help me God" on the application. I also wrote on the form that the U.S. Constitution prohibits religious tests as a qualification for public office.

South Carolina secretary of state Jim Miles returned my application on the grounds I had not filled it out properly. My lawyer then sent it directly to Governor Campbell, who rejected it. When we asked why, the governor's spokesperson replied it would be too burdensome to give reasons for every negative decision. In a deposition taken from Secretary of State Miles in 1994, he was forced to disclose that 33,471 notary applications were approved from 1991 to 1993 and that mine was the only one denied. To my knowledge, I am the only person in the history of South Carolina to be rejected as a notary public.

Governor Campbell completed his final term in office in January 1975, still claiming immunity from having to give a deposition where he might be compelled to state under oath the reason for denying me the notary commission. Then we got help from a most unlikely source. My ACLU lawyer argued successfully in circuit court that if the lawyers for Paula Corbin Jones (whose case led to the Monica Lewinsky case) could depose President Bill Clinton, then former governor Campbell could no longer avoid being deposed. My lawyer took a deposition of eighty-six pages from Governor Campbell on March 3, 1995. Among Campbell's many convoluted responses, here is what he said about why it might be permissible to deny office based on religious beliefs: "Would it be right to have somebody running for public office that was avowed to overthrow and destroy the United States of America, and they didn't believe in a supreme being but they believed in a foreign government, and they call that a religion?"

Shortly after the deposition, my case took an ironic twist. My lawyer, Edmund Robinson, quit my case. In fact, he quit his entire law practice—to enter the seminary. It wasn't what the Religious Right had been praying for. Edmund hadn't become a born-again Christian. He'd long been active in the Unitarian Church and decided to go to Harvard Divinity School. He's now a Unitarian minister in Massachusetts. Armand Derfner, another Charleston lawyer who had worked with the ACLU, took over my case.

On August 2, 1995, the presiding judge of the Fifth Judicial Circuit in the Court of Common Pleas said my petition to be a notary met all the legal requirements. He told the governor to act on my application within thirty days. By that time Governor David Beasley, elected in 1994 with strong Christian Coalition support, had succeeded Governor Campbell. A born-again Christian, Beasley hoped to see creationism taught in public schools.

Secretary of State Miles urged state officials to appeal the Circuit Court decision because he did not think the South Carolina constitutional provision that prohibited atheists from holding public office was religious discrimination. He said, "I believe that language is appropriate because I'm a Christian." Unwilling to go quietly, even after losing a judicial reconsideration appeal, Governor Beasley then appealed to the South Carolina Supreme Court.

An October 31, 1995, headline in the Charleston *Post and Courier* read, "Gov. David Beasley wants the S.C. Supreme Court to decide if office seekers should be forced to believe in a Supreme Being." I responded that I understood how I could be forced to *say* I believe (torture would work!), but Governor Beasley did not clarify how I could actually be forced to believe. My point was that it's proper for government to regulate some behavior, but it's neither proper nor possible to regulate belief. In an interview, I couldn't resist pointing out, "The state considers me qualified to be a professor of mathematics at a public institution, but says I lack the ethical and moral standards to become a notary public. Perhaps the value placed on religious indoctrination over reason and scientific inquiry might help explain the dismal condition of education in South Carolina today, where SAT scores have been among the lowest in the nation for many years."

The South Carolina Supreme Court heard my case in October 1996. A reporter asked me why I thought Governor Beasley was appealing to the Supreme Court. I said, "Governor Beasley must know religious tests for public office are unconstitutional. By trying to exclude nonbelievers, I think he's simply playing to the religious bigotry of a segment of his constituency."

In the same article, Gary Karr, the governor's press secretary, responded that he "denies in the strongest terms that Governor Beasley is a religious bigot and thinks it is a shame that Dr. Silverman would attack the governor's religious beliefs like that." You would think I was trying to prevent Christians from holding public office.

Good news came on May 27, 1997. The Supreme Court unanimously affirmed the circuit court's holding that the South Carolina Constitution violated the First Amendment and the "no religious test" clause of the United States Constitution. This ruling meant that atheists could legally hold any public office in South Carolina, including governor. Nevertheless, Governor Beasley still had a tough call. He didn't want to be the first governor of South Carolina to grant a notary

With Charleston ACLU attorneys Edmund Robinson and Armand Derfner,
celebrating our notary public victory in 1997

commission to an open atheist. On the other hand, he was reluctant to appeal to the U.S. Supreme Court for a couple of reasons. His lawyers had concentrated on the states' rights argument that state officials had sworn to uphold the state constitution without regard to previous U.S. Supreme Court decisions. How could they then ask the federal government to interfere with the unanimous decision of the highest court in the sovereign state of South Carolina?

In addition, the state had recently squandered a substantial amount of taxpayer dollars attempting to keep women out of The Citadel, the state military college. Charleston County had also wasted money in another legal case when they unconstitutionally posted the Ten Commandments in council chambers. And close to $100,000 had already been spent trying to prevent me from becoming a notary public. Officials didn't want to be criticized for wasting even more taxpayer dollars on what would obviously be another fruitless appeal. Finally, on August 8, 1997, Governor Beasley granted me a notary commission.

Receiving my official notary certificate from the Charleston County clerk in 1997

Sharon and I went with great jubilation to the county clerk's office to pick up my notary commission. Sharon took photos of the clerk handing me the license, and then of me raising it over my head in triumph. Now I don't know your definition of a "loser," but the people in the county clerk's office, who knew nothing about my case, must have been having a good laugh about a guy whose high point in life seemed to be getting a notary public license.

Although the Religious Right was ultimately unsuccessful, my case indicated the influence it can exert over politicians. None of the political leaders in South Carolina, and certainly not the lawyers advising them, believed they could prevail legally if I continued to pursue my case. Yet those same politicians demonstrated they would prefer to waste time and money on a lost cause rather than risk the wrath and lose votes of the well-organized Religious Right.

Shortly after becoming a notary public, one of my mathematics students, unfamiliar with my case, saw the notary sign prominently displayed in my office, and asked if I'd gone to law school to become a notary. I told him, "It wasn't quite that simple. Law school would have taken only three years. It took longer for me to receive my notary commission than my PhD in mathematics." Of course, my right to become a notary should not have taken seven years or happened the way it did, but in many ways it was well worth the wait.

Love and Marriage

By far the best outcome of my eight-year political saga was finding Sharon. My cultural and social life had been wrapped around the wonderfully insulated world of academe, and I previously would have rejected Sharon based on her vita alone. She had only a bachelor's degree from Chestnut Hill College, a mediocre Catholic school, and was divorced with three adult children. I used to think a good vita was necessary, but not sufficient, for a good relationship. I've been wrong about many things in my life, but none more than this.

I met Sharon at just the right time with just the right cause. I might have been looking to do something else with my life and Sharon became the catalyst. I began to appreciate my mother's old refrain about me, "You may be smart in book learning, but you don't have an once of common sense." Sharon has more common sense than anyone I know, and I just about always seek her opinion. She's also smarter than I am in "book learning," which doesn't require lots of degrees.

After a year had passed, since we were seeing so much of each other, Sharon brought up the idea of living together. I like to move slowly, so I suggested a plan. The first month we would spend one night a week together, the next month two nights, etc. After seven months, maybe we would decide to live together. Sharon wanted a quicker decision. During my December break from teaching in 1990, I suggested to Sharon that she stay at my place for a few days. She did and never left, and I didn't want her to leave. Sometimes important decisions are made by default.

After living together for ten years, Sharon felt we were getting too old to be boyfriend and girlfriend, and suggested that we get married. I didn't like the idea, so it required discussion. Here were my best arguments against marriage: If it ain't broke, don't fix it; we should be together because we want to be, not because we have to be; marriage is a religious tradition, and I enjoy telling people that we're living in sin;

we support gay marriage, so we should boycott heterosexual marriage until gays can marry.

Sharon didn't counter my arguments, but they didn't convince her either. She added, "We shouldn't get married if you are really that opposed to it." I couldn't tell if she was being nice or clever. We often based decisions on whether one of us wanted something more than the other didn't. Since Sharon wanted us to get married more than I didn't, we decided to go ahead and do it.

But who to perform the wedding ceremony? South Carolina is one of three states where notary publics can marry people. In fact, I've performed twelve nonreligious weddings as a notary public or a Humanist Celebrant. What's statistically surprising is that none has ended in divorce.

Our friend, Jack Parson, became a notary public so he could perform our ceremony. An atheist himself, he thanked me for paving the way in court to his notarydom. The wedding took place at the home in which Sharon and I had been living in sin for ten years. In the presence of friends, we got married at one minute after midnight on January 1, 2000, an easy date for me to remember our millennial anniversary. Sharon wanted me to dress more formally than usual, so she got me a tuxedo T-shirt. Each of us spoke unrehearsed words at the ceremony. I thanked God for his nonexistence, without which I never would have met Sharon. We enjoyed our Ben and Jerry's ice cream wedding cake, after which we went cross-country skiing for our honeymoon at Lone Mountain Ranch in Big Sky, Montana, where we had been going every January, wedding or not.

On January 1, 2001, Sharon surprised me with a wonderful first anniversary present. She had saved the letters I wrote to her between our first brief meeting at the Unitarian Church in May 1990 and my return to Charleston in August. We read them together, and enjoyed reliving the development of our relationship through real letters. I was sorry I hadn't saved Sharon's letters, but I remembered a lot of what she wrote and could fill in the blanks based on my responses to hers. Sharon recognized that I hadn't overpromised what I was like. In one letter, I said, "Don't get the wrong impression from having seen me in a tie and jacket when I spoke at the Unitarian Church. You'll hardly ever see me dressed that way again." And she hardly ever has.

Sharon Fratepietro and I at our home wedding
at 12:01 a.m., 2000

That long-ago summer it had been obvious to both of us that we were falling in love through letters and long-distance phone calls. Our only physical contact had been a brief handshake at the Unitarian Church. I've never been called a sexual prude, but I don't think Sharon and I would have established the kind of intimate relationship we now have if I had stayed in Charleston and let nature take its course. We had the time to establish a genuine friendship before we became lovers.

My first-year anniversary present to Sharon was to tell her, "You know, being married isn't as bad as I thought it would be." She laughed and responded, "That's the most romantic thing you ever said to me." And it probably was.

Before I met Sharon, I could make the same claim as Woody Allen's character in Manhattan, that I hadn't had a relationship with a woman that lasted longer than the one between Adolph Hitler and Eva Braun. Though I don't believe in souls, I'm comfortable saying Sharon has been my soul mate (and my first love) for the past twenty-plus years.

CHAPTER 8

LOCAL SECULAR ACTIVISM

Graduation Day

The College of Charleston, a state institution, regularly began its graduation ceremonies with a prayer. I submitted a petition in 1990 to College president Harry Lightsey, signed by fifty faculty members objecting to the tradition. He agreed to end the practice for the 1990 graduation, but when the media heard about it, the College received many angry letters. Lightsey then reversed himself. What action could I take next? At the graduation, I sat with the other two hundred faculty members dressed in traditional academic garb. Most faculty bowed their heads during the prayer, but I held up an "Atheist on Board" sign, similar to the familiar "Baby on Board" signs. It was a bold yellow protest raised high above a flat black sea of academic caps.

This, to me, was the perfect dissent. Those with heads bowed would not be inconvenienced, but others would silently applaud. That evening, all three local networks began TV coverage of the graduation with a shot of my sign, which I continued to use at College ceremonies. (I've made friends at meetings that begin with a prayer. I look around while most heads are bowed, and invariably catch the eye of other non-prayers.)

The College hired a new president in 1993. Alex Sanders had been a member of the state legislature and chief judge of the South Carolina Court of Appeals. A newspaper article quoted me as being disappointed that we hadn't chosen a president with a stronger academic background. Ever the politician, Sanders then invited Sharon and me to have dinner with him and his wife Zoe. Alex was charming, but it was obvious we were both trying to win each other over. I suggested academic changes and discontinuance of prayer at graduation. Sanders understood the issue and said he would do the correct thing. There was no prayer at the next or future graduations, but Alex would start the ceremony in a way he knew would tweak me a bit. He'd typically begin his address, "As our thirteenth president Harrison Randolph once prayed, 'It's a great day for a graduation.'"

Now that's a prayer I can live with.

Secular Humanists of the Lowcountry

Whenever I received media attention during my "campaigns" for governor and notary public, I got unsigned hate mail and anonymous phone calls. But I also received letters and calls of support and appreciation. Many had thought they were the only atheists in South Carolina, and most were closeted for fear of social and family disapproval. These isolated atheists needed a supportive community, so with my list of local names I suggested meeting to see if there was interest in organizing a nontheistic group. And so in 1994 we formed the Secular Humanists of the Lowcountry (SHL) with a dozen founding members. About the name: Charleston and its surrounding communities are at sea level, which is why the region is called the Lowcountry. And some SHL members liked to be identified as "atheists," while others preferred "humanists" because of the negative public perception of atheists.

An atheist is without a belief in any gods, while a secular humanist is a nonbeliever who strives to be good without god. These are two sides of the same coin. Atheism describes what we don't believe, while humanism describes what we do believe. Today there are increasing numbers of local secular groups around the country. We all have similar principles and values, sometimes written on paper, but not commandments written on stone. We wanted a close-knit community, where we would have opportunities to make our views and activities known to the wider culture.

Because the SHL at the time it was founded was so unusual in the Bible Belt, we received considerable media attention. Eric Frazier, religion writer for the Charleston *Post and Courier*, interviewed me for an article in 1994 about whether atheists celebrate Thanksgiving, a holiday when Americans thank God for their blessings. I told him that we gather with friends and family, just like most Americans, and know whom to thank for our Thanksgiving meal. We thank the farmers who cared for the plants and the migrant workers who harvested them. We thank the workers at the processing plant and the truck drivers who brought the food to the grocery store. And finally, we thank our friends for helping prepare the meal and for being present to share in the festivities.

The newspaper got some angry letters about our members not thanking God, but several secular humanists heard about us for the first time and joined SHL. That would become a pattern for us. Whenever we received media attention, we'd hear from people who disliked us and people who joined us. It was easily worth the trade-off.

Another opportunity arose when one of my math students, James Christian, spoke to me after class. He was a member of First Baptist Church, the oldest Southern Baptist church in the South, and had seen an article about the SHL. James said both Southern Baptists and secular humanists probably had unfair stereotypes of each other, and it might be a good idea to get together for discussions. I heartily agreed, and we arranged for several in each group to meet for brunch at a local deli. One of the participants, Dr. Mitch Carnell, was a Sunday school teacher at First Baptist and also wrote a weekly column for the Charleston *Post and Courier*.

The title of Mitch's piece on September 25, 1995, was "Good Conversation Is Lurking If You Look." He wrote, "We were meeting to discuss religious beliefs or the lack of them. We knew in advance that we not only disagreed with each other, but that our views were directly opposite of each other's. Yet, by all accounts, the event was a rousing success. People not only enjoyed it, but also wanted to continue the discussions. Why? There was mutual respect for the individual."

And that was the key. Both groups chose representatives who knew how to disagree without being disagreeable. We continued to meet periodically, and even gave a name to our group: BASH. The acronym stood for Baptists And Secular Humanists, not the tenor of our meetings.

An article about BASH appeared in the December 3, 1995, Charleston *Post and Courier*. In it, First Baptist Pastor Lamar King referred to the intolerance of some in the Religious Right, and wanted to prove to us that Southern Baptists can be reasonable. They did prove their case. However, shortly thereafter, Lamar King lost his job. Though BASH was not the stated cause, it appeared there weren't enough like-minded Southern Baptists at his church. When theists and nontheists get together, I think there is generally more of an upside for nontheists. We know more about them than they know about us, and none of our people feel threatened when we talk to their people.

Membership in SHL continued to grow and our activities expanded. We had monthly newsletters, speakers, and book club meetings. We had community service projects and took political action when state and local governments illegally promoted religion. We also had potluck dinners and enjoyed socializing with one another. Members were free to partake in as many or few activities as time and comfort level permitted. We tried to create a "big tent," with room for all as long as we treated one another with respect. Some of our members have shirts with my favorite pun, "Secular Humanists of the Lowcountry: A Non-Prophet Organization."

The Charleston *Post and Courier* printed a long "High Profile" feature weekly about distinguished and beloved people in the community. Reporter Sybil Fix decided to break the mold and write a profile about me, which appeared on November 7, 1998. Sybil later told me that the newspaper received more hate mail about this piece than for any other article in its history. Some cancelled subscriptions in protest. The week after the piece appeared, the "Letters to the Editor" section devoted a full page to complaints, with the subheading, "Silverman Profile Riles Readers."

Here are some of the things that riled readers. The profile usually included a standard boxed question that asked, "What guests would you like most to have at a fantasy dinner?" I took the word "fantasy" literally and said, "God, Santa Claus, and the Easter Bunny." Many letters claimed I was making fun of Jesus, whom I did not name and who had probably existed, unlike the other three. Bob Mignone, a math colleague, good friend, and fellow atheist was quoted in the article as saying he had appointed me the spiritual advisor to his children, who were two and five, and that every time I saw them I said, "There is no God." Perhaps my "spiritual advice" worked, since they are both atheists today. Though I don't think I deserve the credit, readers were especially upset that I was pushing helpless little children toward hell.

The High Profile piece began with a comment related to the College of Charleston's purchase of an abandoned Catholic school building.

College of Charleston President Alex Sanders recently got a humorous letter asking that the "plus sign" atop the old Bishop England High School be removed. The letter was vintage Herb Silverman, Sanders knew. And while he agreed the cross couldn't stand atop a secular building, he wasn't going to take it down without making a joke or two about Charleston's most famous atheist. "I said, I will just assign the building to Herb Silverman as his office," Sanders jokes. "With the cross at the top and Herb Silverman at the bottom, I thought that would be an equalizing force. I wrote him back, and told him that if he kept quiet about the cross, no one would be nailed to it."

President Sanders and I had exchanged private e-mails about the matter. Neither of us had been offended by the humor, which he chose to make public. However, there was much community outrage about my referring to the cross as a "plus sign." Indignant writers fumed about how I offended Christians. Nobody took offense (myself included) to Sanders' allusion that I might get nailed to the cross for my behavior.

President Sanders frequently put his humor on public display. He sometimes showed me his written responses to phone calls or letters asking that I be fired. Here's what Sanders wrote to a Christian who told him to fire me or repent for allowing me to teach at the College: "I repent for a lot of things, but Professor Silverman is not one of them. He is a fine professor of mathematics. His personal beliefs, or lack thereof, have nothing to do with his teaching ability. Even if his views did carry over into the classroom, no harm would come of it. The Gospel of our Lord Jesus Christ does not need my protection or yours from Herb Silverman. To suggest that it does is the ultimate blasphemy. Fearing the Lord, as I do, I would not dare suggest any such thing. Why don't we instead pray for Herb? After all, God loves him just as he loves you and me."

Dave Munday, a new religion writer for the *Post and Courier*, wrote a full-page story on February 24, 2002, about how atheists say morality and good works guide their lives, and that we don't need a belief in God to be moral. There were photos of several SHL members picking

My car and I trust reason to get us where
we need to drive.

up trash along a highway, and the article mentioned other good works some of our members did. Whether or not people joined SHL, we wanted to change some hearts and minds of our fellow South Carolinians about how people can be good without god.

Reason and God

When the Secular Humanists of the Lowcountry learned in 2003 that South Carolina offered license plates at no extra charge with the motto "In God We Trust," we looked into challenging it as an unconstitutional government endorsement of religion. An attorney advised us we couldn't win, since that is now our national motto. So one of our members, Bill Dusenberry, suggested we request tags from the Department of Motor Vehicles with the motto "In Reason We Trust." Other organizations and schools had special tags, for which a fee was imposed. We paid the extra fee and our tags were finally approved. Had we been turned down, we were ready to publicize that South Carolina promotes God, but opposes reason.

Atheist Student Group

A student named Kate Martin came to my office in 1998 and asked about starting a group at the College of Charleston similar to the Secular Humanists of the Lowcountry. I was thrilled and agreed to be its faculty advisor. Despite attempts by a few Christian students in the Student Council to oppose giving official club status to the Atheist/Humanist Alliance, the new AHA prevailed. When the group first met, several students talked about friends or roommates who now shunned them because of their nonbelief. These atheist students came to meetings because they needed a supportive community. Gradually attitudes at the College of Charleston have changed and now students worry far less about becoming unpopular because of openly being atheists. I've heard students in 2011 say they joined the club because atheist students are pretty cool. They are, but they were also cool in 1998. I'm encouraged by the younger generation's wider acceptance of the diversity in our society.

Working in a Coalition

In 2001, SHL joined the South Carolina Progressive Network, which formed to counter an increasingly conservative state government and social climate. The Progressive Network contained more than fifty state organizations, including groups like Charleston Peace, the National Association for the Advancement of Colored People (NAACP), Planned Parenthood, Alliance for Full Acceptance, Alliance for Fair Employment, Environmentalists, Inc., S.C. Hispanic Outreach, S.C. AFL-CIO, and South Carolinians for Abolishing the Death Penalty. We didn't agree on all issues, but we were all outside mainstream South Carolina and usually opposed by the Religious Right. We understood that people are more likely to listen to a network than to one lone group.

Here's an example. In 2003, the Progressive Network sponsored a "Meet the Candidates" forum prior to a Charleston City Council election, and each group submitted a question for the candidates. Our question was this: "As you know, City Council starts meetings with a prayer. Since you will represent all your constituents, not just religious believers, will you consider periodically allowing nonbelievers to give the invocation?"

Two candidates indicated they would, and both were elected. One took me to lunch, and told me his religious views were similar to mine but that he didn't want to take the political risk of inviting me to give an invocation. I respected him for his honesty, if not his courage. The other, an African-American who told me he was religious, also invited me to lunch. He wanted my assurance that I wouldn't make fun of religion. He then asked what I thought about reparations for descendants of slaves, which I knew he favored. I told him I thought the government should help people in need, but that I didn't favor reparations. To my surprise, he smiled, gave me a high five, and said: "I like you. You're not just one of those knee-jerk liberals who agree with everything I say."

Councilman Kwadjo Campbell then invited me to give the council invocation on March 25, 2003. I felt this would be an opportunity for atheists to gain some community respect, so I carefully prepared and delivered the following inclusive invocation:

Thank you for this opportunity to invoke a minority point of view. Each of us is a minority in some way. It might be race, religion, sexual orientation, nationality, or any other aspect in which we may be regarded as different. Each of us is also part of some majority. It is when we wear our majority hats that we need to be most mindful of how we treat others. We must pledge our best efforts to help one another, and to defend the rights of all of our citizens and residents.

What divides us is not so much our religious differences in this diverse country, but the degree of commitment we have to equal freedom of conscience for all people. We are gathered today, both religious and secular members of our community, with the shared belief that we must treat our fellow human beings with respect and dignity.

In this invocation, I don't ask you to close your eyes, but to keep your eyes constantly open to the serious problems that city government can solve or improve. I don't ask you to bow your heads, but to look up at what you can accomplish by applying your considerable talents and experience to the issues that confront us.

As you work together on behalf of all who live in this city, may you draw strength and sustenance from one another through reason and compassion. I'd like to close in a bipartisan manner by quoting from two presidents I greatly admire —one a Republican and the other a Democrat.

First, the Republican: "When I do good, I feel good; when I do bad, I feel bad. That is my religion." Abraham Lincoln.

And now, the Democrat: "It's remarkable how much you can accomplish if you don't care who gets the credit." Harry S. Truman.

Nobody who heard my invocation was offended by it. However, when Mayor Joseph P. Riley stood to introduce me before a large crowd, half the council members (seated on the stage at the front of the room) walked out and did not return until I had finished the invocation, just before all recited the Pledge of Allegiance. As the protesting council members said the Pledge, they turned toward me and bellowed the words "under God."

Sharon and I remained at the meeting for about half an hour. As we went to the car, she said the surprise walkout had taken her breath away. I too felt shocked. Just as I thought we were beginning to gain some respect in our community, this had happened. But then I saw how I might be able to turn these lemons into lemonade. The following day I phoned a reporter from the Charleston *Post and Courier*. I told him which council members had walked out and suggested that his readers and I would like to know why. The reporter followed up immediately, and here's how the council members justified their action in an article he wrote for the paper.

Councilman Jimmy Gallant: "The fool says in his heart, there is no God."

Councilman Wendell Gilliard: "An atheist giving an invocation is an affront to our troops, who are fighting for our principles, based on God."

Councilman Robert George: "He can worship a chicken if he wants to, but I'm not going to be around when he does it."

To this last, the reporter printed my response, "Perhaps Councilman George doesn't realize that many of us who stand politely for religious invocations believe that praying to a god makes no more sense than praying to a chicken. At least you can see a chicken."

Several days later, six favorable letters, some from Christians, appeared in the Charleston *Post and Courier*. It was extraordinary to see Christians side with atheists in South Carolina, against other Christians. And there was this letter from Dot Scott, president of the Charleston branch of the NAACP:

> I read with disbelief the actions of our councilmen who walked out of an official meeting during the invocation by Herb Silverman simply because of his religious views. It is most difficult for me, a Christian African-American female, who has probably experienced every kind of prejudice and intolerance imaginable, to understand an act that was not only disrespectful, but also unquestionably rude by folks elected to represent all of the citizens, regardless of race, creed, color, religion or sexual orientation. It is most regrettable that during a time when the fight is so fierce to have all citizens' rights protected and respected, some of us would neglect to do the same for others. When any elected official demonstrates such lack of tolerance, especially while performing his official duties, those of us of conscience must speak out and voice our outrage.

(Four years later, Dot Scott was a guest at a dinner party Sharon and I had. We exchanged stories about how the Religious Right treats our respective constituencies, though clearly African-Americans have it much worse than atheists in South Carolina. She told a shocking story about a fund for families of the nine Charleston firefighters who had died in a furniture store fire on June 18, 2007. Some potential contributors wanted to give only if they could earmark their donations to the *white* firefighters. Dot said that when bad things used to happen in South Carolina, the consoling comment would be "Thank you, Mississippi." She opined that this comment is no longer operative, since South Carolina may now be worse than Mississippi. I looked at her and responded, "Dot, I've lived here long enough to know the real expression, so please feel free to say it correctly." She thanked me for not being offended by the phrase "Thank God for Mississippi," and I thanked her for recognizing that not all people are religious.)

The *Post and Courier* gave me the opportunity to write an op-ed about the council walkout. Here's an excerpt: "In recent years, Charleston has taken steps to become a progressive city that celebrates, rather than fears, its diversity. The walkout, however, vividly shows that we are still engaged in one of the last civil rights struggles in which blatant discrimination is viewed as acceptable behavior. Of course, bigotry exists everywhere, but it is especially lamentable when public acts of intolerance at government functions are later defended in the media by government officials."

CHAPTER 9

NATIONAL SECULAR ACTIVISM

Natural Law Party

With Republicans and Democrats in 1996 praising God in their speeches, I half-jokingly told Sharon I'd support any candidate who didn't end a speech with, "God bless you, and God bless America." My search ended with the acceptance speech delivered on C-SPAN by presidential candidate John Hagelin of the Natural Law Party (NLP). He not only didn't invoke a deity, he spoke sensibly (meaning I agreed with him) on the issues. When I sent him a $25 contribution, I promptly received a fifty-point action plan that defined each problem and his proposed solution. My candidate, a PhD in physics from Harvard, had as his slogan to "bring the light of science into government." The NLP wanted to be more in accord with the laws of nature than the laws of God.

Apparently my $25 contribution impressed the party. I received a call from an NLP organizer who said the party was looking for candidates in South Carolina, and asked if I'd consider being one. When I told her about my previous run, she invited me to a weekend retreat in Boone, North Carolina, for party leaders and potential candidates. I was pleasantly surprised that my atheism didn't dissuade her, so Sharon and I drove to the thousand-acre retreat at Heavenly Mountain, a resort in the "Spiritual Center of America."

At the retreat, I spoke extensively with John Hagelin and vice presidential candidate Mike Tompkins, also a Harvard graduate and a descendent of President John Adams. Both were articulate, supported my past South Carolina constitutional challenge, and encouraged me to be the NLP gubernatorial candidate in 1998.

But there was a downside. Hagelin, Tompkins, and many others either taught at or had graduated from Maharishi University in Fairfield, Iowa. Maharishi Mahesh Yogi founded the school, and most of the thirty-five candidates had been trained in transcendental meditation. Hagelin's plan to bring science into government was by what he called "scientifically verified" transcendental meditation (TM) studies.

TM seemed to be their solution for almost any problem. Nearly all party members supported the claim that violent crime is substantially reduced whenever TM-Sidhi (practitioners who have completed an advanced transcendental meditation program) meditate in urban areas. This would be more believable if the practitioners convinced criminals to replace violence with meditation. Even stranger, based on teachings of "physicist" Maharishi Mahesh Yogi, some believed that advanced TM practitioners could reach higher states of consciousness and perform Vedic flying, literally hovering above the ground.

At the last session of the retreat, I said to John Hagelin and other participants, "In my opinion, the three greatest physicists in my lifetime are Albert Einstein, Richard Feynman, and Stephen Hawking. Each readily admitted to significant research errors. Is anyone here aware of any errors of Maharishi Mahesh Yogi?" Nobody present was willing to deny the doctrine of Maharishi infallibility.

So, to run or not to run? That was the question Sharon and I discussed for most of the 330-mile drive from Boone back to Charleston. We agreed that the NLP emphasized important issues not addressed by major parties, and that its leaders seemed to worship the Maharishi. Sharon's position was clear, that I should not affiliate with this strange group. My position was conflicted. If more reasonable people like myself were to run, then the party might move in a more rational direction. Besides, party leaders told me that as a candidate I would not have to espouse TM unless I became convinced of its efficacy.

In the end, my decision fell along rather conventional political lines. I didn't have the same "fire in the belly" as in my 1990 gubernatorial campaign when I was fighting for the right of atheists to hold public office. Some of my happiest moments were traveling with Sharon to debates and speaking engagements on behalf of that cause. But when Sharon said she would not vote or campaign for any NLP candidate, including me, I decided not to run "so I could spend more time with my family."

Community of Reason

I had been receiving invitations to talk about my Bible Belt activities, mostly from local freethought groups like our own Secular Humanists of the Lowcountry, but also from national organizations I hadn't heard of. They identified themselves by a variety of names—atheists, agnostics, humanists, rationalists, secularists, and more. They all promoted causes I supported, like church-state separation and increasing respect for nonbelievers. However, each organization was doing its own thing without recognizing or cooperating with worthwhile efforts of like-minded groups. I thought this was a shortcoming that needed to be addressed if we were to make a difference in our culture.

One speaking invitation came from Margaret Downey, president of the Freethought Society of Greater Philadelphia. Afterward, she said she was on the board of directors of the national American Humanist Association, and she asked my permission to nominate me for that board. After some discussion about the national organization, I agreed to run and won election to the AHA board in 1998.

At my first AHA board meeting, I proposed we explore joining with other organizations to form a national coalition of like-minded groups. When the motion passed, I sent a letter to the seven national nontheistic organizations I knew about, noting that none of the groups was large enough to make a significant impact. I proposed that by sometimes working together we could show strength in numbers and more effectively counter political and social threats from the religious right. I hoped to form a coalition that would 'someday hold a joint conference in Washington, DC, an event that might be televised on C-SPAN, just like the Christian Coalition's Road to Victory Conference.

Though we disagreed with *everything* the Christian Coalition stood for, they had a terrific model: put aside minor theological differences, work together on important political issues, and grab media attention. That was their plan to change the culture and make politicians take notice. Their strategy of demonizing atheists and secular humanists, while moving this country closer to a theocracy, was working all too well. I'm willing to learn from anyone who has something to teach us.

I was not discouraged when those with considerably more experience in the secular movement warned me that getting freethinkers to cooperate was akin to herding cats. (The animal analogy for religious people is "sheep," as in, "The Lord is my Shepherd.") My two cats put aside personality differences, past grudges, and turf protection when I fed them cat crunchies out of one bowl. I assumed that evoking Pat Robertson and Jerry Falwell would provide the freethought crunchies around which secular organizations could enthusiastically rally.

At a September 2000 meeting in Washington, DC, a dozen leaders representing five organizations met to form a coalition, with me as facilitator. It was a unique and worthwhile experience for these groups simply to sit down and talk to one another. Not surprisingly, we had trouble choosing a name for the coalition. We recognized that "atheist" gets more attention and "humanist" gets more respect from the general public. Since we were not faith based, we settled on the Coalition for the Community of Reason (CCR).

(Here's an interesting distinction between Christians and secularists: Christians have the same unifying word, but fight over theology; secularists have the same unifying theology, but fight over words. At least our wars are only verbal.)

Coalition members shared information and several themes emerged. We wanted cultural and political influence, were concerned about theocratic threats to our secular democracy, and hoped to turn widespread public misunderstanding about our constituency into greater public respect and acceptance. The organizations agreed on cultural and political goals, but often couldn't reach consensus on how best to cooperate to achieve our shared aims. Some favored informal alliances on a project-by-project basis, while others pushed for a more structured model. We reached a standstill.

Secular Coalition for America

In 2002, the Coalition for the Community of Reason evolved into the Secular Coalition for America, a much different coalition even though its members consisted of some former CCR organizations. Instead of a loose confederation, the Secular Coalition became a formal organization with an activist mission: to increase the visibility of and respect for nontheistic viewpoints, and to protect and strengthen the secular character of our government. Because member organizations were educational nonprofits with strict limits on lobbying, we incorporated as a national political advocacy organization to enable unlimited lobbying on behalf of secular Americans for the first time.

Discrimination still exists against blacks, women, gays, and Jews, but neither as overtly nor permissibly as it once was. Politicians know these groups have well-organized advocates and constituencies. Now it was our turn to seek that respect. For too long, our nontheistic constituency had been considered politically inconsequential. We may be the last minority against whom intolerance and discrimination are not only permitted, but also sometimes promoted by political leaders at every level. Surveys show that at least 50 million Americans have no religious preference. The Secular Coalition was formed to advocate for those millions who choose to live without religion.

The Secular Coalition's 10 national organizations cover the spectrum of nonbelievers: American Atheists, American Ethical Union, American Humanist Association, Atheist Alliance of America, Camp Quest, Council for Secular Humanism, Institute for Humanist Studies, Military Association of Atheists and Freethinkers, Secular Student Alliance, and Society for Humanistic Judaism.

Two of these organizations, American Ethical Union (AEU) and Society for Humanistic Judaism (SHJ), have religious designations. Most in this country mistakenly believe that all religions require god beliefs. But by one measure, I might be the most "religious" person in America. I have not one, not two, but three religions. In addition to joining AEU and SHJ, I joined the Unitarian Church in Charleston after I gave a sermon about atheism on February 6, 2005, and most of the congregants said they agreed with what I said.

The Secular Coalition board consists of one leader from each national organization, with me as president. It also has an outstanding advisory board, which includes luminaries like Richard Dawkins, Sam Harris, Wendy Kaminer, Steven Pinker, Salman Rushdie, and Julia Sweeney. The advisory board chair is Woody Kaplan, former volunteer lobbyist and fundraiser for the ACLU, and a tireless force working with Congress and helping to unify Secular Coalition members.

We began with just volunteers. After working for two years to raise enough money for a lobbyist to represent the freethought community on Capitol Hill, the Secular Coalition hired Lori Lipman Brown in August 2005. Lori did an outstanding job changing stereotypes about atheists. She was such a warm and friendly person that even those who disagreed with her positions found it hard to dislike her. Sean Faircloth, who had served a decade in the Maine State Legislature, succeeded Lori as executive director and conceived of our optimistic and we hope realistic plan for a secular decade, which can be found on our Web site (www.secular.org). Sean is now the policy and strategy director of the Richard Dawkins Foundation for Reason and Science, which has helped make the relationship between our two organizations even closer as we cooperate and work together on behalf of all secular Americans. The Secular Coalition has grown to a full-time staff of six, not nearly enough to equal the number of lobbyists representing the powerful forces in the Religious Right, but a good start.

The Secular Coalition collaborates with organizations that are neither theistic nor nontheistic, like the ACLU and Americans United for Separation of Church and State. It also cooperates on selected issues with theistic organizations, like the Interfaith Alliance and the Baptist Joint Committee for Religious Liberty. Working with diverse groups provides the additional benefit of gaining more visibility and respect for our unique perspective. Improving the public perception of secular Americans is as important to many of us as pursuing a particular political agenda. Politicians think they are being tolerant when they express support for all faiths; instead, we hope to hear them express support for all faiths and none, for freedom of conscience for all people.

In 2007, the coalition held a contest to recognize the highest-ranking elected public official without a god belief. We didn't intend to "out" anyone. Before announcing the winner, we confirmed that Rep. Pete Stark (D-CA) was willing to come forward. He became the first member in the history of Congress to acknowledge being an atheist.

A landmark day for the Secular Coalition was our February 26, 2010, meeting with White House officials to discuss issues of concern

Meeting Rep. Pete Stark (D-CA), first open atheist in the U.S. Congress, in 2007

to secular Americans. This historic meeting marked the first time a presidential administration met for a policy briefing with the American nontheist community.

We had also become important enough for some media to grossly distort our mission and what occurred at the White House meeting. A group called "In God We Trust" ripped the Obama administration "for meeting to plot political strategy with 60 atheist activists." Its chairman, Episcopal Bishop Council Nedd, said we represent "some of the most hate-filled, anti-religious groups in the nation."

Then Sean Hannity claimed on Fox News that the Obama administration gave special treatment to atheists that religious groups have not received. I suppose in Hannity's America a two-hour meeting with secular Americans was "special treatment," but not a two-day meeting the previous month for more than sixty religious leaders, sponsored by the White House Office of Faith-Based and Neighborhood Partnerships.

The headline in a press release from the Catholic League for Religious and Civil Rights stated, "Obama Aides Host Catholic Bashers." Its president, Bill Donohue, referred to representatives of the Secular Coalition as "some of the biggest anti-religious zealots in the nation," and said many of us "would crush Christianity" if we could. We don't want to crush Christianity, but we do oppose public policy based solely on ancient theology. The Catholic League ended its diatribe with, "It is important that the public learn of the contents of this meeting. We will do what we can to find out what happened."

What on earth were they expecting—an atheist plot to take over the government? The Catholic League's crack investigative team never thought to contact any of the Secular Coalition representatives at the meeting. So I wrote an article for the Washington Post about the meeting, which was published on February 28 in my "On Faith" column, telling with whom we met and the issues discussed. At the White House

Delivering opening remarks to White House officials on behalf of the Secular Coalition for America in 2010

meeting, we focused on military proselytizing and coercion, childhood medical neglect and abuse, and fixing faith-based initiatives.

Local Turns National

Bill Upshur, a founding member of the Secular Humanists of the Low-country, was one of the finest people I've ever known. He knew how to live, and how to die with courage and grace. When he learned he had terminal esophageal cancer in 2007, he continued to participate in causes as long as possible. He believed, at age seventy-seven, that he had lived a full life. The only time I saw him choke up was when he talked about leaving his beloved wife Jane alone.

Our local group has an annual winter solstice potluck gathering, along with a used book auction. Knowing he didn't have long to live, Bill told me he wanted to donate $20,000 to the Secular Humanists of the Lowcountry. He devised a fun plan to make the donation. Typically books at our auction go for no more than $10. Bill and I engaged in a fake bidding war for Richard Dawkins' book, *The God Delusion*. It started typically with incremental bids of a dollar or two, then soared to $1,000, $5,000, $10,000, and ended with Bill's winning bid of $20,000. I had told nobody, including my wife Sharon, who became increasingly alarmed by my extravagant bids.

When I told Richard Dawkins, he wrote a wonderful note to Bill, which I read to him in the hospital a week before he died. Richard said, "I hope you will not think me impertinent if I say you are my kind of guy. You now possess the most expensive copy of *The God Delusion* in the known universe. Thank you for all you have done for secular causes." My last memory of Bill was his broad smile after hearing Dawkins' words.

Part of Bill's contribution went to an interesting cause. Several secular organizations around the country were putting messages on public billboards. We chose one that said, "Don't believe in God? You are not alone." Our goal was to tell passing motorists that our local organization existed, but we were braced for angry reactions from some religious objectors. The billboard got a lot of publicity and, surprisingly, most of it was favorable. I was pleased that our community, in 2009, was finally gaining acceptance, or at least tolerance.

Since ours was the first such billboard in the South, I got a call from Laurie Goodstein, religion correspondent for the *New York Times*. She asked if she could come down for a couple of days to meet some of our members and also discuss my work with the Secular Coalition for America. We were thrilled by this opportunity.

Goodstein's piece on April 26, 2009, "More Atheists Shout It From the Rooftops," was the second most viewed article that week in the *Times*. The takeaway message was that if it could happen in South Carolina, then it could happen anywhere.

Harriet Johnson and Peter Singer

Two atheists I greatly admire are Peter Singer and Harriet Johnson. Singer is professor of bioethics at the University Center for Human Values at Princeton University. Many credit him with having started the animal rights movement through his 1975 book *Animal Liberation*. Singer is also a controversial and original thinker about human rights, including the right of parents to euthanize hopelessly ill newborns. Harriet Johnson was a local lawyer in Charleston, a member of our secular humanist group, and a national activist for disability rights. She was physically disabled herself, and a talented writer.

In 2001, the College of Charleston invited Singer to give a talk on life and death, a contentious topic, especially for Harriet. When I accompanied Singer to the campus building where he would speak, Harriet was waiting by the door in her wheelchair. What happened between them that day eventually led to an invitation by Peter Singer to debate Harriet Johnson in his class at Princeton University on March 5, 2002. Their encounters at the College of Charleston and at Princeton became the subject of Harriet's 8,000-word *New York Times Magazine* cover story of February 16, 2003, which brought her considerable attention in the disability rights movement and from the general public. I can't describe the initial meeting better than Harriet's own words in that piece:

> What stands out when I recall first meeting Peter Singer in the spring of 2001
> is his apparent immunity to my looks, his apparent lack of discombobulation,
> his immediate ability to deal with me as a person with a particular point of
> view. Singer has been invited to the College of Charleston, not two blocks

from my house. He is to lecture on "Rethinking Life and Death." I have been dispatched by Not Dead Yet, the national organization leading the disability-rights opposition to legalized assisted suicide and disability-based killing. I am to put out a leaflet and do something during the Q. and A.

On arriving almost an hour early to reconnoiter, I find the scene almost entirely peaceful; even the boisterous display of South Carolina spring is muted by gray wisps of Spanish moss and mottled oak bark.

I roll around the corner of the building and am confronted with the unnerving sight of two people I know sitting on a park bench eating veggie pitas with Singer. Sharon is a veteran activist for human rights. Herb is South Carolina's most famous atheist. Good people, I've always thought—now sharing veggie pitas and conversation with a proponent of genocide. I try to beat a retreat, but Herb and Sharon have seen me. Sharon tosses her trash and comes over. After we exchange the usual courtesies, she asks, "Would you like to meet Professor Singer?"

She doesn't have a clue. She probably likes his book on animal rights. "I'll just talk to him in the Q. and A." But Herb, with Singer at his side, is fast approaching. They are looking at me, and Herb is talking, no doubt saying nice things about me. He'll be saying that I'm a disability rights lawyer and that I gave a talk against assisted suicide at his secular humanist group a while back. He didn't agree with everything I said, he'll say, but I was brilliant. Singer appears interested, engaged. I sit where I'm parked. Herb makes an introduction. Singer extends his hand.

I hesitate. I shouldn't shake hands with the Evil One. But he is Herb's guest, and I simply can't snub Herb's guest at the college where Herb teaches. Hereabouts, the rule is that if you're not prepared to shoot on sight, you have to be prepared to shake hands. I give Singer the three fingers on my right hand that still work. "Good afternoon, Mr. Singer. I'm here for Not Dead Yet!" I want to think he flinches just a little. Not Dead Yet did everything possible to disrupt his first week at Princeton. I sent a check to the fund for the 14 arrestees, who included comrades in power chairs. But if Singer flinches, he instantly recovers. He answers my questions about the lecture format. When he says he looks forward to an interesting exchange, he seems entirely sincere.

Harriet expanded on the topic in her funny and pointed memoir, *Too Late to Die Young*, published in 2005. Unfortunately, she died in 2008 at age fifty, leaving an exemplary life of accomplishment despite obstacles most people would find daunting. Her *New York Times* obituary appeared in the paper on June 7.

I had a couple of conversations with Peter Singer after Harriet's piece appeared in the *New York Times Magazine*. He thought it was fair and he admired Harriet's commitment and dedication. I'm sure Peter Singer will never forget Harriet, nor will I.

CHAPTER 10

DISCUSSIONS ON RELIGION

Crusades

My first interesting discussion with non-Jews was at a Billy Graham Crusade in Philadelphia in the early 1960s. When I heard that a "crusade" was going to be held at Convention Hall, I asked the Billy Graham organizers about selling refreshments there, as I had done at sporting events. They declined, but I accepted their invitation to attend. I watched intently as Graham moved an audience in ways I hadn't seen before. At the end, he encouraged people to come forward. I did, out of curiosity. After Graham mumbled a few words about being "saved," waiting pastors each chose one of us to indoctrinate further.

My pastor began by asking if I had accepted Jesus Christ into my life, to which I said no. Additional attempts to close the deal (including warnings of fire and brimstone) met with similar frustration for him. When he learned I was Jewish, he transferred me to a recently converted pastor with a Jewish background. I began with Pastor Two by asking if his parents were alive. When he said, "No," I asked, "Is it painful knowing that your devoted parents are suffering the torments of hell?" When he disagreed, I invited Pastor One into our conversation. The highlight of my evening was watching Pastor One and Pastor Two argue about the afterlife of Pastor Two's Jewish parents.

My mother, who had tried to keep me from attending the crusade, was relieved that I had not converted. She had heard that Billy Graham was a charismatic speaker, but logic for me was considerably more compelling than charisma.

130

I know I'm in a distinct minority, but I decided that being evangelized could be a lot of fun. I've welcomed Jehovah's Witnesses into my house, frequently to their surprise. More often than not, they've left before I was ready to end the discussion.

I once persuaded Sharon to stop with me at a Scientology storefront. The Scientologist in charge invited us to take a personality test. Sharon passed and was asked to join, but he said my personality test revealed I might not be a suitable member. Later Sharon received increasingly urgent mail requests to join their cult, until they finally concluded her case was as hopeless as mine.

I don't know any other Scientology rejects. I thought they were as anxious for members as a caller from an Arthur Murray Dance studio, who once told me I'd win a free dance lesson if I could answer, "Who is buried in Grant's tomb?" I responded, "Lincoln?" She said, "That's close enough. Congratulations, you are the winner of a free dance lesson." I've known many easy graders in my life, but none as lenient as she.

During a visit to California in the mid-1990s, I showed Sharon another side of Judaism. I took her to a free dinner sponsored by Chabad-Lubavitch, an ultra-Orthodox Jewish sect. We couldn't talk to each other at dinner because men and women were at separate tables. After dinner we watched a short film honoring the recently departed Rebbe Schneerson, whose return as messiah many attendees were hoping to witness soon.

The film showed Schneerson, a so-called humanitarian, telling his sect never to make territorial compromise in Israel. Afterward, I asked the host, "Would you be willing to cede a little territory for a 100 percent guarantee of peace?" He looked as if he couldn't believe a Jew would ask such a question and said, "How can we give away a gift God promised to us?" Ever since, I've been pessimistic about peace breaking out in the Middle East, with such uncompromising religious extremists on all sides.

When members of the Unification Church (otherwise known as Moonies) were proselytizing on the College of Charleston campus along with other religious groups, campus authorities told them to leave because they didn't have a faculty sponsor. Lots of Christian groups had sponsors, so I offered the Moonies my services as faculty sponsor. No religious test was required and they gratefully accepted.

When they asked if I was a supporter, I told them I thought their beliefs were bizarre, but that all points of view should be allowed on campus. I didn't want Moonies to gain converts, but I did want students exposed to different beliefs. Most students were Christians who knew nothing of other religions, and I hoped questioning others might inspire some to question their own.

Because I'm outspoken about my religious views, some believers call me an evangelical atheist. In one sense, we're all evangelists for issues that matter to us. The question isn't whether to proselytize, but how and how often? Were I on the "soul saving" team, a fellow believer who stood on a corner shouting epithets at sinning passersby would embarrass me, so I'd never be a screaming atheist or go door-to-door spreading the word of God's nonexistence. I hope, though, that more atheists and humanists will feel comfortable engaging in thoughtful conversations when questioned about their worldview.

What I learned from the Billy Graham Crusade (though I hadn't realized it at the time) was that I'm a counter-evangelist. I don't usually initiate discussions with theists, but I sometimes feel I'm as much on a countermission as they are on a mission. By engaging impassioned religionists in a conversation they never had before, I hope to create a spark that will start them thinking about different paths.

Whatever the outcome, thinking and discovering are good. Most of us grew up believing it was rude to discuss sex, politics, and religion. (Actually, nobody told me not to discuss sex, because sex was not even mentioned in my house.) Politics and sex are no longer taboo, but criticizing a person's faith is still socially unacceptable. Atheists are often called insulting or hateful for critically discussing religion in a way that is commonly accepted in political opinion pieces or restaurant reviews.

Speaking of restaurants, a few years ago, several of us at an atheist convention went out to dinner. While we were eating dessert, a man came over and asked, "Are you an insurance adjuster?" I had no idea what he was talking about. He explained that his colleagues at the next table were insurance adjusters, and they liked the quote on my shirt from someone they hadn't heard of, humanist icon Carl Sagan: "Extraordinary claims require extraordinary evidence." I finally understood what accident reports and religious beliefs have in common.

We had a good laugh and discussed our different worldviews. Theirs was definitely for profit and ours was both nonprofit and nonprophet.

A Civil Right?

In 1966 Tony Geramita and I got a new graduate school roommate. Joe Cavenaugh and I enjoyed singing, but Tony said we had the worst voices he had ever heard. When Joe noticed a church announcement for chorus tryouts, we auditioned. So a Catholic and a Jew tried singing hymns at a Protestant Church. When we were both rejected, I said to Joe loud enough for the director to hear, "I told you he was anti-Semitic." The director rushed over and offered me another chance. I laughed and told him I was kidding. I doubt I'd have been offered a second chance had I said, "I told you he was anti-atheist."

Here's another example where I received an undeserved apology. Shortly after the math department at the College of Charleston hired Pat, an administrative specialist, I excitedly told her on February 2, Groundhog Day, that Punxsutawney Phil had seen his shadow, which meant we were in for six more weeks of winter. When she laughed, I feigned surprise and said, "It's not nice to make fun of someone's religious beliefs. I'm from Pennsylvania, where some of us consider Groundhog Day the holiest day of the year." She then apologized profusely. Now that Pat knows me better, we annually joke about my "holy" day. One year she even gave me an autographed picture of Phil on February 2.

Many atheists don't understand why I "waste" time focusing on nonexistent deities. Since I was once an apathetic atheist, I can identify with such concerns. Then I saw no more need to promote atheism than to promote a round earth. Though a Flat Earth Society still exists, its supporters don't have the political clout of the well-organized Religious Right. If they did, I'd probably join a round-earth organization, especially if some school boards wanted "flat-earth theory" taught in science courses.

Atheists as a class are well educated, productive, and prosperous, but we're not as organized as many minorities with fewer adherents. Atheists are not influential because most remain in the closet out of apathy or fear. And it's easy for atheists to stay in the closet. Blacks and

women can't, while gays and lesbians can lead secret lives only with
great sacrifice. Gays and lesbians have changed public perception simply by having large numbers come out of their closets, and so it could
be with atheists. When people tell me I'm the only atheist they know,
I respond, "No, I'm not. You know hundreds. I'm the only one who
has been public about it."

Attitudes will change rapidly when people learn that they have
friends, neighbors, and even family members who are atheists. We'd
become more effective politically in promoting strict separation of
church and state, and we'd gain more visibility and respect for our
secular viewpoints. We'd also put an end to many stereotypes that religionists have about atheists, which ideally should lead to treating us as
individuals rather than as members of an undesirable class. And that,
to me, is what civil rights are all about.

Advice to Fellow Atheists

Since religious people often tell atheists that we are arrogant and anti-
religious, we should come out softly, or at least wait for the right opportunity. It won't take long. Perhaps you'll be asked which church you
attend or how you'll be celebrating a religious holiday. We can describe
and answer questions about our naturalistic worldview without trying
to convince others to adopt it. If it makes sense to some, they might
convince themselves. The most you might be able to do is plant a seed
of doubt, which could result in a believer getting into an argument
with himself or herself. When you win an argument with yourself, you
save face.

We ought to recognize why religious believers' worldviews may be
more important to them than ours is to us. For most of us, it's a philosophical position or intellectual exercise. For many of them, eternal
life is at stake, which is more important than life itself.

We should not gratuitously bash religion. Most Christians aren't
like the ones who have their own television shows or believe the Bible
is inerrant. We must not stereotype Christians. They don't like it any
more than atheists do.

We can argue whether religion or god belief has been more of a
positive or negative influence in our culture (I'd vote for negative), but

such arguments are unproductive when trying to work with moderate theists who feel they are living ethical and moral lives, and who recognize that atheists are, too.

Many believers seek emotional solace, answers to practical everyday questions, and someone to listen to them. If all we offer are reasons to quit religion, which often includes "quitting" one's community, family, and support system, we won't find many takers.

We shouldn't whine about past injustices or an unhappy religious upbringing. We won't win friends and influence people on the basis of victimhood. They weren't responsible for our childhood.

We should respect the right of people to believe whatever makes sense to them. We need not respect the belief itself, or condone harmful actions based on beliefs, but we all need to work out ways of living together in mutual respect. It helps to seek common ground.

Atheists have more in common with some believers than they realize. We have no god beliefs, but many theists believe in a god who is not engaged in the workings of the world, a god who doesn't judge actions in this life to decide what to do with you in an afterlife. Such a god has little or nothing to say about how we should conduct our lives. Practically speaking, these god believers behave like atheists. I classify as *functional atheists* people whose god beliefs are independent of their actions.

Functional atheists include all deists, who believe a deity started the universe and then retired as deity emeritus. It includes almost all Unitarians as well as many other liberal religionists. It includes all Universalists, who believe that everybody goes to heaven. It also includes those who view God as an impersonal force (25 percent of Americans, according to a 2008 Pew Survey).

So if strength in numbers is meaningful, atheists are well served to ally themselves publicly with the much-larger number of "functional atheists" whenever atheists as a class are maligned. The general public may then begin to view atheists in a more favorable light, or at least in a less unfavorable one.

Advice to Theists

Don't say you feel sorry for us. Some religious believers have told me

they wouldn't see the point of living without belief in God and an afterlife. It sounds like they can't find any joy in this life. Atheists don't
feel sorry for themselves or deprived of something real.

Don't assume atheists are untrustworthy because they don't believe
in a judging God. It only makes us think you would be untrustworthy
if you stopped believing. J. C. Watts, a former conservative member of
Congress from Oklahoma, once said, "Character is doing what's right
when nobody's looking." By that definition, only atheists are capable of
showing good character.

The prefix "a" can mean "anti" or "non." Some atheists may be anti-
theists, but most are nontheists. We don't believe in any gods, but that
doesn't mean we have a problem with others believing. Get to know
us without assuming we hate you. If you hate us, make sure it's for a
reason other than our being atheists. And don't say, "I love you because
you are a child of God and God wants us to love all His children." It
sounds insincere and condescending.

Don't tell us, "I love the sinner, but hate the sin." Many of us see
nothing wrong with what you might consider sinful. Examples include
homosexuality, feminism, physician-assisted suicide, alcohol, abortion
rights, and vaccinations.

Don't assume that everyone around you is a God-fearing Christian,
or even religious. Some may feel uncomfortable if you ask everyone to
bow their heads and participate in your prayer or "grace." This happens
constantly at public and organizational meetings in the South.

Advice to atheists and theists: Let's all listen to "the other."

A Witch, a Catholic, and Me

In the fall of 2004, the director of diversity at the College of Charleston invited Darla Wynne and me to appear in a forum called "Religious Intolerance and Multicultural Awareness." Darla is a Wicca high
priestess who had won a lawsuit on July 22, 2004, against the town
of Great Falls, South Carolina, when the town council refused to stop
offering an explicitly Christian prayer at public meetings. What followed were anonymous acts of vandalism during and after the court
case, from destroying her car to poisoning her pets. Someone behead-
ed Darla's parrot and cut out his heart. Attached was a note, "You're

next!" I felt proud to share the stage with such a courageous woman.

However, shortly after the forum had been announced, the director told me it would be postponed temporarily. A member of the College Board of Trustees objected to a program that featured an atheist and a witch, but no Christian. The director knew the objection was oxymoronic, since the program was about persecution due to religious beliefs outside the mainstream. The mainstream in this community is Christian.

The director managed to find a "persecuted" Catholic student, which allowed the program to run. At the forum, I told my story about challenging the state Constitution and Darla talked about her much-more harrowing ordeal. Then the Catholic mentioned that some Southern Baptist students on campus didn't believe Catholics were real Christians, and how sad that made her feel. During the question and answer period, about 70 percent of the questions were directed to Darla and the remainder to me. Nobody asked the Catholic a question and I think she was uncomfortable on stage.

It turned out to be a worthwhile forum about the value of diversity. A Muslim instead of a Catholic would have been appropriate, but none was found. I'm sorry the Catholic student was put in an awkward position. It was the trustee's fault, not hers. But that, too, was an interesting and unstated lesson about the meaning of diversity.

An Atheist Goes to Bible School

In September 1998, a former math student invited me to participate in an Alpha course, a twelve-week Bible study program at nearby conservative St. Andrew's Episcopal Church. Its purpose, she said, was to learn more about the Bible in an atmosphere where questions would be encouraged. Her minister knew I was an atheist and hoped I'd attend. The course was designed not only to strengthen the faith of believers, but also to provide proof of God's existence and his love for all people.

I recalled with satisfaction our 1995 meetings between Baptists and secular humanists. Those were relatively liberal Southern Baptists, but the leaders of the Alpha course would be less tolerant. They believed every word in the Bible and had recently accused some Episcopalian brethren of heresy for condoning homosexuality.

The weekly meetings at the church began with dinner, prayer, and a brief sermon by the minister. Then the 120 participants, all apparently conservative Christians except me, broke into discussion groups of ten. I was in the group with the minister.

Small talk at dinner helped build rapport. Getting to know an atheist who seemed almost normal appeared to comfort some of them. They no longer pictured a scarlet "A" on my forehead. I think this activity induced them to listen more openly to issues and questions I later raised. Discussions after dinner were based on lessons from our Alpha booklets. The minister introduced a moral lesson each week, along with a biblical passage. Since we had the schedule in advance, I was prepared to give my point of view.

I planned to raise problems with biblical inerrancy. For instance, when the minister spoke of the Prodigal Son, and the generosity and loving kindness of the father toward his wastrel son, I sympathized with the father's slave whose task was to shower the unworthy son with gifts. Many were surprised when I quoted biblical passages that condone slavery. The minister countered that this referred to humane treatment in a society that embraced slavery. I agreed, and said we might wish to examine which passages still make sense and which need to be modified in our freedom-loving society.

When I would quote from a particularly brutal or antiquated Old Testament passage, someone would say that Jesus did away with such harsh rules. I pointed to Matthew 5:18, which said that Jesus didn't come to change one jot or tittle of the old law; I did, however, agree that some of those jots and tittles should be abandoned. But then I asked how we decide which to keep and which to discard. This made the minister uncomfortable, since he believed the Bible is inerrant. He would attempt to interpret such passages in a positive light, often a difficult exercise.

Since the majority in our group were women, the minister tried to find biblical passages that put women in a favorable light. When he mentioned that the proscription against adultery protected women, I said that biblical adultery was restricted to a man's having sex with another man's property—his wife. They were appalled to learn that the penalty for a single man's rape of an unattached virgin was a payment to her father of fifty shekels, followed by marriage to the now-damaged woman he raped (Deuteronomy 22:28–29).

One Old Testament rule the minister believed strongly was that homosexuality is a perversion. He pointed out how God destroyed Sodom and Gomorrah, sparing only the righteous Lot and his family. I asked the women in the class how they would have reacted to the following situation when they were very young: "Your male neighbors want to sexually assault a male stranger visiting your father, but he tells them to leave the stranger alone and to have sex with you instead." Of course, the women were horrified. I showed them (Genesis19:8) that this is the offer of the "righteous" Lot that so pleased God.

The minister tried to provide scientific evidence for biblical stories, claiming that recently found pieces of the wall of Jericho dated to the wall's crumbling in the time of Joshua. I asked if there was also evidence that the sun stood still an extra day at Joshua's request. One of the minister's ardent supporters had heard a scientific explanation for the phenomenon, but couldn't explain it. I replied that cosmologists have shown that the sun *always* stands still and that the Earth rotates around its axis. From facial expressions, it appeared most participants accepted this Copernican view, rather than the biblical one.

The minister's main proof that Jesus is the Son of God was the historical fact of the Resurrection. After citing eyewitness accounts of the Resurrection in the Bible, the minister looked at me and said that even the most hardened skeptics should be satisfied by what the renowned Jewish historian, Josephus, said: "He (Jesus) was the Christ. He appeared to them alive again the third day, as the divine prophets had foretold."

I responded that most scholars doubted the authenticity of this passage, since Josephus, a devout Jew, nowhere else acknowledged the divinity of Jesus. His celebrated work, *The Antiquities of the Jews*, comprises twenty books. Why would Josephus devote only one paragraph to someone he thought was the Messiah? Why would other historians of that era not even mention the most astounding event in the history of the world?

I also pointed out that resurrection sightings were not uncommon in that period and described Mithras, the Persian Messiah from several centuries earlier, whose followers purportedly saw this Son of God rise from the tomb after three days. I don't know if the minister had heard this Persian myth before, but he gave credibility only to Christian myths. Neither of us believed that Mithras rose from the dead.

The minister introduced the necessity of belief with I Corinthians 15:14: "And if Christ be not risen, then is our preaching in vain, and your faith is also in vain." I asked whether he thought Jesus' teachings were not meritorious enough to stand on their own. I also questioned why a benevolent God would condemn people to hell for eternity simply for not believing that he required his son to be tortured and killed on our behalf. After hearing that God loves us so much that he sacrificed his only son to save us, I asked, "Shouldn't we be responsible for our own actions? If I wanted to take the place of a murderer on death row, would justice be served by killing me and freeing the murderer?"

When we discussed how to resist Satan, who the minister said is as real as God (I silently agreed), I gave my solution: "Stop believing in Satan. Nonbelievers are never possessed. By taking personal responsibility, we can't blame Satan for our failings." This conservative group agreed with the notion of personal responsibility, but seemed uncomfortable letting go of Satan. I thought about wearing my happy face T-shirt with the slogan, "Smile, There is No Hell," but I didn't want them to think I was making fun of them.

The most moving session was the final one, when we offered personal impressions and insights. Each student made a reference to me. They were impressed by my biblical knowledge. (I probably knew more from the New Testament than most and more from the Old Testament than anyone, perhaps including the minister who seemed unfamiliar with a number of passages I brought up in discussion.) I enjoyed hearing how I gave them a lot to think about. We spoke of the many things we have in common, and how they also believe most Christians don't place enough emphasis on loving their neighbors. We all appreciated the opportunity to disagree without being disagreeable.

One woman began sobbing and said she had apologized to Jesus and now wished to apologize to me. The previous year she had written a letter to the editor of our local paper criticizing my immoral, atheistic philosophy, and me, personally. She said she had sinned in being so judgmental and no longer thought I was immoral. After thanking her,

I said I thought it was more difficult and more beneficial to ask forgiveness from those you wrong than from Jesus.

Interestingly, nobody mentioned that the course had strengthened his or her faith—as it was intended to do. My closing observation, to their smiles, was a biblical quote. I said that this wonderful shared experience would not have been possible had the group subscribed to the views of Paul (II Corinthians 6:14): "Believers must not commune with unbelievers. What fellowship hath righteousness with unrighteousness, light with darkness, believers with infidels?"

CHAPTER 11

DEBATES ON RELIGION

Sometimes it's hard to tell the difference between a discussion and a debate. Here's how I distinguish them. In discussions we listen to and learn from one another, with give and take. In formal debates we listen mainly to frame counterarguments and score points with an audience. Debaters are unlikely to change their minds based on issues raised. At most, they might modify presentations in future debates to better clarify points.

Many atheists, myself included, have been overly optimistic in believing a rational argument will be sufficient to change minds. I now think the best we can do is make good points in a reasonable and pleasant manner. I emphasize "pleasant" because many in the audience make unconscious judgments based more on personality than on arguments. That was difficult for me to understand, since it's so different from my world of mathematics. Smiling is effective in debates and useless in mathematics.

Most of my debates have been with fundamentalist ministers, with most of the audience from the minister's flock. I hope to plant seeds of doubt with those open to new ideas. Religious discussions and debates can be productive, especially for atheists. A theist is more likely to hear something new from an atheist than the other way around.

I prefer being in the minority during a debate because it's more productive than preaching to the converted. It can also help break stereotypes, especially when some know about atheists only from what they've heard from their preachers. I'm good at keeping my cool, but here's a confession. When an overly enthusiastic Christian from the audience interrupts, shouts, or makes nasty comments, I try to look sad but am secretly delighted. I sometimes get apologies from Christians about inappropriate behavior from other Christians. This gives me the opportunity to say, "There are good and bad Christians as well as good and bad atheists, and we shouldn't stereotype." I also like it when my Christian opponent upsets other Christians in the audience.

Here's one of my favorite e-mails from a student, an atheist who had persuaded his Christian father to attend a debate. "After the debate, I asked my dad for his reactions. He told me that the atheist guy was more of a Christian than the Christian guy. I used this opportunity to explain that characterizing your morality as Christian is not appropriate. Christianity does not hold the market on good or right. Through your conduct and reasoning, you helped my father understand that atheists are not immoral, evil, or devil worshippers. And for that, I thank you. Please keep up your good work."

A Public Radio Debate on Atheists Holding Public Office

This was my first public debate with probably the easiest topic I've argued, and one of the few where I knew the audience would mostly be on my side. In 1990 the Unitarian Church of Charleston held debates in its historic Gage Hall, located in downtown Charleston, and broadcast them statewide on South Carolina Public Radio. The church invited me to debate Rabbi Joel Landau from the local Orthodox Jewish synagogue. The debate was on October 15, 1990, just before my November 6 public television debate with other gubernatorial candidates, described in chapter 7. I knew that the views of many members of this progressive church were similar to mine. Since neither the rabbi nor I was a lawyer, we agreed to talk about moral rather than legal issues.

The rabbi began by quoting Dostoevsky, "Where there is no God, everything is permitted." He acknowledged that belief alone doesn't guarantee goodness, but that "the death of God guaranteed evil." Rabbi Landau added, "Though atheists aren't necessarily immoral, they are most definitely amoral." He also claimed, "Belief in a moral code emanating from God's will, to which we are all accountable, is indispensible to a moral society." And that's why he opposed atheists holding public office.

I argued that we develop moral codes through reason, experience, and compassion. I mentioned we've had so many holy wars because believers can't seem to agree on what God expects or how to interpret holy books. I also argued that we've learned a lot in the last three thousand years, and what was moral when those books were written may not be so moral today.

In the Q&A, most in the audience were on my side. One person said he would vote for me because "anyone in South Carolina who says he's an atheist must be an honest person." Rabbi William Rosenthal from the Reform Jewish synagogue said he supported me more than Rabbi Landau, and that people didn't need to fear God in order to be good. After the Q&A, the audience voted and I won overwhelmingly. I think the only people who voted for Rabbi Landau were those from his congregation.

After the debate, Rabbi Landau invited me to a December conference in Savannah, Georgia, featuring a scholar who would offer mathematical proof that the Bible was written by God. I was intrigued, so Sharon and I made the ninety-mile drive expecting an interesting weekend, and it was. The speaker gave examples of sequences of equidistant letters in the Torah (the Old Testament) that he said predicted future events, including assassinations of leaders. I thought it was nonsense, since the speaker was working backward. He could find sequences to justify events that had occurred, but couldn't predict future events. In other words, he offered only "postdictions" (the hindsight bias that explains claimed predictions of significant events). I felt that I could probably make similar postdictions using *War and Peace* or any other long book.

I didn't know at the time that the speaker was on to something important, not in terms of accuracy but in terms of a best-selling book by another author. Several years later, Michael Drosnin had huge success with his 1997 book, *The Bible Code*. Members of the American Mathematical Society, both religious and nonreligious, reviewed the book, pointing out obvious mathematical flaws. They also showed that postdictions could be found in just about any book.

In his 2002 sequel, *The Bible Code II*, Drosnin made predictions. He said that a Palestinian from Hamas would shoot and kill Yasser Arafat, who instead eventually died from an illness. Drosnin also predicted that Libya would use its weapons of mass destruction to attack the United States. Libya improved relations with the West in 2003 when it gave up all its existing weapons of mass destruction programs. This proves that it's much easier to make postdictions than predictions.

Most at the conference were Orthodox Jews and probably everyone except Sharon was Jewish. She had an opportunity to hear how some Jews talk when they think no Gentiles are present. Since Orthodox Jews consider the body sacred, even after death, I asked one if he supported doing research on dead bodies and donating organs. He agreed with me that these medical advances could save lives, but added, "There are lots of goyim and animals available for such things." I wanted to watch his reaction after Sharon told him she was a Gentile, but she was more interested in learning than in confronting on that fascinating weekend.

Prayer in School

In 1992, I debated John Graham Altman III on whether public schools should sanction prayers for students. Altman was then chairman of the Charleston County School Board and a Bible study teacher at his church. The debate was sponsored by the Charleston Chapter of the ACLU and held at the College of Charleston. Altman argued that the United States was drowning in rampant crime, poverty, broken families, and social dysfunction. He said school prayer may not be a cure-all, but a moral education is a good start in getting the country back to the Judeo-Christian bedrock on which it was founded.

I said I had nothing against students praying in school. Before any math exam, some of my students were likely to pray (though I think studying is more effective). I asked Altman, a conservative, why he wanted government help for prayer. I said our secular government should not tell students when, whether, or what to pray. Prayer should be voluntary, not forced. I ended one portion with a quote from Matthew 6:5, where Jesus cautions his followers not to pray "as the hypocrites, who love to pray standing in the corners of the streets that they may be seen of men. Instead, go into your closet and pray in secret." I then added, "Can you say amen to Jesus, Mr. Altman?"

Altman responded, "Silverman has read the Bible, but he didn't inhale." This was a sarcastic reference to then-presidential candidate Bill Clinton's comment on his marijuana use. The implication, of course, was that I was quoting the Bible out of context. I've learned that when believers have no satisfactory response to biblical quotes about the treatment of women, slavery, child abuse, anti-Semitism, and a host of other issues, they usually say, "You took that quote out of context." I'm rarely able to get them to put the quotes into what they consider proper context, and Altman was no exception.

Liberal religionists often acknowledge that certain passages are either outdated or were never in date, so they should be ignored. That, to me, leads to the slippery slope of secular humanism, where we pick and choose from what makes sense and what should be ignored from different books. It's slippery, but it can be a wonderful and instructive slide.

Can We Be Moral Without God?

My first major debate, with Pastor Conrad "Buster" Brown in 1998, was in the College of Charleston's largest auditorium. More than eight hundred attended, some crowding onto the stage itself, and more were turned away. I can't take credit for the crowd, since the overwhelming majority came from my opponent's East Cooper Baptist megachurch. Most of the students in the audience were Christian, though members of our recently formed Atheist/Humanist Alliance student group were also present.

Debaters usually prepare fairly standard openings. Rebuttals can't be prepared in advance, unless you're pretty confident about an opponent's opening. What follows is my typical opening on the topic of godless morality, where I start by explaining what an atheist is and why I am one.

> First I'll tell you what I don't believe and then, more importantly, what I do believe. I'm an atheist, which means I have no belief in any gods. I can't prove there aren't any gods. I just don't find credible evidence for believing. That's also why I don't believe in astrology or alien abductions by UFOs. It may surprise you to know that Pastor Brown and I are both atheists, with one tiny difference. There are over seven thousand gods that people believe in, and Pastor Brown is an atheist with respect to all gods but one. I just don't make that one exception.
>
> I know I'm in the minority in not believing in the Christian God or any other. I think religion arose out of fear and confusion about the mysteries of nature (like thunder, eclipses, earthquakes, and floods), which people attributed

to acts of the gods. The more we learn about the predictive value of science, the less we need ascribe natural phenomena to supernatural causes. There will always be mysteries, and we can look for evidence to resolve them or say that one of the gods did it. Such a response serves only to isolate the problem from rational discussion. Attributing to a god whatever is unknown is called "the god of the gaps." That just passes the buck from one mystery to an even bigger mystery.

I understand the appeal of religion. Fear of death can lead to a longing for an afterlife, where we can be reunited forever with our loved ones in eternal bliss. Or perhaps we can come back reincarnated as a better person. But it's important to distinguish between the world as we know it and the world as we'd like it to be. Many believe they've had personal experiences with different gods, and that can be comforting. But with all the conflicting religious beliefs in the world, how do people choose the one true religion? As it turns out, there's a remarkable coincidence: the overwhelming majority choose the religion of their parents.

Religious beliefs are learned, not discovered. I learned to believe in the biblical God Yahweh, not Jesus. Why? Because I was born into a Jewish family. Had I been born into a Christian family, I'd likely have believed that Jesus is Lord. It's natural to wonder why the majority of Indians are Hindu, Saudi Arabians are Muslim, and Americans are Christian. It doesn't take long for a thinking person to realize that religious belief is based more on geography than theology. With all the conflicting faith beliefs in the world, they can't all be right. But they can all be wrong.

Science, on the other hand, doesn't rely on faith in divine revelations or interpretations of ancient books by religious authorities. Science does require a willingness to question assumptions critically and search for evidence until a consensus is reached. That's why scientific truths remain the same in Pakistan, the United States, Israel, or India, though their citizens may have very different religious beliefs.

As an atheist, I don't believe in any gods. But that doesn't make me a non-believer. As a secular humanist, I believe in many things. I believe we can gain knowledge of the world through observation, experimentation, reading, and critical thinking; I believe we're part of a natural world, the result of unguided evolutionary change; I believe that ethical values are derived from human needs and interests, and are tested and refined by experience; I believe morality should be based on how our actions affect others; I believe that our deeds are more important than our creeds, and that dogmas should never override compassion for others. I don't think we should give credit to a deity for our accomplishments or blame satanic forces when we behave badly. I believe we should take responsibility for our actions.

So how do we make moral decisions? One criterion is to look at what works well and has withstood the test of time. Just about all religions and philosophies have grounded morality in some version of the Golden Rule, treating others as we would like to be treated. But that's a guideline open to interpretation, not an absolute. Even if we believe in absolutes, we're forced to make human judgments on how to interpret them. For instance, we all agree that murder is wrong. But what do we do about euthanasia, suicide, abortion, war, capital punishment, and stem cell research? Different religions, and even people within the same religion, often disagree.

So how do we decide? In tough decisions, I believe we should be guided by the consequences of our actions to individuals, to our families, and to our community, rather than by what we believe a deity might want. We can make up needs of an imagined god, but we know the needs of real humans. I think morality is a necessary invention of humans to construct a livable society. It requires flexibility because the circumstances under which we live continue to change and we discover what works better.

Should we subscribe to the same beliefs as the biblical writers who lived some two to three thousand years ago in a small corner of the Mediterranean world? My answer is: yes, and no. Some biblical wisdom is worth keeping, like love your neighbor, and don't murder, steal, or lie. These practices are necessary for survival of any culture, with or without religion, and are by no means unique to the Bible. But we need ongoing discussions about moral issues, where we continue to refine our views about how best to minimize human suffering and promote human dignity more effectively.

Some believe we should turn back the clock of moral and ethical development and rely exclusively on religious doctrines written when democracy was nonexistent, when kings ruled by Divine Right, and when fallible religious leaders interpreted so-called infallible holy books for everyone. Such leaders include Islamic fundamentalists who are proponents of sharia law, and Christian Reconstructionists who want our country to be governed according to their strict interpretation of biblical law.

Morality today differs significantly from biblical morality. Throughout history, the Bible has been quoted to justify slavery, anti-Semitism, treating women as property, executing blasphemers and homosexuals, and burning witches and heretics. Some actions deemed moral two thousand years ago are considered immoral today. Morality evolves over time as our understanding of human needs within a culture changes. Even those who believe in biblical inerrancy interpret some passages in a different way today than in centuries past, in a manner more consistent with many secular humanist principles. This shows that we have independent human notions of morality that do not come from the God of the Bible. We make judgments about which portions of a sacred text to take literally, which metaphorically, and which to ignore completely.

Here's a small sample of biblical passages to ignore: in Numbers 31, God orders his invading army to kill all male children and women who have known man, but to keep for themselves the young virgins; Ephesians 6:5 tells slaves to obey their masters and Exodus 2:20 describes when it's permissible to beat them. Nowhere in the Bible is slavery called an abomination. If your parents observed Deuteronomy 21:18–21, you would have been stoned to death had you ever been stubborn or rebellious toward them.

Sometimes the nicest thing you can say about God is that he does not exist.

Christians who claim the one true morality can't seem to agree on what it is. The same goes with other religions. Associating God with morality is problematic, especially when it requires putting love of a god above love of human beings. Reasonable people may disagree on the right thing to do in a given situation, but a supernatural belief system offers nothing particularly moral or ethical that cannot be derived from a secular morality based on reason and compassion.

One biblical character, Abraham, is revered as a prophet in all three monotheistic religions: Judaism, Christianity, and Islam. He is admired for having such great faith that he was willing to kill his son because God told him to do it. I don't think Pastor Brown is a man of this much faith, or at least I hope he's not. But just to make sure, I'll close by asking Pastor Brown this question: "If God commanded you to kill a member of your family or to kill me, would you do it? And, depending on your answer, I might move a bit farther away from you.

Debate participants usually have an opportunity to question each other. One of my favorite questions is, "How would your behavior toward others change if you were no longer to believe in a God who judges your actions?" This to me is a win-win question. If my opponent says he would not change, then God isn't necessary for morality. If he says he would change, then he's not being good for goodness' sake, but for a promise of future rewards. What kind of morality is that?

Pastor Brown answered, "I'm sometimes tempted by women to cheat on my wife, but I resist because I know how much it would hurt Jesus." My response was, "I'm sometimes tempted by women to cheat on my wife, Sharon, but I resist because I know how much it would hurt Sharon." After the debate, several women in the Pastor's church told me they liked my answer a lot more than they liked his, and Pastor Brown's wife didn't look all that happy with his response either.

Our answers represented a significant difference in worldviews. Do we look to please God or humans? This is often a point I try to make, allying secular humanists with liberal religionists on many causes opposed by conservative religionists. Many innocent lives are lost because some believe they are performing God's will.

Pastor Brown's favorite moment came when he referred in his closing to my comment about Charleston having churches on just about every block, with most of them disagreeing on God's word. The debate took place the week before Easter. Pastor Brown said, "Though churches may disagree on some theological issues, we will all soon be shouting for joy, 'Jesus is risen!'" This brought the biggest applause line of the evening, along with smiles, cheers, and foot stomping. I tried not to appear rattled, and simply thought to myself, "The shouting may be real, but the rising isn't."

Alex Sanders, president of the College of Charleston, moderated the debate. The next day he told me I had done an outstanding job, adding, "I couldn't disagree with anything you said." I think this was his way of telling me he was an atheist, though he'd likely deny it if asked.

Academic Freedom

I debated Dr. Richard Johnson on the same topic in 2004. He is a religion professor at Charleston Southern University (CSU), formerly named Baptist College and retaining its strong Baptist affiliation. More interesting than the debate itself were the obstacles both before and after.

Dr. Johnson originally invited me to debate him on his campus, an invitation I readily accepted. But CSU refused permission, so the debate was held at nearby Old Fort Baptist Church, which Dr. Johnson and many CSU students attended. A few days before the debate the minister called to explain that the church had certain rules of decorum, and he told me to make sure my atheist friends would not do anything sacrilegious while in the church. I asked what sort of things he was worried about, but I didn't get a very coherent reply. When the debate ended the minister looked relieved, so I guess none of us committed a sacrilege.

After the debate, Dr. Johnson asked me if he could speak to the Atheist/Humanist Alliance student club at the College of Charleston. I said he would be most welcome, so he appeared and tried, unsuccessfully, to lead some of those students to Jesus. In the Q&A period, a student asked Johnson if he would invite me to speak to his CSU philosophy of religion class. Johnson agreed, but the day before I was to talk, I received an e-mail from him explaining there were "complications," and his administration did not want him to devote class time to my appearance.

I told the religion editor of our local paper how a Christian professor at a Baptist institution had broken his promise to allow me to speak at his university, after I had kept my promise allowing him to speak at mine. I observed that allowing only one point of view on campus reflected poorly on any academic institution. Had the administration at the College of Charleston objected to the religion professor speaking at my institution, I would have fought it and engaged others on campus to help keep academic freedom alive. The chair of the CSU religion department told the reporter that the invitation was rescinded because their "students had heard quite enough from Dr. Silverman recently." I asked what that meant, since I had never been allowed to speak on their campus.

The reporter wrote that the CSU provost declined to explain "how not allowing Silverman to speak in Johnson's classroom fits in with CSU's vision of academic freedom." Johnson also declined comment. I'm sorry his institution put him in such an embarrassing position, and even sorrier that his students are denied opportunities to hear different points of view on campus.

Are We a Christian Nation?

One of my Christian nation debates took place in the Charleston *Post and Courier* in 2005. The religion editor had asked several local leaders, including me, to comment on President George W. Bush's faith-based initiative. My op-ed ended, "The framers of our Godless Constitution (and I'll give $1,000 to anyone who can find the words God or Jesus in it) had the foresight to establish the first secular country. They recognized that religious institutions must rise or fall through voluntary contributions, not through taxes imposed on all citizens. Forcing taxpayers to subsidize religions they may not believe in is no different from forcing them to put money in the collection plates of churches, synagogues or mosques."

I knew my $1,000 offer would spark interest, and that my money would be safe. Skip Johnson, former religion editor for the *Post and Courier*, accepted my challenge and followed up with an op-ed trying to make a case for collecting the reward. Johnson's main constitutional arguments were that it was signed "in the year of our Lord;" it contains the word "oath," a call to God; and it allows the president an extra day to return a bill if the tenth day falls on a Sunday, the day set aside to worship God.

In my next op-ed, I replied that this was the standard way of dating important documents in the eighteenth century, that oaths weren't necessarily a call to God, and that in 1787, as now, people were sometimes given Sunday off to do as they pleased.

I also mentioned that our founders wisely established a secular nation whose authority rests with "We the people" (the first three words of the U.S. Constitution) and not with "Thou the deity." When Johnson responded that we were founded as a Christian nation, I cited unambiguous language to prove otherwise. In 1797, the United States Senate unanimously ratified the Treaty of Tripoli, which stated in part, "The government of the United States is not in any sense founded on the Christian religion."

Next Johnson asked, "Does it really seem like the people who wrote the Constitution intended to keep God out of it?" I responded, "Our founders were a lot wiser than Johnson gives them credit for being. They were careful and thoughtful writers. Had they wanted to put God into the Constitution, they would have."

After this journalistic sparring, the religion editor of the *Post and Courier* wrote, "Next week, we will tell you who, according to our readers, won the debate." Knowing a little about the Bible Belt readers of the paper, I told the editor I would pay the $1,000 if evidence were found to prove my assertion wrong. I would not pay because the majority of letters said I was wrong. The editor understood this.

To my pleasant surprise, eight published letters favored my position, while only six favored Johnson's. When the public editor was asked about the choice of letters printed and omitted, she responded that the religion editor opted not to publish some letters because they were obscene. I asked her if all the obscene letters were from Christians, and she acknowledged that they all favored Johnson's position.

The public falsely assumed that Johnson and I were bitter enemies because we disagreed about a religious claim. So I invited Skip and his wife Sue to have dinner with Sharon and me, and suggested we write an op-ed about our areas of agreement. We went back and forth on ideas and reached agreement on a number of issues. The *Post and Courier* published our joint article, which read,

> We share the following viewpoints, whether we consider them part of the social gospel or secular humanism:
>
> We are concerned with securing justice and fairness in an open, pluralistic and democratic society. We want to eliminate discrimination and intolerance based on race, religion, gender, nationality, class, sexual orientation or ethnicity, and we think it important to personally contribute to the common good of humanity. We believe in helping the disadvantaged and disabled so they will be better able to help themselves. We are committed to the application of reason, science and experience, among other things, to better understand the universe and to solve human problems.
>
> We respect the right to privacy and believe in the right to sexual and reproductive freedom commensurate with acceptance of sexual and reproductive responsibility. We want to protect and enhance the Earth for future generations and to avoid inflicting needless suffering on other living beings. We must never enlist the government to force others to acknowledge or support anyone's religious ideas. We oppose constitutional amendments that would weaken our Bill of Rights, like prohibitions against flag burning or permitting government-sponsored Bible reading in public schools.
>
> We find much wisdom in the Bible, but agree that many of its stories should not be taken as literally true. It is unreasonable to hold ancient writers to modern journalistic standards. Personal theology is not as important to us as is our behavior—the need to love our neighbor. Our actions are not based on rewards or punishments in an expected afterlife. We believe that doing good is its own reward.

The church at its best is among the first to arrive at disasters, and it feeds and clothes hungry people at home and abroad. It builds and maintains universities and hospitals. It has been the catalyst for much of the world's greatest music. But the church at its worst has caused wars and inflicted death, suffering and fear on vast numbers of people.

We believe negotiation and compromise are more effective than war in resolving differences. We oppose any preventive war and think the U.S. should never have attacked and occupied Iraq. War is absolutely the last resort to settle differences, with no exceptions. We think the "War on Drugs" is a misguided and failed policy, just as alcohol prohibition once was. The sale of drugs to adults should be legalized, with more money put into prevention and rehabilitation programs.

In summary, we both follow a progressive and naturalistic life stance that affirms our ability and responsibility to lead meaningful and ethical lives. We think this exercise has been a wonderful experience for both of us. People spend too little time communicating in a positive way with those who have different points of view. It is easier simply to stereotype and demonize those who are different. We have both learned a lot from talking to each other. And, yes, as an added bonus, we have become friends.

The response from readers of the *Post and Courier* was impressive. Of course many Christians disliked what Johnson said, but I heard more positive reaction from local residents about this joint statement of agreement than for anything else I have written. Johnson reported a similar reaction from his friends. A number of Christians stopped me on the street saying what a wonderful idea it was to seek common ground. One writer to the paper said he followed our debate with interest, but found it to be no more than an academic exercise of little real consequence. In contrast, he found the joint letter to be "the most profound and uplifting to grace the Faith and Values section."

I had a similar experience after a debate with Jack Hoey of Seacoast Church in Charleston. The September 29, 2011 debate to an overflow crowd of more than 600 people, most from his evangelical church, was on "Does God Exist, and Does it Matter?" Several days after the debate, a letter appeared in the Charleston Post and Courier that said debates between atheists and Christians are fine, but added: "I challenge Herb Silverman and Jack Hoey to find a project they both support and can work on together. Finding one won't be difficult; these are men of values and principle." I liked the challenge and contacted Hoey to discuss projects on which his church and the Secular Humanists of the Lowcountry could cooperate. We, of course, didn't want to work on any of their programs that had an evangelistic component. We agreed that our first joint secular project would be to help prepare and maintain a community garden in a depressed neighborhood. To paraphrase Ecclesiastes, "There is a time to confront, and a time to cooperate."

I had another "Christian nation" debate at the University of South Carolina's Darla Moore Business School on October 29, 2009, sponsored by the Pastafarians student group, with about three hundred attendees. My opponent was Chaplain E. Ray Moore, president of Frontline Ministries and founder of the Exodus Mandate Project, "a Christian ministry to encourage and assist Christian families to leave government schools for the Promised Land of Christian schools or home schooling."

Moore argued that though we were founded as a Christian nation, liberal court judges have retreated from the principles of our founders. I pointed out that Moore might have been hearkening back to the first Pilgrims and Puritans who settled here and established Christian colonies, where those of the "wrong" religion were excluded from government participation and persecuted. Such church-state unions led to the Salem witch trials.

I said that the framers of our U.S. Constitution and Bill of Rights wanted no part of the religious intolerance and bloodshed they saw in Europe or in our own early theocratic colonies. They wisely established the first government in history to separate church and state. While forming a new federal government, a minority faction at the Constitutional Convention of 1787 sought some recognition of Christianity. But more enlightened founders like our own Charles Pinckney, a South Carolina delegate to the Constitutional Convention, disagreed, and he even recommended language prohibiting religious tests for federal office. This became Article 6 of the U.S. Constitution, adopted in 1789 as a purely secular document.

I also quoted Robert E. Lee, who in 1856 wrote a letter to his wife, saying, "Is it not strange that the descendants of those Pilgrim Fathers who crossed the Atlantic to preserve their own freedom of opinion have always proved themselves intolerant of the spiritual liberty of others?"

There have been numerous amendments proposed to turn our secular country into a Bible-based Christian nation; but thanks to people like Lee, all such attempts at official establishment have failed.

I added that our founders wrote the Constitution as a secular document because they didn't want the new federal government to have authority over, or meddle in, religion. Our secular laws are based on the human principle of "justice for all," and our civil government enforces these laws through a secular criminal justice system.

When Chaplain Moore said that separation of church and state is a myth used as a club against religious people, I countered that government neutrality is not government hostility toward religion. I closed by pointing out that the essence of religious liberty comes from Thomas Jefferson, who said, "It does me no injury for my neighbor to say there are twenty gods or no god. It neither picks my pocket nor breaks my leg."

Here is what Moore said about the debate on his blog: "Through this experience I learned several lessons: Never enter into a debate or forum against such a skillful debater as Dr. Herb Silverman without thorough preparation. Have real conviction on the topic of America's Christian foundation. My purpose was to persuade Christians of the importance of this issue. A Christian people robbed of their heritage are easily manipulated by every kind of doctrine. Be prayerful and seek God's assistance every step of the way."

Does God Exist?

A group of Christian faculty at the University of North Carolina at Wilmington invited me to debate William Lane Craig on March 23, 2010. I knew Craig by reputation to be one of the most experienced and smooth Christian apologist debaters in the country. He had engaged many accomplished debaters, including Christopher Hitchens, Daniel Dennett, and Episcopal bishop John Shelby Spong. I wanted to debate whether we can be moral without God, but Craig chose to debate God's existence. I prefer more practical discussions on how best to conduct our lives rather than philosophical questions about the existence of a deity, but I agreed to the topic. Craig is a philosopher and an evangelist, and I think he's more interested in preparing people for an afterlife than on how best to live in this life.

The debate cosponsors were the Christian Faculty Commons and the Inter-Varsity Christian Fellowship, a group of Christian students. They invited Craig and me to have breakfast with them on the morning of the debate at the Salt Shaker Bookstore and Café, whose purpose is to provide Christ-honoring products and communicate the Gospel to the lost. (Probably I was the only "lost" at breakfast.) The Christian faculty members were polite and engaged me in small talk. They clearly viewed Craig as an evangelical star and were grateful he had agreed to pay them a visit.

About an hour before the 7 p.m. debate, information tables were set up outside the hall. An array of supporters sold Craig's books, CDs, and tapes, while on my table I placed free Secular Coalition for America brochures. A lot more people bought Craig's wares than picked mine up for free.

To prepare for this formal debate on whether God exists, I read transcripts of some of Craig's previous debates and was ready to rebut his arguments. We each would have an opening, two rebuttals, a closing, and a Q&A session with the audience. There would be plenty of time to make our points.

In Craig's opening, he asserted as an atheist I needed to prove his God does not exist. In my opening, I said an atheist is someone without a belief in any gods, not someone who has to furnish proofs for the nonexistence of the 7,000-plus gods in which people believe. I said to the audience: "Suppose I tell you that the universe was created just 10 minutes ago, and that a supernatural being planted false memories in all of you. You can't disprove it, can you? But you don't believe me. You would rightly want evidence, and would examine my evidence carefully. You would be under no obligation to prove that such a supernatural being does not exist. We can't prove that unicorns and leprechauns don't exist, but we still don't believe in them. The burden of proof is on those who assert a belief, not on those who deny it."

Throughout the debate, Craig and I went back and forth on this point. He kept insisting I hadn't proved his God didn't exist, while I explained why Craig's six alleged proofs (cosmological, ontological, teleological, objective morality, historicity of resurrection, and direct experience) didn't constitute credible evidence.

Craig rarely deviates in debates from his standard arguments, found on his Web site. The first four originated with ancient philosophers and Craig dressed them up a bit with scientific jargon. I doubt that anyone who didn't already believe would be convinced by his scientific arguments. I brought in scientific evidence mostly to counter what Craig had said. It was quite a stretch for Craig to posit a generic god's existence based on what we know about the Big Bang, but such arguments are far removed from Craig's main goal to bring Jesus into people's hearts. I felt that Craig was far more interested in his last two proofs (resurrection and direct experience), which felt like sermons to me. I expect he first wanted to sound erudite and dazzle his audience with historical and scientific factoids, before his "come to Jesus" moments.

Craig claimed there are objective moral truths, which can only come from God. He cited opposition to slavery and genocide as examples. After I quoted biblical passages that justified such immoral behavior, Craig gave a rather strange response. He acknowledged that the God of the Bible was responsible for genocide and other atrocities, but he said that God doesn't stand under the same moral duties we do. Craig added, "It would be wrong if I were to whip out a gun and shoot someone for no reason at all. But if God wants to strike me dead right now, that's his prerogative. God is the giver of life, and he has the prerogative to give and take life as he sees fit."

Such an argument reminded me of my childhood thoughts that God either did not exist, or if he did he was worse than Hitler. The former seemed to me more humane and more likely to be true, both then and now. Even as a child, I would not have accepted Craig's view that a good creator is justified in torturing his creation, and that he deserves to be praised for all his actions. Feared, maybe, but not praised.

Of crucial importance to conservative Christians is belief in a historical resurrection of Jesus. Craig's evidence came only from the Bible. I pointed out that the Gospels were written thirty-five to sixty-five years after Jesus's death, with no evidence that anything in the New Testament was written by anyone who had met Jesus.

And Jesus wasn't the only New Testament figure to rise from the grave around that time. According to Matthew 27, graves opened and lots of resurrected Jews went to Jerusalem and were seen by many. Again there are no nonbiblical sources to confirm this event. I said we would have expected to hear something from the resurrected and their relatives, like what it's like being dead, how long they stayed in Jerusalem, and whether they returned to their graves. A more likely explanation is that early Christians simply invented resurrection stories to conform to religious beliefs of other traditions.

I also mentioned another resurrection version believed by many Christians. After Jesus died, but before he went to heaven, Jesus stopped in the United States. This story was chiseled on gold plates in Egyptian hieroglyphics and buried in Palmyra, New York. In 1827, the angel Moroni led Joseph Smith to the gold plates and a magic stone. When Smith put the magic stone into his hat and buried his face in the hat, he was able to translate the plates into English. I asked Craig if he believed the Book of Mormon was true, and if he thinks Mormons are Christians. Craig didn't respond.

As for Dr. Craig's assertion that the resurrection must be true because the disciples were willing to die for their beliefs, I gave a two-word response: 9/11.

The real sermon portion of the debate came when Craig spoke about how God could be immediately known and experienced. Craig described how he had opened his heart and let Jesus in, and Jesus changed his life. Craig then told the audience, to much applause, "The same can happen to you if you give yourself over to Jesus. You can know God exists wholly apart from arguments simply by immediately experiencing him. This was the way people in the Bible knew God."

This argument was a bit tricky for me to navigate. I didn't want to make fun of Craig's beliefs, but this debate was supposed to be about evidence. I mentioned that I didn't dispute Dr. Craig's sincerity. I added that his personal and moving testimony seemed like the "evidence" most meaningful and convincing for him, from which all his other arguments followed. But there are people just as convinced of their evidence for different religious beliefs. However personally consequential such stories are, I don't accept them as evidence for the existence of any gods. I then quoted from Dr. Craig's book *Reasonable Faith*: "Even if there's no evidence for the truth of the Bible, even if there's evidence against it, we are still required to believe. We can know the truth whether we have rational arguments or not."

I said that the value I place in evidence and Dr. Craig places in faith is one significant way we differ. Faith is a belief with an absence of evidence; science requires the presence of evidence. If data conflicts with a scientific proposition, scientists throw out the proposition; if data conflicts with a faith belief, believers often throw out the data.

Another substantive issue on which we disagreed was Craig's view of heaven and hell. Perhaps because of my mathematical bent, I asked him, "How much better is the worst person in heaven than the best person in hell?" Craig responded to what he knew would be his biggest applause line: "We can't be saved by good works, since we're all miserable sinners. The only way to be saved is through accepting Jesus as your personal savior." I'm not antireligion in general, but I'm uncomfortable with people whose worldview places belief above behavior.

William Lane Craig and I stayed at the same hotel, and I saw him in the lobby the morning after the debate. He was waiting for transportation to take him to the University of North Carolina at Charlotte for his next debate on the same topic. I took this opportunity to ask him a couple of questions he had avoided answering during our debate. I asked if he thought Mormons were real Christians, and he said, "No. They are a cult." I then asked Craig how he made moral decisions based on his objective morality, and I got this rather puzzling reply: "Pretty much the same way you do." I would have liked to follow up on this answer, but Craig's car arrived to whisk him away. I had the feeling that Craig felt more comfortable talking to me publicly than privately.

William Lane Craig enjoys being the center of attention on stage. But I won't cast the first stone at him. I do, too.

Does Science Make Belief in God Harder or Easier?

This was the topic I debated during "Darwin Week" on February 8, 2011, at the College of Charleston. My able opponent was Dr. Karl Giberson, physics professor at Eastern Nazarene College in Boston, and vice president of the BioLogos forum founded by Dr. Francis Collins, known for his leadership of the Human Genome Project. The mission of BioLogos includes showing "the compatibility of Christian faith with scientific discoveries about the origins of the universe and life."

The auditorium held two hundred, but many students wound up sitting on the floor and stage, while others had to be turned away for lack of space. The debate was in the Lincoln-Douglas format, which allowed ample time for us to question each other. Dr. Giberson opened by claiming how unlikely it would be for mathematicians to discover by chance how simple and beautiful our natural laws are, and this constitutes scientific evidence for a creator. I replied it's nice to know that God set the universe in motion so that some 13.7 billion years later mathematicians would appear as his crowning achievement. I asked Giberson if God also arranged for an asteroid to hit the earth and wipe out dinosaurs so humans could evolve 55 million years later. He acknowledged that if the universe were again set in motion, humans in our present form might never exist, but opined that the laws were fine-tuned enough so that there would be some form of intelligent creatures.

A few Christians in the audience cringed at the thought that God's plan might have led to a chimpanzee Jesus coming to save other chimpanzees from sin. Giberson said he didn't believe that God tinkers much with natural laws, one notable exception being the miracle of the resurrection of Jesus from the dead, though my opponent had no nonbiblical source for this event.

Giberson laughed when I referred to him during the debate as a theological combination of the Dalai Lama and Pat Robertson. I said that he and the Dalai Lama are both intelligent men who value science. I quoted the Dalai Lama, "If science proves some belief of Buddhism is wrong, then Buddhism will have to change," and added that Giberson could probably say the same about Christianity. But Giberson doesn't believe in reincarnation because he wasn't born into a Buddhist family, and the Dalai Lama doesn't believe in the resurrection of Jesus because he wasn't born into a Christian family.

Reverend Pat Robertson and Dr. Giberson are both Christian evangelists who recognize there are conflicts between science and the Bible, and they both look for ways to keep Christians in the fold. Robertson tells Christians to believe all miracles of the Bible, even if they conflict with scientific evidence. Giberson tells Christians not to believe the many biblical miracles that science can demonstrably prove to be false, but he says they should believe in the resurrection miracle because it is essential to Christianity.

Giberson had a tough position to defend in this debate, and he did the best he could. He seemed to be saying he's a Christian and believes in evolution so others can also believe in evolution and remain a Christian. But I pointed out that a person could believe in evolution and reincarnation, evolution and alien abduction, or evolution and astrology. There's an abundance of scientific evidence for evolution, but evidence for those other beliefs is sorely lacking.

I wish all Christians accepted science to the degree Giberson does, but I don't think he gave any credible evidence for belief in any gods. He was the most liberal Christian I've debated, and in my mind the closest to being an atheist. He seemed to hold the minimal belief required to remain teaching at his Christian institution. A few months after the debate, Karl left Eastern Nazarene College to "create more time for writing." Perhaps, but I can at least fantasize that the strength of my arguments might have had something to do with his career change. I found Karl Giberson to be an extremely warm person, and someone I would be proud to call a friend.

Oxford University Debate

What do I have in common with Mahatma Gandhi, Nelson Mandela, Malcolm X, Richard Nixon, and Mother Teresa? We all spoke at the Oxford Union at Oxford University in England, the most famous debating society in the world.

I took part in a debate there on May 26, 2005, about whether American religion undermines American values. My opponents (there were three on each side) were Rich Lowry, editor of the *National Review*; Eric Metaxas, author of forty books and writer for former Watergate conspirator and conservative Christian Charles Colson; and Joe Loconte, a William E. Simon Fellow in Religion at the Heritage Foundation. Author Michael Lind from my side cancelled, leaving Welton Gaddy, a Baptist minister and president of the national Interfaith Alliance, and me. A student opened the debate for each side.

This was easily my favorite debate, not so much for the debate itself but for the unique experience. The age-old format at the Oxford Union is highly formal and ritualized. Debaters wear tuxedos or long gowns, and the students who run the debate also wear formal attire.

Debating at the Oxford Union in 2005. Rev. Welton Gaddy is on my right; Rich Lowry (leaning forward) and Joe Loconte are on my left.

I had never before worn a tuxedo. Sharon, who knows how to find such things, led me to a store in a Charleston mall where I could rent one. It was early May, and I found my shaggy, white-bearded self waiting for service behind a line of high school seniors preparing for their upcoming prom. They knew how to try on a tuxedo, but I hadn't a clue. Fortunately, the sales clerk helped dress me.

We packed the tuxedo and flew to London several days early, taking the opportunity to do some sightseeing before our train ride to Oxford. The evening of the debate all participants, student leaders, and guests enjoyed an elaborate, formal dinner with lots of good wine. At the appointed time, we ceremoniously walked into the historic debate hall to audience applause.

This debate was easier to prepare for than most, because of its format. Each debater spoke for twelve minutes, and we didn't get to rebut or question opponents.

Dr. Welton Gaddy gave a fact-based, convincing argument supporting our case. I followed Rich Lowry, who had complained about the problems of being a conservative in New York City. My opening sentence made even Lowry laugh: "You just heard Richard Lowry mention what it's like to be a conservative in New York City; now I'll talk about what it's like to be an atheist in South Carolina." I then described some of my experiences, to much laughter from the audience.

In trying to show how tolerant and diverse Christianity is in America, Lowry said that a committed Christian like Howard Dean (former governor of Vermont) left one Christian sect to join another because of a dispute over a bicycle path. I speculated that Howard Dean was probably not a committed Christian, but had to pretend in order to get elected. Lowry told me after the debate that he agreed with me on this point. (Dean had failed in his 2004 bid to gain the presidential nomination. He lost, of course, to another professed Christian.)

My biggest applause came when I said: "In the melting pot called America, we are one nation under the Constitution (or maybe under Canada), but not one nation under God. Given how the Religious Right opposes the teaching of evolution or any scientific and social view that conflicts with a literal interpretation of the Bible, we are really becoming one nation *undereducated*. And this is not an American value to be proud of."

When the debate ended, the audience of students, professors, and guests voted with their feet according to which door they chose to leave the hall. Despite my opponents' side outnumbering ours by three to two, our side won the debate.

When we got home, I received a nice e-mail from Richard Tydeman, then student president of the Oxford Union Society. He said, "I thought it was a fantastic debate and you made a great speech which went down extremely well (as you will have noticed!). Congratulations also on winning, of course, and I hope you and Sharon both had a good time in Britain overall, too." We did.

After my comment about Howard Dean, I thought more about the apparent political requirement in America to profess belief, especially of a Christian nature. Though there are hundreds of Christian denominations, I had previously broken them roughly into conservative, liberal, and cultural. To these, I now add a fourth category: political—one who thinks an unwritten requirement for public office is to profess deeply held Christian beliefs.

In 2008, Americans showed how diverse they could be when they elected as president a black Christian instead of the usual white Christian. Barack Obama was once an agnostic, but became a Christian in time to run for public office. I believe he even made a political choice for minister, Reverend Jeremiah Wright, whom Obama abandoned when it began to hurt him politically.

In 2010, my home state of South Carolina showed how diverse it could be when it elected as governor its first female Sikh Christian, instead of the usual white male Christian. Governor Nikki Haley, whose parents had immigrated to this country from India, was raised as a Sikh, and became a Christian before running for public office. When she first became a candidate, her Web site said, "I believe in the power and grace of Almighty God." She later felt the need to change the Web site to, "My faith in Christ has a profound impact on my daily life. Being a Christian is not about words, but about living for Christ every day." A cynic might say, "Maybe it's also about winning elections."

I don't know for sure what Dean, Obama, and Haley really believe, but I suspect they are all political Christians. I think it says something sad about our politicians and the electorate that many politicians feel they must pretend to be religious.

CHAPTER 12

ESSAYS ON RELIGION

Why I Love the Bible

The "Good Book" really is a good book. Maybe not great, but good. Some atheists attack it because of its believers. Christians often use the cliché, "Love the sinner, but hate the sin." In practice, lots of them hate both. Atheists, however, should distinguish between the quality of a book and the behavior of its adherents.

After several false fire alarms at a hotel, I jokingly said to a friend while waiting for the all clear, "One of these times we'll ignore the alarm when there's a fire—just like in the 'biblical story' of the boy who cried wolf." Of course my friend pointed out the story was from Aesop, not the Bible, to which I responded that Aesop wrote the better book. Both feature talking animals, with moral lessons and universal truths. Leaving aside the question of which book imparts better advice, at least Aesop's stories are recognized as fables. The same can be said of the *Iliad* and the *Odyssey*, though they were once religious texts for some.

For better or worse, the Bible and the religions it spawned have deeply influenced our culture and the world. To be educated, we need to know the Bible, understand why so many love it, and learn how to communicate better with those who do.

The Bible has many boring, violent, silly, and repetitive sections. My elementary school teachers began each day reading a portion to us. When one had her students take turns reading, I selected a portion with an endless array of "begats," much to the amusement of my classmates. Pennsylvania state law then required the Bible to be read without comment, but my teacher's facial expression conveyed her displeasure.

Scholars have written books about political and cultural influences under which the Bible was conceived, atheists have written books about atrocious and contradictory biblical passages, and theists have written books justifying those passages as the inerrant word of God. The book I've not seen is a biblical equivalent of Aesop's fables, with different yet positive moral lessons from biblical stories. To inspire someone to write a biblical fables book, I'll start with ten fables from Genesis, the first of sixty-six books in the Bible. My messages may be considerably different from those of religious people, or even other atheists, but they can serve as a good starting point for discussions about the Bible.

1. The Matchmaker Fable

God notices that the first man he created is lonely. He parades a bunch of animals in front of Adam, but Adam remains lonely. God then fashions another human from Adam's rib, with similar but not identical body parts. Adam prefers Eve to all the other animals.

The Moral: Humans and most other species are social animals. Solitude has its rewards, but so does the company of others. It's good to associate and cooperate with people whose values you share. Learn about other kinds, but recognize those with whom you can communicate well and trust.

2. The Snake Fable

God tells Adam he may eat anything in a garden but the fruit from one tree, saying he will die on the day he eats it. A cunning snake convinces Eve that her eyes will open after eating the forbidden fruit and she will know good and evil. Eve eats, likes what she sees, and encourages Adam to partake. They discover many things, presumably including sex, and so God banishes Adam and Eve from the garden and tells them they need to work for a living.

The Moral: God makes blind obedience the supreme virtue, assuming ignorance is bliss. God either lied or was mistaken when he said humans would die on the day they received knowledge. So don't blindly believe, even if you pay a price for independent thought. Better to have freedom without a guarantee of security than to have security without freedom.

3. The Cain and Abel Fable

Adam and Eve's two sons bring offerings to God, but God gives no reason for accepting Abel's and rejecting Cain's. Cain gets angry and kills Abel. When God asks Cain where Abel is, Cain responds, "Am I my brother's keeper?" God curses Cain, who must now wander the earth, but God places a protective mark on Cain.

The Moral: The first worship ceremony is followed immediately by the first murder, which shows we must not put our love and worship of a God above our love for human beings, especially when God's favoritism can be so arbitrary. Cain belatedly learns that humans should look out for one another, making each of us our brother and sister's keeper. God recognizes his culpability in the first murder and puts a mark on Cain as a sign to those he meets that they must not do to Cain what Cain did to Abel.

4. The Flood Fable

God decides to destroy almost all of Earth's inhabitants in a flood because humans are wicked. He instructs an obedient, 600-year-old Noah to build an ark for his family and pairs of all species. When the genocide is complete and the waters recede, all leave the ark and Noah sacrifices an animal to appease God's wrath. God likes this sweet odor of burnt flesh and promises never again to destroy the earth by flood. Noah gets drunk, one of his sons takes sexual advantage of him, and humans remain as wicked as ever.

The Moral: God learns that his expectations for humans were unrealistic and genocide solves nothing. Never indiscriminately destroy the innocent along with the guilty. God should have been concerned about a compliant Noah who showed no empathy for the lives of others. Older doesn't necessarily mean wiser, even with 600 years of experience.

5. The Tower of Babel Fable

Men in the city of Babel decide to build a tower to heaven. God thwarts this activity by confusing their language, and the men are scattered throughout the world.

The Moral: Leaders must not become as insecure as God, who prevented others from cooperating and moving upward together. Also, there is value in diversity. Each of us must decide when to go along with the crowd and when to set out on a road not taken.

6. The Sodom and Gomorrah Fable

God tells Abraham he plans to destroy the city of Sodom because of its wickedness. Abraham convinces God to reconsider if fifty, then forty-five, thirty, twenty, or even ten righteous people can be found. Abraham's nephew Lot is the lone righteous person found, so God spares only Lot and his family from the fire and brimstone that obliterate Sodom and Gomorrah. God tells them not to look back, but Lot's wife peeks, so God turns her into a pillar of salt. Lot and his two daughters flee and live in a cave. Lot's daughters want children, but there are no eligible men around to impregnate them. So they take turns getting their father drunk and having sex with him.

The Moral: Abraham is morally superior to Noah in fable 4, since he tried to talk God out of mass destruction. It takes courage to stand up to authority, especially one bent on genocide. God teaches the value of looking forward to a fresh start without dwelling on the past, but what he did to Lot's wife for a brief look backward was, shall we say, overkill. People in new and frightening environments are likely to act in ways formerly unthinkable. Lot's motherless daughters, believing all other men dead, chose what they thought the most practical path for the survival of the species—make love, not war.

7. The Binding of Isaac Fable

God commands Abraham to sacrifice Isaac, the son he loves. Abraham acquiesces, but God stops Abraham as he lifts his knife. God provides a lamb to take Isaac's place.

The Moral: God tests Abraham, who fails the test. Nobody should commit an atrocity, no matter who makes the request. Abraham's willingness to kill his son creates a dysfunctional family. Neither Abraham's son Isaac nor his wife Sarah ever speak to Abraham again in the Bible. It is better to do good than to have faith.

8. The Jacob and Esau Fable

A "birthright" normally passes from father to oldest son. Jacob convinces his tired and hungry older brother Esau to trade his birthright for a meal. Years later, a blind and faltering Isaac plans to give his best blessing to his favorite son, Esau. However, Isaac's wife Rebekah tricks him into mistakenly blessing Jacob, Rebekah's favorite son. When Esau learns of the deception, he vows to take revenge. Jacob flees, but eventually wants to return and so he sends gifts to his brother. Esau forgives Jacob, and the brothers reconcile.

The Moral: We shouldn't prey on the weaknesses of family members, as Jacob and Rebekah did. On the other hand, a future leader should be a thinker and planner like Jacob, rather than prone to foolish choices, as Esau was. Esau makes the wise decision to forgive his brother, rather than seek revenge. Violence breeds violence.

9. The Joseph and Coat Fable

Of his twelve sons, Jacob favors Joseph. He gives Joseph a coat of many colors and Joseph tells his brothers of his dream that they will one day serve him. Joseph's envious brothers plot to kill him, but one of the brothers, Judah, persuades them instead to sell Joseph into slavery. Joseph becomes a slave in Egypt and improves his lot by interpreting the Pharaoh's dreams. Joseph and the Pharaoh conspire to buy and hoard grain before a famine, after which they sell it back to starving inhabitants for enormous profit. Joseph's brothers no longer recognize him when they beg Joseph to sell them food. Joseph accuses his brothers of being spies, holds them hostage for several days, and later falsely blames one for theft. Finally, Joseph reveals who he is and the brothers reconcile.

The Moral: As often occurs in families, Jacob picks up some of the bad habits of his father, and suffers for openly favoring one child over another. We learn about degrees of horrendous behavior, with Judas appearing the most reasonable brother because he favors selling Joseph into slavery instead of killing him. Joseph, similarly, feels the need to torment his brothers before eventually disclosing his identity and dropping the trumped up charges. We learn in this fable not to flaunt a favored status, as Joseph does, and not to overreact from envy, as Joseph's brothers do.

10. The Onanism Fable

Judah, Joseph's brother in the previous fable, has three sons—Er,

Onan, and Shelah. Er marries Tamar, but God kills Er. Following tradition, Judah tells the son next in line, Onan, to have sex with Tamar and produce offspring who will inherit Er's property. Onan wants to remain Er's heir, so he pulls out of Tamar just in time to ejaculate on the ground. God then kills Onan, so Judah fears Tamar is jinxed and banishes her from the household instead of bringing her to his remaining son. Still wanting an heir, Tamar dresses as a prostitute at the side of a road and offers her services to a willing and unsuspecting Judah. When Judah sees a pregnant Tamar several months later, he calls her a whore and condemns her to be burned to death. After Tamar produces incontrovertible evidence that Judah is the father, he repents and says, "She is more righteous than I, since I refused to give her my son Shelah."

The Moral: Marriages arranged by authority figures for the sole purpose of increasing property can lead to death and destruction. Couples should be honest with each other about their sexual relationships, which Onan was not. Judah, at least, is willing to admit his error when confronted with proof. Tamar is the most admirable character because she is not a hypocrite and attains her goal the only way possible in a culture ruled by men.

My ten fables are abridged and there are many more in Genesis alone. Atheists almost never put the character "God" in a good light, and God's behavior is particularly egregious in Genesis. But God learns from some of his early mistakes and in later fables we can even "praise God" on occasions when it's warranted. Such praise would show that atheists don't hate God any more than they hate Zeus.

Here's why I think a biblical fables book could benefit both children and adults. Students are required to write book reports not only to provide evidence that they have read the book, but because it helps them focus on key parts from which to draw inferences. Ideally, a discussion follows between teacher and students about disparate or contradictory understandings of the same passage. One of the best ways to read the Bible is by identifying and writing about its fables. An atheist's insights would be different from those of either liberal or conservative religionists. But if we start with the assumption that the Bible is a good and important book to read, this common bond might earn atheists more respect within the religious community, and help atheists communicate their differences more effectively with at least some theists.

Kindergarten Questions for God

All I Really Need to Know, I Learned in Kindergarten was a best-selling book by Robert Fulghum. The Jesuits put it, "Give me a child until the age of seven, and I will give you the man." In *The God Delusion*, Richard Dawkins points out that following blindly what parents or other authority figures told you may have had survival benefits because experience taught elders the dangers to avoid. But as we move from child to adult, we need to learn which lessons of our parents to keep, modify, or discard.

We shouldn't shield children from learning about beliefs of others. Some are reprimanded for asking questions about God that make adults uncomfortable, and some are given "age-appropriate" answers. For fundamentalists, a "correct" answer for a kindergartener is equally correct for an adult. Some kindergarten questions are not easy for adults to answer. I've had adult discussions about each of the ten questions below.

1. Who Created God?
This is the first question my rabbi refused to answer, and I understand why. There is no reasonable answer to give a child or adult, only a faith-based answer. If everything has a cause, then God has a cause. If God can exist without a cause, then so can our universe.

2. What Was God Doing before He Created Humans?
Whether believers think the universe is several thousand or several billion years old, they still believe God predates it by billions of years (or eternity, whatever that means). If God's primary concern is with us, he sure waited a long time before saying to himself, "I'm lonely. I think I'll create human beings to mess around with."

3. Since We Are Created in God's Image, Does He Look or Act Like Us?
Even children find it difficult to picture God as an old man with a white beard (a slimmed down version of Santa Claus). If he's perfect, why did he create us so flawed?

4. Why Did God Stop Talking to Humans (Me)?

We think people are crazy if they claim to have actual conversations with God. Were those so-called ancient prophets also crazy? Or did they just make up stuff so people would follow them? Adherents of all three monotheistic religions honor Abraham for his unwavering faith when he hears God tell him to kill his son, yet today we institutionalize people who hear the same voice (and request).

5. Why Do Bad Things Happen to Good People?

There is no satisfying answer if you believe in a good and powerful god. To paraphrase God's response to Job: "Who the hell do you think you are to question me? Were you there when I did all this incredible universe stuff, you puny little ignorant jerk?"

6. Does God Ever Change His Mind When We Pray?

Whether or not we believe everything is predetermined, it seems like heresy to ask God for something he hadn't planned on giving. Doesn't he already know what's best? I just can't picture God slapping his forehead and saying to himself, "Good point, Herb. I hadn't thought of it in that clever way of yours."

7. Why Is Belief So Important to God When He Judges Us?

Children are praised or punished for how they act, not what they think. They are taught that actions speak louder than words, and I would add that words speak louder than thoughts. Wouldn't a benevolent deity focus on our being kind to the people he allegedly loves? Is God's ego so fragile that he confines his ultimate wrath and vindictive acts to those who disbelieve in his existence or don't properly worship him?

8. How Much Better Is the Worst Person in Heaven than the Best Person in Hell?

Our binary divisions are usually quite arbitrary. People may vote when they are eighteen and buy alcohol when they are twenty-one, but they are not permitted to do either on the day before. We recognize such rules for what they are—distinctions without a real difference. Not so when it comes to the cutoff between an eternity of bliss and an eternity of torture.

9. Will I Be the Same Person in Heaven as I Am on Earth?
If I can sin on earth, but not in heaven, then I will be a different person. Who will I be? And if I can sin in heaven will I *still* be in danger of being cast into hell?

10. Why Are There Other Religions?
All my neighbors stay with the religions of their childhood and believe the others are false. After all these millennia, can't a benevolent God help us get it right?

Positive Atheism

In January 2005, a Charleston television station invited me to appear on a local show called *Talkback Live* about a legislative bill to place a Ten Commandments plaque on the State Capitol grounds. When I arrived at the station, the producer told me the bad word on my T-shirt was unfit for a family news show. He asked me to cover the T-shirt with a jacket so that viewers would be protected from its message, "Smile, there is no hell."

Isn't it interesting that a family news show would censor "hell," a word of primary biblical significance to most fundamentalist Christians? Yet "Smile, there is no hell" is an important message of positive atheism. We don't believe in hell or eternal punishment, and that's worth smiling about.

Positive atheism sounds like an oxymoron. After all, atheism really is a negative word. It means not having a belief in any gods. But negative isn't always bad. Other negative words are *independent, nondiscrimination,* and *antidote.* Religious people describe their deity with negative terms (infinite, unlimited, infallible). And 80 percent of the Ten Commandments (the eight "thou shalt nots") are negative. Negative protestors founded what is now the dominant religion in this country. They are *Protest*ants.

Here's an example of negative atheism. If a religious person says, "I'll pray for you," a negative response would be, "OK, I'll think for both of us." But this hurtful reply would only offend a presumably well-meaning person. I think the best response is, "Thank you." However, if the opportunity presented itself, I might get into a discussion about the

My notary certificate on the wall. I'm wearing the shirt that was too shocking to be shown on local TV during an interview in 2005.

efficacy of prayer with questions like: Why would an all-knowing, all-loving god change his mind because you asked him to? Or why would a god who ignored the prayers of millions of Holocaust victims take a special interest in a football game? But I would only engage a person who seemed receptive to such a discussion.

Pope Herb I

I was invited by the American Atheists organization to speak at a peaceful protest on April 16, 2008, when Pope Benedict XVI was visiting President Bush in the White House. Here are my remarks in Lafayette Park, across from the White House:

A Catholic News Service article mentioned that Pope Benedict XVI would pay close attention to what people say in the United States. "This pope is a great listener," said papal spokesman Father Federico Lombardi. Wonderful! Here's what I want to tell him: Pope Benedict, I'd like to defend you against some scurrilous allegations. I don't believe you are the Antichrist, as many Christians do—including Pastor John Hagee, who also called the Catholic Church the whore of Babylon and a cult. It's not the whore of Babylon and it's no more a cult than Mormonism, Islam, Jehovah's Witnesses, Scientology, or any other religion that values faith more than reason.

I was thrilled when you said, "A world marked by so much injustice, innocent suffering and cynicism of power cannot be the work of a good God. A God with responsibility for such a world would not be a just God, much less a good God." Unfortunately, you didn't claim these as your own words, but as arguments used by atheists. Still, I give you credit for accurately portraying my view.

As a card-carrying member of the American Civil Liberties Union, I support your right to promote your beliefs, just as I supported the rights of the American Nazi Party to march in Skokie. The best counter to bad or hateful speech is good speech, not censorship. If you agree about the importance of dialogue among those with whom you disagree, I hope you'll engage with some of us to better understand our perspective.

I consider it progress that you seek ways to cooperate rather than continue fighting against factions with whom you have doctrinal differences. Unfortunately, your cooperation with other Christians is for the purpose of defending the faith against secularism, which you call a fundamental problem of modern society. You even made it the goal of your papacy to counteract secularism, claiming atheism was responsible for some of the greatest forms of cruelty in history, citing leaders like Stalin and Mao.

The cruelty under such regimes was made possible not because its leaders were atheists, but because its leaders were granted unquestioned power and loyalty. Dissenters were banished, imprisoned, or killed. Such actions, whether propagated by secular or religious regimes, are inexcusable. Democratic countries that tolerate dissent are the ones most likely to promote human rights for all. These happen to be the secular governments you decry, not the theocratic governments you apparently would like us to emulate.

Our godless Constitution gives us the right to worship one, many, or no gods. We proudly promote freedom of conscience for all people. We will defend secularism against theocratic attacks, whether such attacks come from fundamentalist Islam or from your church. Such attacks motivate us even more to keep our government secular.

You said you are greatly disturbed because atheists put their faith in human reason and freedom. I would be, as well, if human reason and freedom had led to atheist crusades, atheist inquisitions, atheist witch burnings, or atheist suicide bombers.

You said in an encyclical that many reject religious faith because they no longer find the prospect of an eternal afterlife attractive. Not true. We don't find an eternal afterlife unattractive; we just find it *unbelievable*. You say that fear of God is at the root of modern atheism. But how can we fear a God whose existence we don't accept? *We do* fear many of God's defenders, those inspired by God to destroy infidels and heretics.

You also decry moral relativism, which undermines your absolutist pronouncements. Yes, we tolerate other points of view and are willing to change when evidence warrants. Otherwise, we'd be stuck defending some outlandish claims written thousands of years ago. We are mindful of the words in Lord Acton's famous April 3, 1887 letter to the Archbishop of Canterbury in opposition to papal infallibility: "Power tends to corrupt, and absolute power corrupts absolutely."

Even your own church has shown inclinations toward relativism. In 1990, as Cardinal Ratzinger, you still maintained that the actions of the Church at the time of Galileo were justified because of ethical and social consequences of Galileo's teaching. However, in 2000, your papal predecessor finally apologized for the church's treatment of Galileo. Though several hundred years late, this is still progress away from absolutism. Your church also apologized in 2000 for excesses in the Inquisition, for witch burning, and for its silence during the Holocaust. I guess it's better late than never.

I would like to suggest that you take action on a few obvious items so another pope doesn't have to apologize for them. If you care about human rights, please support stem cell research that likely will lead to cures for many diseases. And stop denigrating gays and lesbians simply because they want a loving sexual relationship. Even though you oppose a woman's right to choose, do you want a future pope to apologize for all who died from AIDS because your church preferred death without condoms to life with condoms? Comprehensive sex education programs make abortions more rare, and you must know that contraception is more effective than the so-called rhythm method.

Your church can look rather foolish when its reasons keep changing to maintain its conclusions. It used to accept the wisdom of St. Bonaventure, who said, "Since only the male was made in the image of God, only the male can receive the godlike office of priest." After such claims of female inferiority became a bit embarrassing even to the Church, the story became, "Only males can hold positions of leadership in the Church because all the apostles were male." By that reasoning, I am more qualified to be pope than you. All the apostles were married Jews, just like me. So either your church must again change its reasoning or I would like future consideration to become Pope Herb I.

The Constitution and the Bible

What can be more different for atheists than a godless Constitution and a god-awful Bible? Lots, actually, and we oversimplify when we think of them only as reason vs. faith. Recognizing their many similarities can enhance communication between those whose worldviews may be worlds apart.

Each document is open to interpretation, with conservatives more likely to focus on "original intent," and liberals on societal changes. Though we don't always know original intent, we know political and social climates that inspired portions of the Bible and Constitution. Both were built on earlier works, modified to suit the times, and written for present and future generations. Before final approval, committees debated and voted on passages to include or exclude. Most Americans believe both documents were inspired and blessed by God. Religionists deify their holy books for obvious reasons. Liberals and conservatives "deify" those who wrote the Constitution, so both sides quote selectively from founders like George Washington, Thomas Jefferson, and James Madison when it suits their purposes.

Conservative religionists and civil libertarians have supported "Hang Ten" displays on public buildings, though different tens: the Ten Commandments and the first ten constitutional amendments that make up the Bill of Rights. What these have in common are society's overwhelming support and ignorance of their contents. Most Commandment enthusiasts can't name them, while many Americans respond unfavorably when they are read the Bill of Rights without being told where they come from. Both contain anachronisms. The Tenth Commandment tells us not to covet our neighbor's slaves, oxen, wife, or other property; the Third Amendment tells us in times of peace that we need not quarter any soldier in our house without our consent.

Agreed-upon interpretive bodies make binding decisions about both documents. The U.S. Supreme Court is the ultimate decider on constitutional law, while each religion determines who will decide belief and interpretation. Both constitutional and biblical leaders often choose citations to justify preconceived outcomes. We expect secular judges to be more objective than biblical judges, but how do we explain the spate of 5–4 Supreme Court decisions? A case can be made that some judges interpret the Constitution the way poet William Blake wrote about that other document, "Both read the Bible day and night, but thou reads't black where I read white."

Like all analogies, the Constitution/Bible one is flawed. Writers of the Constitution understood it to be an imperfect document and made provisions for future generations to amend it. Alas, conservative religionists permit no such biblical escape clause, and I think I know why. When we pick and choose from so-called holy books, we recognize them to be products of fallible humans, not of an infallible deity.

Thomas Jefferson, in effect, amended the Christian Bible. He wrote his own version, leaving out miracle stories and keeping only what made sense to him. He referred to what remained as "diamonds in a dunghill." Not surprisingly, the religious right of his day attacked Jefferson for being an infidel and a filthy atheist.

Ten Commandments

While liberal religionists know the Bible contains some false and anachronistic passages, most believe the Ten Commandments are among the finest guidelines for a virtuous life. But few can name them, and even fewer have thought through their implications for our pluralistic, democratic, and freedom-loving society.

The First Commandment, "Thou shalt have no other gods before me," conflicts with the First Amendment to our Constitution that guarantees freedom of religion—the right to worship one, several, or no gods. The next three Commandments (no graven images, not taking God's name in vain, keeping the Sabbath day holy) refer to specific kinds of worship directed toward a God who punishes several generations of children because their fathers did not believe. These first four are religious edicts that have nothing to do with ethical behavior. They describe how to worship and pay homage to a jealous and vindictive God.

Those who refer to these commandments as our Judeo-Christian heritage should realize they long predate Christianity. Jesus was a Jew and would be considered a false god by his people, not one to be worshipped, and the Sabbath would be on Saturday, not Sunday.

The Fifth Commandment, about honoring parents, should not be so unconditional as to condone child abuse. Unfortunately, there is no commandment about parents honoring their children or treating them humanely.

The next four (proscriptions against murder, adultery, stealing, and lying) obviously have merit, and existed in cultures long before Moses. Yet even they are open to interpretation. Is abortion murder? Euthanasia? War? Capital punishment? People can tolerate diverse opinions, unless convinced they are acting as God's messenger.

The Tenth Commandment, "Thou shalt not covet thy neighbor's house, wife, slaves, ox, donkey, or any other property," condones slavery and treating women as property. Furthermore, the American system of capitalism relies on coveting our neighbor's possessions.

The Ten Commandments are notable for what they omit. Instead of condemning covetousness and threatening to punish children if their parents don't worship in the correct way, why don't they condemn slavery, racism, sexual assault, child and spouse abuse, and torture? After a few moments' thought, any of us could come up with a better set of rules to live by than the Ten Commandments.

These Commandments from Exodus 20 are only 10 of the 613 in the Hebrew Bible. The Catholic Ten Commandments are somewhat different, omitting the one about not having graven images and splitting the coveting commandment into two.

The most interesting commandments are in Exodus 34:12–28, the only place the Hebrew Bible refers to the Ten Commandments. It concludes, "Moses was there with the Lord forty days and forty nights without eating bread or drinking water. And he wrote on the tablets the words of the covenant—the Ten Commandments." However, religions don't promote these because they are particularly anachronistic. The sage advice includes: "Thou shalt not offer the blood of my sacrifice with leaven; the firstborn of a donkey shalt thou redeem with a lamb; the sacrifice of the festival of the Passover shall not be left until the morning; the best of the first fruits you shall bring to the house of the Lord your God." And here's my personal favorite: "Thou shalt not boil a kid in its mother's milk."

However puzzling these Commandments, I think it's better to refrain from boiling a kid in its mother's milk than to justify owning slaves or treating women as property. (Incidentally, the Jewish Kosher laws about not eating meat and milk at the same meal are extrapolated from the "boiling kid" Commandment.)

Whatever people feel about these Commandments, they have the free speech right to promote any or all versions. However, nobody may enlist the government to promulgate a particular religious view. Posting one of the versions of the Ten Commandments in government buildings allies the government with two creeds, Judaism and Christianity, and sends a message to Americans of other faiths or no faith that they are second-class citizens.

In 1998, in Charleston County, South Carolina, where I live, fiscally conservative councilman Tim Scott insisted on posting a Ten Commandments plaque on the wall of County Council chambers, ignoring advice that he would lose the anticipated legal challenge. Scott responded that the display was needed to remind residents of moral absolutes. As expected, the court declared the display unconstitutional and taxpayers were left with a substantial bill for legal costs.

After the plaque went up, the Charleston *Post and Courier* asked Councilman Scott if he could name all the Commandments. He couldn't. Scott was not laughed off the political stage. He continued to serve on County Council, where he became its chairman in 2007. He was elected to the South Carolina House of Representatives in 2008 and to the United States House of Representatives in 2010. He is now my congressional representative, though I can't say he represents my views.

Despite the political victories of Scott and those who share his beliefs, the metaphorical wall separating church and state remains standing, though with increasing fragility. While controversies abound, at least on such public postings, I propose a simple solution that both honors our democratic principles and reminds us of the curbs on governmental abuse of power.

Let's display our Bill of Rights on public buildings. We would still be posting ten (rights, not commandments), and we Americans can all support and celebrate these ten. Or can we?

CHAPTER 14

BLOGGING FOR THE
WASHINGTON POST

In May 2009, I became a panelist for "On Faith," an online forum about religion produced by the *Washington Post*. I'm not the only atheist on the panel. Others include Richard Dawkins, Daniel Dennett, Sam Harris, and Susan Jacoby (coincidentally, all members of the Secular Coalition for America Advisory Board). The *Post* panel includes conservative religionists Chuck Colson, Richard Land, Cal Thomas, and Rick Warren; liberal religionists Karen Armstrong, Welton Gaddy, Barry Lynn, and John Shelby Spong; New Age religionist Deepak Chopra; and other distinguished panelists representing pretty much a full spectrum of religious and nonreligious views.

Sally Quinn of the *Washington Post* poses questions for panelists, and panelists also pitch story ideas. I enjoy contributing, and have posted more than a hundred pieces.

Just a few days after the 2008 elections, but before becoming a regular panelist, I was invited as president of the Secular Coalition for America to be a guest voice for "On Faith." The following piece, titled "For Secular Americans, Lip Service Beats No Service," was my "mad as hell and I'm not going to take it anymore" moment.

About a month before this recent election, some local progressives in South Carolina asked if I would help Democrat Linda Ketner in her congressional campaign against conservative incumbent Republican Henry Brown. At first, they thought I was joking when I said I didn't even plan to vote for her and would leave that portion of my ballot blank. They ticked off a number of issues on which Ketner was better than her opponent. I agreed, even adding a couple of my own. My problem with Ketner was a thirty-second TV ad in which she proclaimed her love of God three times.

I told my friends I have gradually begun withdrawing support from otherwise acceptable candidates who make personal religious beliefs a focal point of their campaigns. In taking a longer view, I described how the Religious Right has moved beyond merely saving souls to becoming a formidable political force. My friends discounted this reasoning. The Religious Right may have been thrown a few crumbs by politicians, they said, but mainly all they received in return for their support was lip service. When my companions asked if I, an atheist, would settle for so little, I replied without hesitation: "YES! We'll take lip service!"

I would be thrilled to see politicians court us by accepting invitations to speak at atheist and humanist conferences, as they do at religious events. I would love to hear them say we were founded as a secular nation with no mention of any gods in our Constitution, and speak about the value of separating religion from government. I'd be delighted to hear them defend atheists and agnostics from our detractors, reminding Americans that freedom of conscience extends to citizens of all faiths and none.

Yes, even if their words changed nothing about public policy, lip service would be a wonderful new dimension in the relationship between politicians and secular Americans—it would mean public acknowledgement that we *exist*. It might even lead to the occasional political crumb: an elected official hiring advisors who are openly humanist, for example. Just this minimal level of recognition could go a long way toward changing the hearts and minds of people who assume god belief to be a prerequisite for morality and ethical behavior.

Why would secular Americans like me set the bar so low? Because we have no direction to go but up. Political candidates are happy to accept our contributions, our volunteer hours, and our votes—as long as we put bags over our heads. ("Thanks," they say quietly. "You understand why I can't....") They behave this way partly because they underestimate our numbers, partly because polls show that Americans fear and distrust atheists, and partly because they think we have nowhere else to go.

What has generally been viewed as the most scurrilous activity of the 2008 campaign season occurred in North Carolina when an ad put out by incumbent Senator Elizabeth Dole's campaign accused opponent Kay Hagan of associating with known atheists who held a fundraiser for her. The ad implied that Hagan herself might be "godless" and that she might have promised something in return for the support of such "vile, radical liberals." Hagan's campaign responded that she is not an atheist, and, in fact, is an active Christian.

That just sets the record straight; no problem so far. But then Hagan filed a lawsuit, claiming defamation of her good name and reputation in the community.

To see why atheists might reply, "A plague on both your houses," consider this unrealistic hypothetical: Candidate A accuses Candidate B of consorting with Jews, and possibly even being one. Candidate B says she is a Christian, not a Jew, and files a defamation lawsuit because of the assumed damage to her reputation in the community. Of course, no Candidate A in this country, at least not in this century, would attempt such an accusation; and no Candidate B would react as if the label "Jew" were understood by all to be an insult. You may substitute just about any other minority for "Jew" in this scenario to get a sense of the secular community's reaction to the squabbling between Dole and Hagan. If merely associating with nonreligious Americans is political suicide and being mistaken for one of us constitutes "defamation," it's not hard to imagine many North Carolina voters making the same painful choice I did on November 4: leaving that part of the ballot blank.

More than 16 percent (over 50 million) of Americans are nontheistic. There are more atheists and agnostics than there are Jews, Presbyterians, Mormons, Jehovah's Witnesses, Buddhists, Hindus, Muslims, Russian and Greek Orthodox *combined* in the United States. Some of these atheists and agnostics were Elizabeth Dole's constituents, and now they are Kay Hagan's. In fact, secular Americans are a significant and growing part of every politician's constituency and they deserve— and are beginning to insist on—the same consideration politicians give to other citizens. Lip service is where it will begin. Perhaps, one day, respect will follow.

This piece I wrote for "On Faith" had an interesting consequence. Several months after the 2008 election, I was seated next to former candidate Linda Ketner (she had lost the election) at a League of Women Voters program. We had never met before, and when Linda heard my name, she suggested that we slip out to the lobby so she could buy me a drink. At the bar, Linda told me she had seen my "On Faith" article and found it enlightening, but she asked me to elaborate. I said, "When you were campaigning, I would not have had a problem in your replying to a *question* about your religious beliefs. But how would you feel if I were running for office and had a thirty-second TV ad in which I mentioned three times that I was heterosexual?" Linda, an open lesbian, got it and said she would not make the same mistake were she to run again for public office. She made my day.

CHAPTER 15

Mathematics and Teaching

How to Teach, and How to Learn from Bad Teachers

I write about teaching with some trepidation, because I still can't get out of my mind an aphorism I heard decades ago: "Those who can, do; those who can't, teach; and those who can't teach, teach others to teach."

Though I've taught for more than forty years, I never took a course on how to teach. Such courses aren't required to teach at the college level. Academic controversy has long endured over whether prospective teachers should concentrate more on learning the content of the subject or on learning how to teach. While both are important, my focus is on content. I think the best way to learn to teach is to teach.

When I was teaching at Clark University, several math majors told me in 1971 that they wanted to teach math in public schools, but not all the required math education courses were offered. I worked out a program with the education department at Clark and I wound up teaching a certifiable education course on "teaching mathematics." I had students take turns preparing and teaching particular topics, while the rest of us in the class acted like students. We then critiqued the teacher's performance. We all had fun in this class, occasionally even throwing spitballs.

To my surprise, the students told me it was the most useful education course they had ever taken in preparing them to teach. This wasn't so much a compliment as it was criticism of their other education courses, which they considered totally useless. Interestingly, I was qualified to certify these college students to teach in public school, but

I wasn't "qualified" to teach in public school myself. Had I taken my own course for credit, I would have been on the road to certification. Such was the education bureaucracy in 1971, and it hasn't improved today as much as I had hoped it would.

Long before knowing I'd become a teacher, I unconsciously prepared for the profession by mentally critiquing my own teachers. Some I wanted to emulate, but with most I thought about how I would do it better. It's a bit unsettling to realize that some of my worst teachers turned out to be some of my best. I don't mean simply that I didn't have the sophistication to appreciate quality teaching until years later, though in several cases that was true. Some were just unprepared, disorganized, uncaring, rotten teachers. What I didn't learn from them, I had to learn on my own; what I learned on my own, I understood better and retained longer.

A special salute goes to my fifth-grade teacher, to whom I took an instant dislike. In one assignment, she gave a list of ten words and asked us to write a sentence for each. I saw the ambiguity in her request and thought I was especially clever when I incorporated all ten words into a single sentence. I suspect my rather long sentence contained numerous grammatical errors, but that was not my teacher's objection. She punished me and had me write ten separate sentences using each word once. So I defiantly followed the letter, but not the spirit, of her assignment. For example, my sentence for the word "across" would be, "Across is a very nice word." I made sure not to give a clue as to whether I knew the meaning of the word. Again, I was punished.

OK, I confess. I could be pretty insufferable. But my punishment, to do math problems while classmates were drawing, was just the motivation I needed. This obnoxious little kid was inspired by his teacher to *enjoy* mathematics because he saw that she hated it. I also had the mathematical incentive to get thrown regularly into the "briar patch." One never knows all the forces that come into play in choosing a career, but I think this bad fifth-grade teacher might have played some role in my becoming a math professor. I hope her math phobia didn't turn too many students off math forever.

I had another how-not-to-teach moment the following year when our sixth-grade class took a trip to Fels Planetarium in the Franklin Institute in Philadelphia. We attended a lecture by someone we had been told was a famous scientist. When he finished his presentation and asked for questions, my curiosity overcame my shyness. I wanted some perspective on this mysterious room that seemed to contain countless optical illusions. Wondering how many feet above the ground the planetarium ceiling was, I took a deep breath, pointed to the ceiling, and asked, "How high is the sky?" The famous scientist responded with laughter, which encouraged my classmates to join in. When the laughter finally subsided, he replied condescendingly that the sky was all around us—and he quickly moved to the next question, leaving my humiliation behind.

I've sometimes related this story to students who told me they were afraid to ask dumb questions in class. I'd say, "There is no such thing as a dumb question." I don't really believe this, but better to ask dumb questions than to remain dumb.

My final how-not-to-teach lesson occurred at, of all places, the Department of Motor Vehicles. I had a driver's license from Pennsylvania, and needed one from New York so I could drive in Syracuse while at the university there. The week before I was scheduled to teach my first class as a graduate student, I went to the DMV and asked a guard where I needed to go. She pointed to a sign in front of me. Obviously annoyed with my question, she added, "How many times do I have to tell you people the same damn thing?" I've been asked some of the same questions by countless students, but I've always remembered that the question was new to the student who asked it and that every student deserved the same respectful answer as the first person who asked me.

I'm not trying to make a case for bad teachers, even though we can often learn more from them. Some of my worst teachers were also some of my worst teachers, and I never did learn their subjects on my own or from anyone else. There is no magic bullet for teaching. Whatever we do or don't do probably will be beneficial to some students and harmful to others. This is not to say that all teachers are created equal.

Different teachers have different styles and philosophies. Some try to make sure that each student has a positive experience and finds learning fun; some try to show that learning can be rewarding because it requires hard work; some try to challenge students by setting unattainable goals for them; and some encourage students to set their own goals. Most teachers have attempted many of these approaches at different times, for different courses, and for different students. Some are at peace with what they do, some are still searching, and some are at peace with searching.

So far I've not distinguished between teaching at the college level and teaching at lower levels, though I think a good elementary school teacher can make a more significant difference than a good college teacher. There may be something to calling us college "professors" rather than college "teachers," since we probably do more professing than teaching. College professors generally expect their students to be sufficiently motivated to learn, though this is often not the case; at lower levels, good teachers spend considerable time encouraging students to want to learn.

At all levels and courses, teachers should have goals. Here are mine, which are not nearly as easy as they sound. I tell my math students there are three things I hope they will learn: how to read, how to know right from wrong, and how to question.

On how to read: Most math students are satisfied if they can solve assigned problems without reading the text or understanding the concepts. But learning to read and understanding some of the subtleties and implications require critical thinking, not merely memorizing. I incorporate questions in my exams that can't be solved merely by doing problems at the end of a chapter.

On knowing right from wrong: This is not a moral issue. Some students will include correct mathematical statements mixed in with garbage, hoping for a significant amount of partial credit. I tell them they will get some credit if they begin a problem correctly, recognize where they are stuck, and say what needs to be done to complete the problem. Not so if they merely add nonsense in an attempt to complete a proof.

On how to question: Mathematics needs to be questioned—not only its internal logic, but also the reasons we are led where we are. Does the conclusion seem reasonable? Did we expect it? Did the steps seem natural or artificial? Can we state intuitively what we have proved? Can we generalize the result? I want my students to have more questions going out of my course than going in. The more we know, the more we know what we don't know.

I also want students to learn that wrong answers can often be as useful as right answers. For example, to find out what integer between 1 and 100 I am thinking of, you need ask only seven yes or no questions. The first is whether the number is between 1 and 50. As you can see, you get as much useful information from a "No" as from a "Yes."

I've had mixed success with the following kind of interchange, whose purpose is to teach students to be precise with their questions. Student: "Can I ask you a question?" Me: "You just did." Student: "Can I ask you another question?" Me: "You just did."

After such an exchange, one satisfactory follow-up is for the student to ask the question without asking permission to ask. Another is to say, "Can I ask you two questions?" I then smile, and say, "What's your second question?" Unfortunately, some students just think I'm being an asshole and they don't ask any more questions.

Over the years, I've changed how I teach. But that change hasn't always been for the better. When I was younger and teaching in Massachusetts, I could get away with saying things I can't say now to a class in South Carolina. I always try to motivate a topic, but here are two (now politically incorrect) motivations I no longer use.

Geometric progressions: I'd ask for a woman volunteer in the class who would answer yes to the following question: "If I gave you $1,000, would you sleep with me?" (I'd almost always get a taker. If not, I'd raise my offer until I did.) I'd then say, "And just for my amusement, would you give me a penny in return?" The student, of course, would agree. I would then offer $1,000 a day for a month, with the student just giving me two pennies the next day, four pennies the next, etc. After the student agrees, I tell her at the end of the month she will be able to use her $30,000 as a down payment for more than $21 million she would owe me. I'd then teach a motivated class the underlying mathematics, without an exchange of money or other favors.

Limits: I'd have a male student (Harry) on one side of the room and a female student (Sally) on the other. I would then tell Harry to walk half the distance toward Sally; then half again, and again. After several such movements, I'd say to the class: "Harry will never quite reach Sally, but he will at some point be close enough for all practical purposes." I'd then introduce the difficult concept of limits in calculus, which requires a careful definition of "close enough" in infinite processes.

Now for three course motivations I can still use.

Thinking outside the box: I ask for a volunteer to guess which hand my penny is in. When he guesses, say, the left hand, I show him the penny in my right hand. I then put my hands behind my back, bring them to the front, and ask him to guess again. Each time he guesses one hand, I show him the penny in the other hand. After a while, he catches on that I have a penny in both hands, because it's more likely that I'm cheating than that he guessed wrong so many consecutive times.

Conditional probability: This is about how an outcome of one event can change the likelihood of another. I conduct a raffle, where each of one hundred people holds one ticket. What's the probability of your winning? Answer: 1/100. I then tear up one ticket, throw it away, and ask, "What's the probability of your winning now?" Almost all students say, "1/99." So I tear up another ticket and ask again. Most will say, "1/98." I then ask, "Does that mean if I tear up 99 tickets that you will be certain of winning?" At this point, they recognize that their reasoning had been faulty, and they need to find the flaw. Of course, your probability of winning increases on each round *only* if yours was not one of the torn up tickets. We then get into the mathematics behind such conditional probabilities.

Television show: This is from the popular game show, *Let's Make a Deal*. You're given the choice of three doors. Behind one is a car, and behind the other two are goats. You pick a door, say No. 1, and the host, who knows what's behind all the doors, opens another door, say No. 3, which has a goat. He then gives you the choice of sticking with door No. 1 or switching to door No. 2. What should you do?

Most incorrectly believe the two unopened doors are equally probable to have the car. But ask yourself this question: how likely was your first guess to be correct? It was 1/3. Regardless of which door you pick, the host will always open a door with a goat, eliminating one of the two bad doors. Since the chance of winning with your original choice remains 1/3, you double your chances of winning to 2/3 if you switch to the remaining door.

The fun of mathematics comes in discovering solutions, not in memorizing procedures. Notice that these solutions tend to be counterintuitive. A problem that defies intuition is one of the best motivators.

Solving such problems and then understanding why your old intuition was wrong is what budding mathematicians most enjoy doing.

What Do Mathematicians Do?

I'm living proof that you don't have to be a genius to be a mathematician. And you shouldn't feel comfortable being innumerate. Well-educated people sometimes tell me they are math dummies or that their eyes glaze over when they see a bunch of numbers. These same people would never say matter-of-factly, "I don't know how to read or write" or "My eyes glaze over when I see a bunch of words." C. P. Snow, an outstanding writer and scientist, deplored our "two cultures," which he wrote about in the 1950s. He said that not knowing the meaning of "mass" or "acceleration" is the scientific equivalent of not being able to read. A bit harsh, perhaps, but ignorance is not bliss. We're all ignorant about many things, whether due to time constraints, indifference, or difficulty in learning. So I hope what follows will be a painless, even enjoyable, journey that will inspire you to understand mathematics a little differently.

You don't have to be a mathematician to appreciate what a mathematician does, or to think like one. Before telling you what a mathematician does, I'll tell you what a mathematician does not do. Being a mathematician has little to do with balancing checkbooks or adding and multiplying numbers. Even the branch of mathematics called "number theory" doesn't deal with numbers in the usual sense. A number theorist gets excited by a proof that every positive integer is the sum of no more than four squares, but he or she has no interest or special ability in multiplying eight-digit numbers.

The mathematician Leopold Kronecker once said, "God created the integers, all else is the work of man." This is a statement more about the axiomatic approach than about numbers or theology. It means that to build a system you have to start somewhere, to accept something. All mathematical systems begin with certain assumptions—which may be called axioms, postulates, hypotheses, or premises. A mathematician is interested in the conclusions that may be deduced from assumptions, regardless of whether the assumptions are true. So a perfectly valid and logical proof may have nothing to do with reality. Part of the beauty of mathematics is seeing the strange and mysterious places that apparently simple and innocuous assumptions may lead.

Case in point: The geometry that students learn in high school is usually not called "Euclidean" geometry because no other geometry but Euclidean is taught. Euclidean geometry contains five reasonable axioms, like "all right angles are equal" and "there is exactly one straight line between two points." Euclid's fifth axiom, known as the "parallel axiom," says that for a point not on a straight line you can draw exactly one line parallel to the original line that passes through the point. Mathematicians often create new systems by either adding or taking away an axiom from a known system. By eliminating Euclid's fifth axiom, mathematicians developed systems known appropriately as non-Euclidean geometries. In these other geometries, the angles in a triangle need not add up to 180 degrees as they do in Euclidean geometry.

Is this hypothesis changing merely a useless game? Even if it is, mathematicians can justify it on aesthetic and artistic grounds if the subsequent reasoning is deep, innovative, and creative. This particular story has a happy ending even for the most practical individual. Einstein developed his general theory of relativity by making use of the theoretical mathematics of non-Euclidean geometry, and applying it to what we now understand to be a non-Euclidean, four-dimensional universe consisting of three-dimensional space and one-dimensional time. Euclidean geometry, however, still works just fine here on planet Earth. ("Superstring theory" might eventually reconcile quantum mechanics with general relativity, though the theoretical mathematics behind it requires at least a ten-dimensional universe. Sounds impossible, but so did a four-dimensional universe in the days of Euclid.)

A mathematical proof is a logical step-by-step approach in its final formulation, but almost never in its creation. Mathematicians usually begin with vague guesses about incompletely posed questions and jump to unwarranted conclusions that require a careful proof. Weeks of labor might show a particular approach can't possibly solve the problem, and a reformulation is needed. Proofs of difficult theorems are usually a combination of insight and luck, along with hours of hard work.

With mathematicians, as with musicians, inspiration and insight may substitute for experience. That's why child prodigies are more likely found in math or music than in history or sociology. That's also why antisocial behavior or inability to function in the real world is less of a detriment in mathematics or music. Yet mathematics is a sociable science, in that mathematicians gain insights by discussing problems and concepts with one another. Mathematicians may seek solutions to specific problems, or build theories to fit results into a more general framework that point us in new directions. Most do some of each, but are usually stronger in one. Problem solvers and theory builders often work together to produce mathematics whose significance is greater than the sum of its parts.

To grossly oversimplify, there are basically two areas (with many subareas) of mathematics: pure (theoretical) and applied mathematics. The pure mathematician takes a "math for math's sake" approach, while the applied mathematician attempts to solve real world problems. Creative tension between pure and applied enhances both. The pure mathematics of one generation often becomes the applied mathematics of another, as was the case with non-Euclidean geometry.

Paul Erdos, one of the finest mathematicians ever, captured the strong aesthetic sense in mathematics with reference to what he called *The Book*. This is an imaginary book in which God has written down the most elegant, clever, and beautiful mathematical proofs. Erdos's highest praise for a proof would be, "This one's from *The Book*." Erdos was an atheist who referred to God as the "Supreme Fascist" because God made it so difficult to discover proofs from *The Book*. Erdos added, "You don't have to believe in God, but you should believe in *The Book*."

And now the time has come to stop gossiping about mathematics and mathematicians and do a problem in mathematics—or, more precisely, show how a mathematician deals with an arithmetic problem. Since mathematics is not a spectator sport, I invite you to join in the solution of the following problem:

A tennis tournament has a hundred participants. Each pairs off with another. Only the winners of the first round continue to the second round, only the winners of the second compete in the third, etc. If there is an odd number of players in a given round, then one player sits out that round (gets a bye) and returns for the following round. The process continues until there is a champion. How many tennis matches altogether will be played?

A suitable, but not the best, way to solve the problem is to add the number of tennis matches in each round as follows:
Round 1: 50 matches; Round 2: 25 matches; Round 3: 12 (one bye) Round 4: 6 (one bye); Round 5: 3 (one bye); Round 6: 2 matches; and Round 7: 1 final match.

Adding, we get: 50 + 25 + 12 + 6 + 3 + 2 + 1 = 99.

This is the answer, but not a satisfying approach for a mathematician. A mathematician would want to know how many matches would be needed if there were 7,593 participants (or any other number) instead of 100. What would be a reasonable guess? A mathematician would probably guess (conjecture) 7,592, one fewer than the number of participants, because that's what it was in the case of 100. But that conjecture would have to be proved. We could go through the same laborious process, and confirm the conjecture for the special case of 7,593 participants. But even if we did, we wouldn't have proved with certainty what would happen if we had 12,345 participants. The more different numbers for which our conjecture works, the more likely we are to believe the conjecture is true. But still the conjecture would remain unproved.

Now this is important in mathematics, and in life: "belief" is not the same as "proof." Some beliefs are eventually shown to be false. For the original problem, we need a different method to solve our conjecture. Often the best approach is to ask the right questions. So here's a better line of thought, which consists of just two questions: How many losers are there in each tennis match? (Exactly one). How many losers are there in the tournament? (Ninety-nine, since all but one is a loser). Mission accomplished!

This is the kind of solution a mathematician seeks. It is general because it can be adapted to any number of players. We have 12,344 matches (losers) for 12,345 participants. And for *n* participants, whatever the number *n*, there would be *n-1* matches. This is also an elegant solution because it is short, devoid of messy arithmetic, and provides us with insight. You can "count," without doing any calculations, that 71,962 matches would be needed to find a winner from 71,963 participants. And the answer makes sense to you. This is the kind of solution that might even be in *The Book*. You can't ask for anything more.

Except that mathematicians are never satisfied. More questions may now be posed, to put the problem in an even more general framework. What if there is a double-elimination tournament (where participants play until they lose two games)? What if n players are allowed to lose m games, for any numbers m and n? What if . . . ?

So now you know how a mathematician thinks, and when you might want to apply such thinking to nonmathematical things. Here's the moral of this chapter. Before trying to solve a problem, whether in mathematics or in life, it's a good idea to take a few minutes for reflection on the important questions related to the problem. Often the best way to learn and understand something is by first asking questions about it. That's what mathematicians do, and you can, too.

CHAPTER 16

Mathematics and God

God and the Green Cheese Theory

The most popular cartoon on the door of mathematicians is by Sidney Harris. One mathematician is explaining his multistep proof, while the other interrupts, "I think you should be more explicit here in step two," which says, "Then a miracle occurs."

A small minority of mathematicians and scientists may believe in miracles, but they recognize them as (by definition) devoid of scientific evidence. We cringe whenever anyone denigrates evolution as "just a theory." From Darwin on, countless peer-reviewed scientific papers have supported evolution. I have neither the expertise nor the inclination to add to that body of work, so I will focus on logic and mathematics to make my points. No mathematical prerequisite required.

Mathematicians and scientists don't use the word *theory* the way laymen do in casual conversation, as in "I have a *theory* that the moon is made of green cheese." This ludicrous statement is a hypothesis, not a scientific theory, and easily dismissed. Scientists elevate a hypothesis to a theory only after using rules of procedure to analyze, predict, or otherwise explain specific phenomena.

Among the theories of evolution, gravity, and geometric functions, only evolution is considered controversial. The "controversy" is religious and political, not scientific, and all three theories are well established, yet incomplete. Geometric functions may sound unfamiliar because it's an obscure field in which I do research. Findings on it appear regularly in refereed mathematics journals. Were there no longer any unsolved problems, geometric function theory would be complete (no longer a theory) and those of us doing research in this field might move to another branch of mathematics. The Religious Right doesn't denigrate geometric function theory because it has no known implications to a biblical worldview. Not so with the theory of evolution.

It's possible for true conclusions to come from an invalid argument. Consider, for example, these arguments with the same two hypotheses:

All men are mortal. Socrates is a man. *Therefore, Socrates is mortal.*
All men are mortal. Socrates is a man. *Therefore, I am an atheist.*

Both conclusions are true, but only the first argument is valid, because the conclusion may logically be deduced from the hypotheses.

Some religious arguments may be valid, but lead to false conclusions because of a false hypothesis. For instance, a valid argument that disproves evolution can begin with a God Hypothesis: God exists. He wrote every word in the Bible, which is literally true. *Therefore, the Earth is less than 10,000 years old.*

Along the same vein, here's a valid argument for the moon being made of green cheese: All lights that shine in the night are made of green cheese. The moon is a light that shines in the night. *Therefore, the moon is made of green cheese.*

God IS Great

Christopher Hitchens, best-selling author of *God Is Not Great: How Religion Poisons Everything*, debated "Is God Great?" with Rev. Al Sharpton at the New York City Public Library on May 9, 2007. Sharpton, of course, could not convince Hitchens that God exists, let alone that he is great. Had I participated, Hitchens would have recognized my argument below for the affirmative position as far superior to Sharpton's:

> If I say everyone in this room is a billionaire, you can easily disprove this claim by pointing out that you are not a billionaire. But you can't disprove my claim that everyone in this room who is ten feet tall is a billionaire. To falsify this claim, you would have to produce a ten-foot tall person who is not a billionaire. Similarly, if I say all gods are great, there is only one way to disprove my claim. You would have to produce a god who is not great. Since we agree that no such god exists, the debate is over. I win!

The validity of my argument relies solely on logic. An argument is valid if and only if its conclusion follows from its premises. For instance, here's a true statement: "If the moon is made of green cheese, then I'm a monkey's uncle." On the other hand, this statement is false: If the moon contains iron and silicon (it does), then I'm a monkey's uncle.

While we're talking about the moon, here's a popular myth that illustrates an important point. When Neil Armstrong walked on the moon, his first words were, "That's one small step for man, one giant leap for mankind." As he was leaving the moon, he also uttered words into an open microphone that few people heard, "Good luck, Mr. Gorsky." When Armstrong returned to earth, the press asked him who Mr. Gorsky was. Armstrong just smiled and said it was a personal moment. Finally, a few years ago a reporter asked him again. This time, Armstrong agreed to explain, saying that everyone involved had died and there was no chance of anyone's being embarrassed.

As a child, Armstrong lived next door to the Gorskys. One afternoon when Armstrong and his brother were playing baseball, his brother hit a ball over the fence into the Gorskys' yard. When Neil went to retrieve the ball, he discovered it had landed under their open bedroom window. As he picked up the ball, he heard Mrs. Gorsky say, "Blow job? I'll give you a blow job when the kid next door walks on the moon!"

However apocryphal the story, Mrs. Gorsky constructed what she thought would be a valid argument to avoid ever performing the act (at least with her husband). On July 20, 1969, the day her unlikely premise (and promise) came true, Mrs. Gorsky was obligated to fulfill her husband's request. It would have been more prudent for Mrs. Gorsky to promise such favors only when the Messiah finally made an appearance.

My fantasy "God Is Great" victory over Christopher Hitchens comes from his inability to produce a god who is not great. But all would not have been lost for him. The title of his book, "God Is Not Great" is equally valid, since nobody can produce a god who is great. Every god that exists is great, and every god that exists is not great. The previous sentence is true only because no gods have been proven to exist.

Three Equals One

This is an equation Catholics "understand." Three Gods equal one

God. Atheists take pride in critical thinking rather than appealing to church authority. However, most religious people are critical thinkers about other religions, if not their own. We must not oversimplify by partitioning humanity into critical and noncritical thinkers.

None of us can or even wants to analyze all of our assumptions, or how and why everything works. We have our own interests, skills, and priorities. But critical thinking requires us to at least know what we don't know. I know I can't give a coherent explanation of why airplanes don't fall to the ground, yet I'm not afraid to fly because there is enough empirical data to assure me. And, yes, at some level I appeal to the authority of physicists and engineers who are satisfied with the scientific explanation.

I've occasionally asked my beginning college mathematics students why we don't allow division by zero. The most frequent reply is, "My teacher told me it can't be done."

Regardless of a mathematician's theological views, such appeal to authority is unacceptable. Here's a more satisfactory explanation. From the axioms for our number system, we can prove that any number times zero is equal to zero. If division by zero were permissible, then all numbers would be the same, rendering mathematics useless. To see this, $3 \times 0 = 1 \times 0$. Dividing both sides by zero shows that $3 = 1$, a better argument for Catholics than I've heard from them.

Now I'm inspired to learn why planes don't crash.

Mathematics and Objective Morality

One of the many arguments for God's existence is that objective morality can come only from God. There have been countless articles about the meaning of morality, whether it's objective or subjective, and whether it's God made or human made. I won't give a philosophical discourse, but I will pose a mathematical hypothesis.

If we could somehow prove an objective morality, there are essentially two kinds of mathematical proofs: *constructive* and *existential*. Here's a constructive proof that between any two numbers there's another number. We construct the number by taking the average of the two. So a number between 7 and 8 is 7.5. Around 300 BCE, Euclid proved that there are infinitely many prime numbers (a number whose only divisors are 1 and itself). His proof was *existential* in that it didn't furnish us with a method to actually construct such an infinite list. We only know in theory that such a list must exist.

It's not important to understand Euclid's proof, which relies on the unique factorization of prime numbers, just that it provides a useful analogy for morality. Suppose we could carefully define "morality," along with a set of axioms on which we all agree. Then we might, and I stress *might*, be able to show that there must be some sort of objective morality. But it would most certainly be an existence proof, not a constructive proof. In other words, it would be a theoretical objective morality and not one that we could apply to our daily lives.

People have always promoted different constructive moralities that contradict one another, handed down by various gods or religious authorities, all having the objective Truth with a capital "T." And deviations often have had dire consequences for heretics. Such inflexibility and certainty represents for me the worst form of morality.

Silverman's Wager

Blaise Pascal (1623–1662) and Herb Silverman (1942–) have had two common interests: mathematics, which led to our mutual profession, and theology, which led to our wagers. Though a Christian, Pascal was also a doubter. In Number 233 of his *Pensées* he says, "If there is a God, He is infinitely incomprehensible, since, having neither parts nor limits, He has no affinity to us. We are then incapable of knowing either what He is or if He is." Pascal later added, "Reason can decide nothing here." He then concluded, in his now-famous wager, that belief in God was the only rational choice to make.

Pascal's Wager: If God does not exist, we lose nothing by believing in him; while if he does exist, we lose everything by not believing.

Before stating my own wager, I'll comment on Pascal's. His first conditional statement could just as well refer to the Tooth Fairy or the pot of gold at the end of the rainbow. Were we to devote our entire life to such fruitless searches, we would be left with an unproductive and wasted life—certainly a loss.

His second conditional statement is even more problematic. Pascal assumes the only existing god would be his Christian version—one who rewards believers with eternal bliss and punishes nonbelievers with eternal damnation. Moreover, it would either be a god who could not distinguish between genuine and feigned belief, or one who rewards hypocrites for pretending a faith that they lack.

I agree with Pascal that no god is comprehensible. But suppose I posit the existence of a creator who cares about human beings and elects to spend an eternity with a chosen few. What selection criteria would such a supreme being adopt? I expect this divine scientist would prefer a "personal relationship" with intelligent, honest, rational people who require evidence before holding a belief. Pascal undoubtedly would have agreed with me that our most promising math students ask provocative questions until convinced by rational arguments, while our dullest students mindlessly regurgitate what they think we want them to say. Wouldn't a supreme teacher concur? My kind of Supreme Being would favor eternal discourse with a Carl Sagan, not a Jerry Falwell.

Such a superior intellect would presumably be bored by and want little contact with humans who so confidently draw unwarranted conclusions about his unproved existence. This brilliant designer would be as appalled as I am by those who profess and glorify blind faith. With that kind of deity in mind, I modestly make my own wager. It is almost a plagiarism. I change none of Pascal's words, except that his last "not" appears earlier in the wager. But what a difference a "not" makes!

Silverman's Wager: If God does not exist, we lose nothing by *not* believing in him; while if he does exist, we lose everything by believing.

Math Quiz about Godless Americans

Assume there are 300 million Americans, and 16 percent are without any religion. Of these 16 percent, 19 percent believe in some god. Of the 84 percent who identify with a religion, 11 percent don't have any god beliefs. Here's the question: How many godless Americans are there?

Answer: 300 million, but only 66.6 million know they are godless.

CHAPTER 17

RELIGIOUS TRAVELS

Travel Gene

My wife Sharon has the travel gene. She would happily visit any country that doesn't require her to wear a burqa. Travel is not my passion as it is hers. Sharon knows what I like and she plans trips we both enjoy. I like to exercise, so we've had nice hiking and cross-country skiing trips. But since my religious journey is a major theme in this book, I'll focus on religion-related travel.

Singapore and India

It is customary for academics working in the same field to collaborate on research and publish papers on their findings. Over the years I've had the pleasure of working with mathematicians around the world. One colleague gave me a standing invitation to talk at his university in Singapore, which I accepted in January 1997, when I was also scheduled to give a series of mathematics talks in nearby India.

Sharon and I felt somewhat apprehensive about visiting Singapore because of the country's questionable record on civil liberties, which included caning, capital punishment for drug offenses, and press censorship. My first impression of Singapore was how clean it was. Many notices warned of severe fines for littering, spitting, and not flushing a public toilet. It was illegal to sell chewing gum. Even a habitual jaywalker like me only crossed with the light, knowing I could be fined or arrested for an infraction. I think this is what Sharon liked best about Singapore, since at home I frequently jaywalk and pace impatiently on the other side while she waits at the stoplight.

I asked my colleague, who was born in India and had taught in the United States and several other countries, for his assessment of the political climate in Singapore. He said he would prefer to see more criticism of the government tolerated, but that his overall quality of life had never been better. He added that Singapore was the only country in the world where he felt his four daughters could safely walk the streets alone at night.

During a bus tour, the guide proudly extolled the virtues of Singapore, which included its *lack* of freedom of the press, speech, and religion. I was appalled by his comments, but I admired his candor. The guide said most religions were allowed, but not those that the government viewed as potentially disruptive, like Jehovah's Witnesses. I'm no fan of that sect, but I was curious about why they had been singled out.

The following day, after my talk at the university, I was invited to meet the dean of sciences. He had earned his PhD at Duke University in North Carolina and spent much of his career in the West. After a brief discussion about the Carolinas, he asked for my opinion of Singapore. I mentioned a few positives and then raised the freedom of religion issue. He brought up Jehovah's Witnesses and cited the reason for exclusion. Military service is compulsory in Singapore and Jehovah's Witnesses refuse to serve. I asked about other conscientious objectors and the dean said the son of a member of Parliament had been one. He served a six-month prison sentence and then returned to society as a respected citizen who had proven the courage of his convictions.

The dean didn't like this religious restriction, but he agreed to abide by the laws. He added that he didn't like some of the laws or harsh penalties, but at least Singapore's citizens were given adequate warning and penalties were applied fairly, regardless of status. He didn't mention the United States, where we both understood that status counts much more than it should.

The dean told me the government accommodated some religious practices that would otherwise be forbidden. He cited the burning of paper money on a holiday when Chinese "send" the money to their ancestors. Normally, this would be a violation of Singapore's restrictive pollution laws. The dean didn't like other restrictions, like those on pornography. He felt that any form of censorship was detrimental to a quality education. I was pleased that he felt free to tell a foreigner he had just met about his disagreements over government policies.

Our flight from Singapore to Madras (now Chennai), India, took us from what looked like the world's cleanest and most efficiently run country to one of the world's dirtiest and most chaotic. We arrived at midnight and waited more than two hours in sweltering heat along with two hundred other passengers until our luggage was unloaded. A patient colleague who picked us up said this was typical. We had to push through swarms of people at the airport to get into his car and head for our host institution, Madras Christian College. Air pollution was visible, though not as obvious as the mounds of garbage lining the roads. What we most noticed, even at that hour, were the continually honking horns and near collisions with auto rickshaws, motor scooters, buses, bicycles, and even roaming cows.

Our host was proud of the college guesthouse, the finest on campus, where he took "Madame Sharon" and me. When Sharon and I walked in, she pulled down the blanket on the bed and was shocked by a huge cockroach that seemed paralyzed in mutual shock at seeing her. She wanted to leave immediately and find a cockroach-free hotel. I convinced her that we should stay, rather than be viewed as ugly Americans. We did stay for several days, as scheduled, and Sharon grew fond of the guesthouse and the location, where monkeys cavorted outside the college's classroom windows. Our hosts appreciated our visit and could not have been more solicitous of our comfort.

Sharon and I were impressed that Christian, Hindu, and Muslim students and faculty learned and taught in harmony at Madras Christian College. Their kindness and respect for one another was apparent. Sharon suggested we contribute a scholarship for a student who could not otherwise afford tuition. This was not as generous as it sounds. Tuition was only $80 per year, with the annual faculty salary ranging from $1,000 to $3,000. Our $500 donation provided a scholarship in perpetuity.

We also traveled around India to five other universities, where I gave math talks. Several introductions of me were embarrassingly long and flattering. One notable exception was from a cordial host who, I assume, thought "too" and "very" were interchangeable: "Professor Silverman has been doing research in complex analysis for too long a time." I think he might have accidentally stumbled onto the truth.

Wherever we went our hosts were extremely kind, considerate, and deferential. We couldn't convince them to call us Herb and Sharon instead of "Professor Silverman" and "Madame Sharon." Our funniest dining experience, at least for me, occurred when my math colleagues brought their wives along to a fine restaurant. Men and women sat at separate tables. Since none of the wives spoke English, I talked with colleagues at my table while Sharon conversed with smiles and gestures at her table.

A scary moment for me occurred at Allahabad University, where we attended a memorial for a math professor who had recently died. Although I had not known the man, I was asked as a guest to sit on the stage during the tributes. Several mathematicians spoke glowingly of his accomplishments, though it was difficult for me to understand details because of bad acoustics and thick Indian accents. It was swelteringly hot, and I became increasingly uncomfortable on stage. Finally, the moderator announced the good news that he would introduce the final speaker. The unexpected bad news was that I was the one introduced. The moderator motioned me to the podium for a final tribute to this beloved colleague I had never before heard of and whose name I didn't remember.

I couldn't decline, so I nervously got up to speak. My speech went pretty well, under the circumstances. I said something like this: "Our esteemed colleague may be gone, but it's obvious from your presence today and your tremendous tributes to him that he will continue to live in our hearts. His mathematical contributions will also live, and we will remain inspired by his work to reach even greater heights. What a wonderful life after death he has achieved through everyone here."

India Insights

Unfortunately, the Hindu caste system was alive and well during that trip in 1997. The remedy for a person born into a lower caste (because of alleged misdeeds in a previous life) was to accept his or her lot, do good deeds, and hope for a better life in the next reincarnation. Government-sponsored affirmative action programs attempted to help Dalits (Untouchables), but there appeared to be no effective way to end the caste system. I thought Hindu Dalits might want to convert to another religion (or better yet, no religion), where behavior in a past life could not be used as justification for discrimination in this one—in fact, many have done so.

The widespread belief in astrology also surprised me. Newspaper advertisements for arranged marriages often required, in addition to the proper caste, the horoscope of the potential mate. Astrology was even taught at some universities, frequently incorporated into astronomy courses. I asked a colleague what he thought of such practices and he said, "That's a bunch of nonsense." I was relieved until he added, "They never get the time of birth right, so how can they expect to get accurate readings?"

I found the poverty in India overwhelming, with some people vying for a good place to sleep in an alley. The saddest sight was in Monkey Park near Delhi University. Every day at a regular time monkeys gathered and people threw them bananas and other food, while impoverished children waited on the side to pick up monkey leftovers.

The Baha'i House of Worship in New Delhi was a welcome change after the distressing scene in Monkey Park. I disagree with the Baha'i theology that God revealed himself through a series of divine messengers, including Abraham, Krishna, Zoroaster, Moses, Buddha, Jesus, and Muhammad, but I like that Baha'is seek common ground for all religions and beliefs. Their priorities are to work for world peace and to eliminate racism and poverty. As I left and offered a small contribution, I heard something I never expected to hear from any religion (or secular organization): "I'm sorry. But we can't accept a donation from you. We consider it an honor to contribute, and only members of the faith are afforded this privilege." No wonder they avoid entering politics.

I *was* allowed to contribute to the Periyar Self-Respect Center in Madras, run by atheists and humanists. Their primary goals are to eliminate the caste system, improve the status of women, and combat superstition created by religion. They sponsor education programs and hold free clinics for women's health and family planning. I happily contributed to this worthwhile center.

Sharon and I have many lasting memories of India: magnificent temples next to streets strewn with garbage; wonderful meals for under $1.50; a televangelist-style elephant who "blessed" us after we deposited money on his trunk. But no report on India can be complete without a remark on toilets. The dearth of clean Western toilets is certainly more problematic for women than for men, but I'll never forget asking about toilet facilities in a restaurant in Varanasi. The owner ushered me out of the restaurant, escorted me around the back, and pointed to a stone wall. As I was laughing and peeing, a friendly cow sidled up right next to me. And that's no bull!

Contrast

Perhaps it's unfair to compare such different countries as Singapore and India. Singapore is carefully managed with fewer than three million people. India is poor with more than a billion people, steeped in traditions and cultural factions. What both countries have in common are many fine, hard-working students who value education and consider it a privilege to go to a university.

Wherever we went in India, people assumed the system was corrupt and poorly paid bureaucrats depended on bribes to supplement their incomes. In Singapore, politicians were paid well and less prone to corruption and bribery. Every rule, whether I agreed with it or not, had a rationale. For example, when I asked a Singapore official about a heavy fine for feeding birds in a particular public place, he told me that the birds had previously polluted the area. The policy encouraged the birds to remain in their natural habitat where food was readily available.

It's an oversimplification to say that there is not enough freedom in Singapore and too much freedom in India. Both the good and bad aspects of "Big Brother" are present in Singapore and absent in India. It's presumptuous for me to expect the political values I cherish to be desirable, or even workable, in a different culture. There is much to admire in both countries, and both have more religious freedom than do neighboring countries like Indonesia, Myanmar, China, and Pakistan.

Israel

In June of 1999, two years before Bruce Feiler's best-selling book *Walking the Bible*, Sharon and I followed a somewhat similar route. Our friend Marty Perlmutter, head of Jewish Studies at the College of

Charleston, arranged for fifteen students, a few faculty members, and several other interested participants to take a Hebrew Bible study trip to Israel, Jordan, and the Sinai area of Egypt. As we visited historic locations, we discussed the history, culture, and religion of ancient Israel and its neighbors. We experienced the diverse physical environments reflected in biblical texts. This trip combined two pleasures for me, walking and arguing. Sharon urged me not to upset others by making fun of biblical passages. As it turned out, this wasn't a problem.

Most in our group were Jews (primarily atheists), with a few Christians (believers, but not fundamentalists). We began our readings from Samuel and Kings, which Marty pointed out were the first books in the Bible for which there is evidence that some characters had existed. There was no archaeological evidence for buildings erected by Solomon, and all we could say about David and Solomon is that their legend endures. Marty's comments made several Christians uncomfortable, but nobody complained.

We also read Richard E. Friedman's book, *Who Wrote the Bible?* The book tries to distinguish among the various biblical authors and their political motives. In this "documentary hypothesis," we read that scholars assigned the names J, P, E, and D to four different authors of the Torah. The author of the document associated with the divine name Yahweh/Jehovah is called J; the document referring to God with the Hebrew name Elohim is E; the writer of legal sections and matters concerning priests is P; and the source found only in Deuteronomy is D.

This sounds somewhat parallel to the four New Testament gospels and their four made-up author names (Mathew, Mark, Luke, and John), with one significant difference. The four gospels are in separate books, with sometimes contradictory versions of events. The four writers of the Hebrew Bible also tell contradictory stories, but they are interwoven instead of separated because tradition says all five books of the Torah had but one author, Moses (who somehow managed to describe his own death in both Numbers and Deuteronomy).

The redactor(s), meaning the person(s) who joined the five books of Moses, deserve considerable credit for skillfully combining alternative explanations and turning them into one story that satisfied all factions. Contradictory stories remained because they represented different traditions and could not be excluded without offending influential sects. Scholars like Friedman use various methods to "un-redact" the Bible and separate it into its distinct authors. They note different writing styles, different values placed on biblical characters, different political motivations, and different portrayals of God. For instance, J describes an anthropomorphic God who grieves, regrets, and smells food, while P's God is a transcendent controller of the universe.

In his book, Friedman graphically displays two different versions of the flood story (Genesis 6:5–8:22). He puts in bold type the passages ascribed to P and in regular type the passages ascribed to J. If you read each source separately from beginning to end, you see two complete, coherent accounts with different vocabulary and concerns. But read as a whole, the story is a mass of contradictions: one pair of each kind versus seven pairs of clean animals and one of unclean; a flood lasting 40 days versus a flood lasting 360 days; Noah sending out a raven versus Noah sending a dove, and so on.

Just as important as our text studies were the biblical insights we gained from our journey. We visited the Dead Sea, the lowest point on the Earth's surface and too salty to sustain life. Sodom is the first biblical story about an actual place. I had always wondered why Lot's wife turned into a pillar of salt, of all things. Standing at the Dead Sea, I understood, noting that some salt formations were almost shaped like human beings.

It was hot in the Middle East in June and I almost always wore shorts. Our group visited various churches, some of which excluded me because of the requirement for men to wear long pants. However, one church only stipulated that knees be covered. So I pulled my shorts below my knees, revealing my underwear, and asked the gatekeeper jokingly, "Would this be OK?" To my surprise, my alteration was permitted and I entered the church, much to the amusement of others in our group.

I did wear long pants on the Friday evening we visited the Western Wall in the Old City in Jerusalem. According to Jewish tradition, this is what remains of the Second Jerusalem Temple and it is considered the holiest site for Jews. Modest attire was required to watch the spectacle of bringing in the Sabbath. As is the case with Orthodox Jews at holy moments, male and female are separated. And, of course, the real action

On the way to church in Israel, with my knees
covered as required

took place on the male side. I was pulled into a group of *Hasidic* men
and we danced in circles for several minutes.

We were not supposed to look at women peering over the barrier at
our holy act, but I managed to glimpse Sharon on the women's side.
All in all, my participation in this Western Wall ritual was a worthwhile
experience, but not something I would want to do on a regular basis.
In the spirit of the occasion, the next morning I recited the only prayer
Sharon ever heard me deliver: "Thank God I was not born a woman."
This is an actual daily morning prayer of Orthodox male Jews. There is
no comparable prayer for women.

Wherever we traveled by car, Israeli soldiers stopped us and made us
wait at numerous checkpoints. Our waits were minor, but I could see
how frustrating it must be for Palestinians to frequently endure much
longer waits and intrusive questions.

One day in the Sinai area, our group heard reports of nearby Palestinian bombs. We stayed undercover until the all-clear siren forty-five minutes later. I also felt sympathy for Israelis. I think secular Israelis and secular Palestinians might be able to resolve the Middle East crisis. Unfortunately, land for many religious Jews, Muslims, and Christians is more important than peace because of God's "promise." God shouldn't be in the real estate business, especially since he promised the same territory to different people.

The high point of my trip, both literally and figuratively, was trekking with several others to the top of Mount Sinai in Egypt. The climb was not difficult and when I reached the summit I had a vision, just like another Jew with a white beard. My vision was not one that even the mythical Moses could have imagined. At the very pinnacle, I beheld a Bedouin selling Snickers bars. This clash of cultures wonderfully illustrated the mixture of the sacred and profane. I bought a Snickers bar and a bottle of water from the Bedouin's candy stand, and enjoyed them while feeling awestruck at the sunset over the stark, magnificent desert below.

Then it was time to return. After descending Mount Sinai, Moses is described in the Bible as having rays of divine light beaming from his face. Since the Hebrew letters are the same for "beaming" and "horns," a Greek translation had Moses with horns. Many medieval artworks depict a horned Moses, most famously Michelangelo's sculpture. This is one of the reasons Jews are believed to be children of the Devil.

Before leaving the summit, I bought three more Snickers bars to share with Sharon and others below. Though a little red from the sun, I reached the bottom with neither beams nor horns. As I jokingly looked up for a sign, I tripped on a rock and lost one of my three Snickers bars. Perhaps that was the sign. My Moses moment was not like Charlton Heston's in *The Ten Commandments*. It was like Mel Brooks' in *The History of the World: Part I*, when he descends the mountain with three tablets shouting, " I have fifteen . . . [he drops and shatters one tablet] I have ten commandments!"

I then realized that the true meaning of "Snickers" is, well, snickering. I understood that today's Jews don't identify primarily with the Orthodox or Conservative or even with the Reform Jewish community. Our current history and our common heritage is Humoristic Judaism.

It's Woody Allen saying he would become a believer if God would send an unmistakable sign—like a substantial deposit in his name in a Swiss bank account. That would probably work for me, too.

Sharon said this visit to Israel was her most interesting trip ever. Unfortunately the Middle East situation has grown too dangerous for the College of Charleston to promote such Bible study trips today. Maybe someday, but not "God willing."

CHAPTER 18

JEWISH STUDIES ATHEIST BRUNCH TALK

Marty Perlmutter, who led our trip to Israel, has been director of the College of Charleston Jewish Studies Program for more than a quarter century, and he is justifiably proud of its growth and diversity. Each semester the program presents a public forum at which Orthodox, Conservative, and Reform rabbis meet to discuss Jewish perspectives on an issue of general interest. This displays a variety of opinion within Judaism and the value of dialogue among different sects. Marty also arranges for distinguished speakers at monthly Jewish Studies brunches, most from out of town, but some local. These events help bring together the college and broader South Carolina communities.

Sharon told Marty she liked the programs, but that they weren't quite diverse enough. She suggested inviting me to speak at a Sunday brunch on Jewish atheism. Marty was open to the idea, but worried that I might offend religious Jews who regularly attend, some of whom are significant contributors to the program. I told Marty how I've disagreed with many conservative speakers he's brought in, and added, "Your brunches would be pretty boring if nobody ever disagreed with the speaker. Isn't disagreement the essence of Judaism?"

Marty still worried about inviting such an open atheist, and said, "In making your case for secular Judaism, would you agree not to denounce religion in general?" I told Marty I never do that. I also promised him I wouldn't "out" any local Jewish atheists. Marty was a little nervous, but he agreed to schedule me.

I was excited about speaking to a group quite different from my typical audience. I usually give talks to fellow secularists, where I'm preaching to the "choir," or I'm in debates where most in the audience have their minds made up beforehand. Many at my brunch talk, delivered on December 6, 2009, were willing to take a wait-and-see attitude.

My main goals were to show that you don't have to believe in God to be a good Jew, and that secular Jews are an important and growing part of Judaism. I also wanted to make the case for why we would all be better off if atheists in general, and atheist Jews in particular, came out of the closet.

In my talk I mentioned one class of Jews I had once been ashamed of, those who pretended they were not Jewish, especially when they changed their names and tried to pass as Gentiles. I later developed more compassion for such Jews after reading Susan Jacoby's memoir about her family, *Half-Jew*. Her mother was Catholic, the religion in which Susan was raised, but Susan became an atheist in her teens. She didn't discover until she was in college that her father was Jewish. At first she was upset that the family had kept it a secret, but Susan later learned that her father just wanted to protect her from the anti-Semitism he had endured. While exploring Judaism and her roots, Susan described a conversation she had with a Conservative rabbi, who tried to make a case for her becoming a Jew. The rabbi said to Susan, "You can be a Jewish atheist. It's not outside Jewish history." "Half-Jewish," she reminded the rabbi. The rabbi countered, "Don't you think it's your Jewish half that made you an atheist?" This rabbi understood that questioning the sacred books was part of the rabbinical tradition. In that sense, secular Jews are also part of Jewish tradition.

While Jews are now quite open about their Judaism, I mentioned that Jewish atheism is accepted privately but rarely mentioned publicly. The American Religious Identity Survey showed that between 1988 and 2008 the percentage of Jews who considered themselves secular jumped from 20 percent to 37 percent. Theological ideas about God are generally private matters in Judaism and not enforced by a religious establishment. I told the audience that when Rabbi Anthony Holz, from our nearby Kahai Kadosh Beth Elohim Reform Synagogue, spoke to our local secular humanist group, one of our members asked him how many in his congregation were atheists. He said, "I don't know. We don't ask such embarrassing questions." Rabbi Holz just laughed when another member asked, "Which answer would be more embarrassing?"

I said that Christianity requires a special belief about Jesus, but no God belief is required for Jews. When we think of well-known Christians, Billy Graham, the Pope, and Mother Teresa come to mind. Or maybe Pat Robertson and Jerry Falwell. Well-known Jews are usually intellectuals like Albert Einstein and Sigmund Freud, or comedians like Woody Allen, Mel Brooks, and Larry David, or perhaps the most trusted broadcaster on television today, Jonathan Leibowitz. Of course my audience didn't recognize Leibowitz until I mentioned his television name, Jon Stewart, from *The Daily Show*. What all these Jews have in common is that they are secular and have openly criticized or made fun of religion. I'm hard-pressed to name a pious Jew, past or present, who's a household name in this country (other than Jesus).

People are often puzzled about why as an atheist, I still identify strongly with Judaism. In addition to my cultural roots, I pointed out that denying my Judaism might sound like I'm ashamed of who I am. When I stopped believing in God, I didn't stop believing in the ethical and moral principles of Judaism. I did, however, stop performing rituals no longer meaningful to me. I had to admit that my Jewish juices flowed most deeply when anti-Semitism was present. Having relatives who died in the Holocaust, I was not about to give Hitler a posthumous victory by killing off my Jewish persona.

I said I had been a wandering Jew, identifying with no congregation or branch, until I found a home with Humanistic Judaism, founded by Rabbi Sherwin Wine in 1969 as a means for nonreligious Jews to form communities and more easily connect with their Jewish identity. Humanistic Judaism focuses on Jewish culture and history, rather than belief in God. Its rituals and ceremonies don't have prayers or invocations to a deity. It emphasizes that people are responsible for shaping their own lives, that ethics and morality should serve human needs, and that actions should be based on their consequences rather than on preordained rules or commandments. Humanistic Jews read the Torah critically, much the way we read philosophers and political writers. We embrace ideas that make sense to us, reject ideas that are anachronistic, and ignore ideas that seem silly. Jews have been called people of the Book, meaning the Torah, but I like to think of us as people of *many* books.

I mentioned that the College of Charleston Jewish Studies Program began in 1984 because of the generous gift of local philanthropist Henry Yaschik. Henry was openly secular and would periodically ask me how smart people could believe in God. I told the audience that the speaker scheduled to appear the month after my program was David Benatar, an Orthodox Jew who has written about his god beliefs, which are similar to mine. The previous month's brunch speaker had been Stephen Whitfield, who spoke about Jews active in the civil rights movement. When privately I had asked him what percentage of those Jews were secular, he said, "Almost all of them." Whitfield had given me permission to mention publicly that he, too, is a secular Jew.

In my brunch speech I said there had been quite a few other secular speakers at Jewish Studies brunch programs, whether they were public about it or not. I told the audience that I am hoping secular Jews will become a well-recognized community and that secularists in general will no longer be denigrated in this country.

I had assured Marty I wouldn't make fun of religious Jews, but I described an interesting play I'd recently seen in London that did. *Two Thousand Years* by Mike Leigh is about a present-day, secular Jewish family in London, with a shy son in his midtwenties who lives at home. He's pretty much of a social misfit, but the rest of the family tolerates his behavior until one day, apparently out of nowhere, he starts wearing a yarmulke. This sends his father into shock. He shouts, "It's like having a *Muslim* in the house!" His grandfather breaks into laughter and nicknames his grandson "the Rabbi." The grandfather had been a socialist who grew up on a kibbutz in Israel, and he continues to fulminate about how the Zionism he once supported was hijacked by religious extremists.

The son has clearly been yearning for a sense of identity and hopes his religious "conversion" will bring him the satisfaction he craves. It doesn't. After the family reaction, the son at first just wants them all to leave him alone. But then he becomes uncharacteristically defiant and asks his relatives what it means for them to be a Jew. Their answers are enlightening: "I was born a Jew." "I can't imagine not being a Jew." "I'm committed to social justice." "I like to argue."

The father says he's Jewish because he likes Jewish jokes, which he tells continually. Here's one of them: A reporter asks the following question of an American, a Russian, a North Korean, and an Israeli: "Excuse me, what is your opinion of the meat shortage?" The American says, "What's a shortage?" The Russian says, "What's meat?" The North Korean says, "What's an opinion?" And the Israeli says, "What's excuse me?"

None of these family rationales for being Jewish satisfies the son. Even the family members don't seem particularly convinced by their own answers. Yet they all view the religious son as somehow less Jewish than they are. Their Jewish equivalent of "real men don't eat quiche" is "real Jews don't wear yarmulkes."

After a lot of conversation, the son grows comfortable standing up (probably for the first time) to strong and accomplished family members. The last scene shows him without a yarmulke, confidently playing chess with his father. This indicates the son's return to secular Judaism and that he has finally become a *mensch* (an admirable person) in the eyes of his family.

Since Jewish humor is such an integral part of Judaism, I thought it fitting to end my talk with three Jewish jokes appropriate for secular Jews.

The first is about a Jewish atheist who hears that the best school in town happens to be Catholic, so he enrolls his son. Things are going well until one day the boy comes home and says, "I just learned all about the Father, the Son, and the Holy Ghost." The boy's father is barely able to control his rage. He grabs his son by the shoulders and says, "Joey, this is very important, so listen carefully. There is only ONE God—and we don't believe in Him!"

Then there was the journalist from the *Jerusalem Post* who lived in an apartment overlooking the Western Wall. After several weeks, he realized that whenever he looked at the wall he saw the same old Jew praying vigorously. Sensing a story, the journalist said to the old man, "You pray at the wall every day. What are you praying for?" The man replied, "In the morning, I pray for world peace; in the afternoon, I pray for the brotherhood of man; in the evening, I pray for the eradication of illness and disease from the earth." The journalist asked, "And how long have you been doing this?" The old man said, "Every day, for twenty-seven years." Amazed, the journalist asked how it felt to pray every day for those things. The old Jew replied, "How does it feel? It feels like I'm talking to a wall."

And finally, some members of an Orthodox synagogue think they should stand during a particular prayer, but others think they should sit. They argue back and forth, yet can't reach consensus. So they agree to send one member, Jonathan, to the next town where there is a learned rabbi whose opinion they all respect. When Jonathan arrives, he asks Rabbi Levy if the tradition is to stand. Rabbi Levy says, "No." So then Jonathan says, "Good. Then the tradition is to sit." Again, Rabbi Levy says, "No." Frustrated, Jonathan pleads with Rabbi Levy, "Please help us find a solution. Members of our congregation do nothing but argue about whether to stand or sit." Rabbi Levy smiles, and says, "Aha! THAT is the tradition."

I then invited the audience to argue with me in the Q&A that followed my talk. Some mentioned that my talk helped them change their minds about what it means to be a Jew. That was the kind of reaction I was hoping to hear. Changing minds is one of my favorite things, including my own when the evidence warrants it.

CHAPTER 19

FAMILY REVISITED

Death and Dependency

In June 1986, I got a call from my mother, who said, "Come home. Your father is probably dying." I flew from Charleston to Philadelphia and went directly to the hospital. My mother, who had not spent a day without my father for forty-eight years, was remarkably calm. She worried about whether the insurance would cover the hospital bills. We checked and it appeared we had at least several more days of hospital coverage. My father had been hospitalized for more than a week, but he hadn't wanted me to know because I might become unnecessarily worried. He never liked to talk about his health problems, and neither do I about mine (not that I have any). As a child, my mother would become distraught over any minor problem, so I learned to keep quiet.

The doctor confirmed that my father, who had had heart problems for several years, was dying and nothing much could be done for him. He was floating in and out of consciousness, but unable to comprehend what was happening. At that point my mother wanted it over, though I'm not sure if her decision was based more on ending his suffering or running out of insurance coverage. I also wanted it over, as I would my own life under similar circumstances. (I've even half-joked with Sharon about pulling the plug on me if my mind goes, like if I start believing in God.)

My mother and I both told the doctor we would like it to be over as soon as possible. When the doctor said my father wanted to stay alive, my mother went to my father and said, "Sam, it's time for it to be over. Don't you agree?" My father weakly nodded yes, but that wasn't good enough for the doctor. My mother and father were used to my mother being the decider, and now she felt exasperated that the doctor didn't understand how their relationship worked.

I took the doctor aside and said, "My mother has loved my father for forty-eight years and I'm worried that she won't recover from watching him suffer like this." The doctor said, "We're giving him morphine to ease his pain." When I suggested a higher dosage, the doctor said that might prove fatal. I then tried a different tack. "If you're worried about legal recriminations among family members, please don't. We just want it over and we'll sign any papers. So please be kind enough to give my father more morphine." The doctor said, "I know you're acting in the best interests of your father and I'll do what I legally can. Would you and your mother like to say what might be some final words to your father?" Before doing so, I said to the doctor, "Thank you. Thank you."

I went back to my mother in the waiting room and told her it might be over soon, and that the doctor suggested we say goodbye to my father while he was conscious. I saw him first and couldn't tell if he was conscious. Regardless, I said, "I'm sorry we didn't talk more. I know you are a good man." There was no reaction. My mother next told my father she loved him, and we left the room. The doctor then examined him privately and returned to tell us, "He's calmer now than he was earlier." I took that as a sign the doctor had administered more morphine. Within a couple of hours, my father was dead.

My mother began to cry, as I had expected. I tried to cry, too, mainly because I knew it would please my mother, but I couldn't. I'm not much of a crier, and I don't think I ever had very strong feelings for my father, one way or another.

On the drive home, my mother made two interesting comments, one unusual and one not. Here is the one that wasn't. "I'm sorry your father died on a Friday. We can't bury him on a Saturday, so we'll have to pay extra for a Sunday burial." Jewish tradition requires burial the day after death, except not on Saturday (*Shabbas*) or Jewish holidays. My mother's surprising comment was, "They gave your father blood transfusions last week. I hope he didn't have AIDS when he died."

My father's *shiva* took place in Aunt Eleanor's apartment. When the Orthodox wing of the family arrived, they became outraged. A sixteen-year old kid from this wing bellowed, "How can you leave these mirrors uncovered? Take them down immediately or cover them with sheets!"

He was technically correct from an Orthodox standpoint. The rationale is that looking in a mirror is a sign of vanity and must be avoided when mourning the dead. The son's behavior was religious fundamentalism, typical of all stripes that often can't see the forest for the trees. In many cases, neither the trees nor the forest make any sense. *Shiva* is meant to comfort the bereaved, not piss them off. My mother and Eleanor felt guilty about this infraction and apologized for the oversight. I felt like taking a mirror down and breaking it over the little Orthodox bastard's head. I'm usually not that emotional and never prone to violence of any kind, so I did nothing.

One of Eleanor's friends came to the *shiva* with her daughter. The daughter and I exchanged a few pleasantries, and that was that. The next day, Eleanor's friend told Eleanor that the daughter liked me. Eleanor immediately told my mother, who became very excited. She had frequently asked me, "Are you seeing anyone?" I would say "No," whether I was or not. I'd always kept my mother out of my personal life. Perhaps my mother thought I was gay, which she would be too ashamed to ask about, or that nobody would be interested in me. I can understand the latter view. No sensible person would be interested in someone with the personality I put on display around my mother. I rarely asked questions, offered opinions, or volunteered information. I'd generally respond to questions with the civilian equivalent of name, rank, and serial number.

Much to my mother's dismay about missing out on a wonderful opportunity, I never followed up with that nice Jewish girl I met at the *shiva*.

Ever since the 1958 brouhaha at the *shiva* for my Uncle Max, who married Steffi the *shiksa*, I hadn't seen that branch of the family. I knew that Steffi's sons Bob and Allen had become lawyers, but I didn't know my mother sometimes called Bob for free legal advice. She invited him to my father's funeral, where I saw him for the first time in twenty-eight years. We had a nice, but short, exchange. I wanted to apologize for the undeserved treatment his family had received from the rest of the family, but not in front of all those people.

I later learned that my mother had asked Bob at the *shiva* to draw up a will for her, which he agreed to do. Remuneration was neither asked for nor offered. When I told my mother that Bob was a professional lawyer and she should have offered to pay for his services, she brushed off my suggestion. "He's family. Why should he take money from family?" So this is how Bob was welcomed back into the fold. My mother had also tried to get Steffi's younger son Allen to do some free legal work, and couldn't understand why he had such a negative attitude toward the family.

Becoming Part of the Family

I was relieved that my father died before my mother, because she'd be able to take care of herself and he wouldn't have been. Still, I saw vulnerability in my mother I hadn't seen before. My father had been responsible for their finances and she wasn't sure what to do. Most of their money had been earning interest in a local bank, with the rest in short-term certificates of deposit. I had recently learned about mutual funds and suggested that she invest a portion, as I had done. For the first time in memory, my mother took my advice.

As I was leaving, I told my mother I'd call in a few days to see how she was getting along. That didn't sound like much, but I had rarely phoned her before. Over the past couple of decades, she would call me weekly. My mother appreciated my concern and said, "I may have lost a husband, but I feel like I gained a son."

I knew there would be some tricky waters ahead to navigate. My mother might have recognized that she now needed me more than I needed her. I was willing to accept the responsibility of helping her because she was a widow in need, but I still didn't want to get close or confide in her. In May, I sent her the first Mother's Day card she had ever received. She thanked me, but I wondered if she had noticed I chose a card with a little ditty that did not include the word "love." I didn't write anything on the card, other than "Herb." My mother might have gained a son, but not a very affectionate one.

I had kept an emotional distance from my mother when I was young, mostly to disengage from her controlling behavior. My resentments and frustrations over the years slowly had been replaced by pity for her. I saw how my mother had worried about me, but I never before thought that she might one day need me, or that I might have a reason to worry about her. Eleanor and my father had been the two people in Fannie's life. With my father dead, I knew she would rely even more on Eleanor, but also on me.

Widows Eleanor and Fannie began seeing a lot more of each other. Surprisingly, they argued frequently. Eleanor couldn't drive, so my mother would drive the three miles from her apartment to Eleanor's apartment. Eleanor would periodically complain to Fannie that she wasn't dressed up to the standard of other residents in Eleanor's up-scale building, and then Fannie would sulk and not visit Eleanor for a couple of weeks.

Sometimes Eleanor and Fannie disagreed over trivial matters and wouldn't speak for days. At a particularly angry moment, Eleanor phoned me to say how cruel my mother had been when Eleanor had taken my side in a dispute. Eleanor had told Fannie, "You shouldn't smother Herb so. He's a good boy and you should give him more independence." Fannie responded, "You have no right to tell me how to raise a child. You weren't even able to have one of your own." That made Eleanor cry for days. After several miscarriages, a doctor had told Eleanor that she could never carry a baby to term.

I agreed that my mother's remarks were unkind, but I reminded Eleanor that Fannie made those hurtful comments more than twenty-five years ago. "You're both different now," I added, "and you should both let go of such past resentments." I felt strange defending my mother against remarks by Eleanor, but my defense went unheeded. In my family, there is no statute of limitations on behavior.

Meanwhile, the low-fee mutual fund I had recommended to my mother was doing well, and she asked me to suggest another. This continued until she had about a dozen funds. I wanted her to consolidate for simplicity, since most were invested in similar stocks and bonds, but she preferred having each small investment in a different fund for her to track. And track she did, daily writing the value of each. After a couple of years, she had list after list on reams of meaningless paper. I told her to throw them out, but I don't think she ever threw anything away, especially if it was money related.

Atlantic City casinos became another source of revenue for my mother, who developed a surefire winning strategy. A free casino bus would take senior citizens from Philadelphia to Atlantic City, and drop them for the day with $20 in chips and a voucher for lunch. My

My mother, Fannie Silverman, and her sister,
Eleanor Roth, in 1997

mother would cash in the chips, eat the lunch, and wait for the return bus to Philadelphia. Mathematician Edward Thorpe wrote a popular book about blackjack called *Beat the Dealer*. Fannie could have written a book called *Bore the Dealer*. Unlike Thorpe's strategy, my mother's scheme worked 100 percent of the time. Who says there's no such thing as a free lunch, or a free $20? When casinos caught Thorpe playing, they immediately threw him out. Authorities wouldn't dare touch my winning mother.

Introducing Sharon

When Sharon and I began living together in 1990, I didn't tell my mother. I spoke more frequently to Eleanor after my father died, but I didn't tell her about Sharon, either. We specialized in one topic—Fannie. Eleanor would complain about how frustrated she was by Fannie's controlling behavior. She'd give examples, knowing I'd understand because I'd experienced similar incidents. Since Eleanor cared more about appearance than Fannie, I didn't mention how I disliked that my mother kept "presentable" clothes for me to wear during my annual visits to Philadelphia. Each year she had me try on the same tie and jacket she had bought for me to wear at funerals. This was the same outfit I had worn for Uncle Norman and my father, and which she expected me to wear for hers when the time came. It continued to fit, so at least I hadn't gained much weight over two decades. When I was seventeen, my mother reluctantly passed on my bar mitzvah suit to a relative because I could no longer fit into what I wore at thirteen.

During a 1994 phone conversation, I revealed to Eleanor that I was happily living with Sharon. Eleanor thought I should tell my mother. I said I was concerned that she would try to interfere too much and, besides, Sharon Fratepietro wasn't Jewish. Eleanor said, "That doesn't matter like it did in the olden days, and your mother would be so happy to know you finally found someone to take care of you in your old age." This oft-repeated bromide appeared to be the family view of marriage, and their marriages seemed to reflect that view. I had a more interesting relationship with Sharon than any of my relatives could conceive of for themselves. I told Eleanor I'd think about telling my mother and asked that she not say anything to her. Eleanor agreed and seemed pleased that I confided in her in a way I couldn't confide in my mother.

But it was the telephone company, rather than Eleanor, that convinced me to tell my mother. She used to call me only after 11 p.m., when rates were cheaper, and I'd always answer. When the phone company began giving the same low rate after 5 p.m., I couldn't further restrict Sharon from answering the phone. So I asked Sharon to tell my mother she was the maid in case she answered a call from my mother. Sharon doesn't like to lie about anything, but she reluctantly agreed. She also lobbied for me to be honest about our living arrangement as she became increasingly uncomfortable being the "maid." So I finally called my mother and told her about Sharon. After a gasp and a long pause, the first words out of my mother's mouth were, "I was puzzled by all those maids. I know you're not that neat."

The last time my mother approved of my appearance, at my bar mitzvah in 1955 when I was beardless.

Sharon and I then planned a Philadelphia trip to meet "Mom." Sharon thought I had prepared her well for the visit, but she still got some surprises. After exchanging brief pleasantries with Sharon, my mother directed her to my bar mitzvah and graduation photos prominently on display in the living room. Fannie asked, "Wasn't Herb handsome then?" Sharon said, "He's handsome now, too." My mother shook her head and corrected Sharon. "No he's not. Look at that beard! He didn't have a beard then." Sharon resisted saying what we were both thinking: "Not many thirteen-year-olds do."

On every visit since 1968, my mother had criticized my beard and tried to convince me to shave it off. Her dislikes usually lasted forever. One exception was Fannie's finally liking a *shiksa*. Sharon treated Fannie more like a loving daughter than I ever had as a loving son.

My relatives who met Sharon also liked her. Part of it was Sharon's warm personality, but I expect another component was amazement that I had found someone nice who liked me. A few family members talked about how their views on mixed marriages had changed over the years. I learned that my mother's parents had once moved to a different neighborhood when they saw eight-year-old Fannie becoming friends with a Gentile boy.

Times may have changed, but not completely. When an elderly Orthodox relative heard I was getting married to Sharon, she had only one question, "Is she Jewish?" When she got the dreaded response, this relative refused to even meet Sharon. We married late in life, and can laugh about and feel sorry for this relative. But that kind of attitude has split apart many families. A more moderate family member, who knew Sharon and I were both atheists, said, "So, why couldn't you marry a *Jewish* atheist?"

With each visit, Sharon discovered more idiosyncrasies about my mother. Fannie would sit in her apartment for long periods next to the window facing the street to make sure nobody would steal her eighteen-year-old car parked outside. As an extra precaution, she had installed a steel bar that attaches to a car's steering wheel to prevent theft. Twice daily, Fannie went outside to clean the car with a rag and fuzzy duster.

Sharon noted my mother's declining health and convinced me that we should visit more frequently. We even got her cards for Mother's Day and signed them "Love."

In 1998, Fannie realized that she needed to go into a retirement home. Of course she first checked the prices of all facilities and chose the cheapest one that had a significant number of Jewish residents. Before moving, Fannie sold her car. She tried to sell the antitheft bar to the same buyer for an additional $30. He refused, so Fannie kept it.

The day before the move, Sharon and I flew to Philadelphia to help. Unfortunately, nothing had been packed. The apartment was crammed with belongings Fannie had been hoarding for years. We knew she would insist on taking every worthless item with her, though there wasn't nearly enough room in her new and smaller apartment.

The move in some ways was more difficult for Sharon than for Fannie. To keep Fannie busy, I drove her to the new home with a few packed boxes, and then took her to a restaurant far away for a long lunch while Sharon packed.

Fannie had accumulated decades of useless stuff, including shoe polish, scouring powder, string, pens and pencils, paper clips, and rubber bands. Sharon found napkins, sugar, salt, and pepper packets, taken from restaurants because they were free. And there was much more. Expecting Fannie's imminent return, Sharon rushed about the apartment, stuffing pounds of trash into huge plastic garbage bags. Periodically she hurried outside to toss them into the dumpster behind the building, all the while worrying that Fannie might suddenly return and catch her in the act. Sharon threw out much more than she packed, and hoped Fannie wouldn't notice after the move. She didn't.

Once in her new retirement apartment, my mother tried to sell the steel antitheft bar to her elderly neighbors, nearly all of whom were too old to drive. The relationship between Fannie and Eleanor continued to deteriorate. Initially they'd visit each other by taking a bus that traveled between their two apartments, but the service was soon discontinued. Neither Fannie nor Eleanor wanted to pay the "outrageous" sum of $5 for a taxi between places, so they rarely saw each other. I pleaded in vain, and even offered to pay for the taxis. They had been best friends their entire lives, and Fannie didn't have anyone else. But they now communicated daily by phone, though the calls were not always friendly.

One day, after several months in her retirement apartment, my mother did not answer Eleanor's repeated phone calls. Suspecting the worst, Eleanor notified the manager of the retirement complex, who let herself into Fannie's apartment and found her unconscious on the floor. Fannie had collapsed with a major stroke and was rushed to the hospital. Sharon and I flew to Philadelphia and the doctor told us that there was no hope for recovery. I showed the doctor my mother's living will and pointed out the merits of giving her more morphine. She died the next day. Though the cause was listed as stroke, I can't help but think a contributing factor was that Fannie finally needed to dip into savings to pay the increased monthly rent at the retirement home. She had become quite upset about no longer being able to make a profit from her social security checks.

Years before, Fannie had had the foresight to persuade Eleanor and the two husbands to prepay a bargain price for adjoining gravesites and headstones. But fortunately for her peace of mind, my mother didn't foresee that she would die on a Friday, requiring the same expensive Sunday funeral that her husband had needed.

Insight into My Father

I didn't think about my father much when he died. My thoughts instead were with my mother, how she would cope and how my involvement with her would change. My parents had always seemed compatible and comfortable with each other, but I don't think I ever understood their relationship very well. In some ways, it appeared to me that my mother treated my father as if he were her son. She would tell both of us what to do, but I was the more rebellious "son." They had been married forty-eight years, but I was still surprised by how much my mother missed and needed my father after his death.

It was only when my mother died that I began to think about my father. At the *shiva* for her, I was alone for a while with Aunt Ethel, my father's youngest sister and his only sibling who was still alive. When I asked Ethel what my father had been like as a child, I gained more insight into his personality in that one conversation than in all the time I had spent with my parents.

My father's father, Herman, died before I was born, and my parents never talked about him in front of me. Herman was a cantor at a small Orthodox synagogue and very authoritarian. According to Ethel, his children didn't like to be around him. He shouted a lot, beat his kids, and would sometimes strike his wife when he got drunk. My father's mother, Sadie, was a sweet woman who never had an unkind word to say about anybody, and never raised her voice. She and the children were happiest when Herman left town to serve as a visiting cantor. My father, according to Ethel, suffered the most emotional scars from this violent childhood. Little Sammy would sit silently in a corner for hours after his father went on a tirade.

Sadie died when I was about five. I had seen her only when my parents and I visited Ethel, her husband Harry, and their daughter Rosalie. They all lived with Sadie, or more accurately, Sadie was then living with them in the same house in which Ethel and Sam had grown up. I would play with cousin Rosalie and my brief encounters with Sadie were always positive, though I can recall saying only two words to her, "Thank you." She'd give Rosalie and me delicious, fresh-baked cookies, which we would gobble up.

Sam didn't learn from his father how to be a good father, but he learned how not to be a bad father. He never raised his voice or hand to me, and never gave me a reason to fear him. When I misbehaved, my mother never said to me what I heard other mothers say to their children, "Just wait 'til your father gets home." I would not have understood the implication. Sam's personality was more like his mother's than his father's, which was fortunate for me.

In some ways, I had acted toward Sam as Sam had acted toward his father, but Sam's father deserved such detachment more than Sam did. I only appreciated posthumously how difficult a life Sam had, and how he was trying to do the best he could with the cards he had been dealt. I regret not having made an attempt to get closer to him. Neither of us seemed to have had the appropriate social skills to communicate more effectively with each other and I heard no suggestions from anyone on how we might have tried.

If Sam learned from his father how not to be a bad father, perhaps I learned from Sam how not to be a father at all. I didn't even relate well to children when I was one myself. As an adult, I thrive mainly on issue-oriented conversations. I viewed communication with children as nothing but small talk. I also thought of parenting as the ultimate loss of independence. You can divorce a spouse if you grow apart, but you can't divorce a child. Children are forever, or at least until eighteen. Genes aside, I expect there would have been a high probability of my not bonding with my own child, had I had one, since I almost never relate to children. Perhaps I would have bonded when she or he became eighteen, but my road not taken was probably a wiser choice.

I Get a New Mother

I didn't remain an orphan for long. Immediately after my mother died, Eleanor went into a deep depression, blaming herself for not noticing how sick Fannie had been. Suddenly in Eleanor's eyes, Fannie had become perfect. Criticism of her was now verboten, even though it had been the main topic of conversation between Eleanor and me in recent years. Eleanor decided to take on the role of being the mother I had just lost, but not the mother that Eleanor sounded like when she was criticizing Fannie's foibles. Eleanor became the mother of Fannie's foibles.

Immediately after her death, I wanted to give my mother's furniture to charity, but Eleanor insisted we sell it. A dealer answered our ad and proposed a lump-sum purchase. When he offered his best price, Eleanor began to cry and left the room. The dealer told me he understood how difficult it was to sell belongings that brought back fond memories of a loved one. I resisted telling him he could stop Eleanor's tears by offering another couple hundred dollars. Eleanor decided to sell the belongings piecemeal and eventually sold it all for $150 more than the dealer offered. I told Eleanor to keep the proceeds she had worked so hard to get, but she insisted my mother would have wanted me to have it.

My lawyer cousin, Bob Silverman, came to my mother's funeral and I asked him if he'd be willing to probate my mother's will. I told him I expected to pay for his time, but he turned down my offer of payment. (I found another way to express my appreciation with a gift to his family.) That started my present relationship with Bob, who quickly became my favorite family member and the one with whom I could most easily converse.

Sharon and I continued the practice of visiting Philadelphia, only now to see Eleanor (my surrogate mother) instead of Fannie. We'd usually fly in on Friday to have dinner with Bob and his wife Sandy, and then see Eleanor all day Saturday. We wouldn't tell Eleanor about seeing Bob on Friday. She was still suspicious of Bob, even suggesting that he had gone to Fannie's *shiva* just for the free food.

Were there Jewish saints, I'd propose Bob as a candidate. When I finally got to apologize for the disgraceful way the family had treated his side of the family, Bob brushed it off, saying those were different times. I said I didn't think he had missed much because I had found family gatherings so boring. Bob, however, wanted to talk about happy times in the old neighborhood. Since he's five years older than I am, he remembered things I had either forgotten or ignored. He was always more sociable than I and valued the alleged good times. Bob is the sort of person who thrives on family closeness, but he was excluded for many years from the kind of gatherings I was trying to avoid. Had our parents been switched, Bob would have been an ideal family member, and I would happily have kept the same distance from the family as his brother Allen had.

More Eleanor

Eleanor is now in her nineties and beset with many physical problems, yet she still tries to be a good mother to me and a good mother-in-law to Sharon. She tells us we don't eat enough or that I don't dress correctly. Sharon and I both find this funny, unlike how I felt half a century earlier when I'd hear it from Fannie. When we visit, Sharon and I usually join Eleanor for lunch in the retirement facility where she now lives. Recently, Eleanor told me to come after lunch because Sharon doesn't eat enough to justify the eight-dollar cost for it. So we visited Eleanor after lunch, and planned to stay with her all afternoon and take her to dinner.

After a couple of hours, Eleanor said to me, "You might want to go back to your hotel before dinner so Sharon can freshen up." I assumed Eleanor was tired and needed a nap, but on the way back to our hotel Sharon had a different and more accurate take. She knew about the "dress code" Eleanor used to try to impose on Fannie, and Sharon said, "She wants me to change into a better outfit." This was particularly amusing because most residents at the retirement facility had such poor vision that they could barely see Sharon, let alone what she was wearing. Sharon looked fine to me and didn't have better clothes to wear, but she did brush her hair before dinner.

After dinner, for no apparent reason except a sense of guilt, Eleanor felt compelled to tell me a secret she'd kept since Fannie had died fourteen years before. She had broken her promise to Fannie. "I just couldn't ask the undertaker to do it," Eleanor said. "Even now I feel terrible. I just couldn't ask him to pull out her gold teeth for me to sell."

A perfectly plausible request in my family.

CHAPTER 20

CAN THIS MARRIAGE
BE SAVED?

My friends often wonder how Sharon puts up with me. Apparently I have some idiosyncrasies that my friends enjoy, but not so much that they would want to live with me. That's OK, because I wouldn't want to live with any of them either. Aside from Sharon's being a generally tolerant person, I'm fortunate that she had a difficult first marriage. From her previous sample of size "one," she thinks I come off looking pretty good. One of my best qualities, Sharon says, is that every morning I bring her coffee in bed. As husbandly duties go, that's a pretty simple one that I wouldn't think deserves such gratitude. It must be because I get the coffee/milk ratio just right.

Sharon and her first husband had three children. I get along well with them, primarily because they were adults when we met. They all live in Toronto with their spouses and children. When we get together, I'm a little uncomfortable around the six grandchildren (my grand stepchildren or my step grandchildren?). Sharon encourages me to talk to them, and I try my best, but it's not easy given my personality.

Sharon and I resolved some minor problems early in our relationship, like who does what around the house. She was doing about 98 percent of the work. On the other hand, I thought most of my 2 percent was unnecessary, since I had been doing considerably less for myself when I was living alone. Though I had a strong case, I didn't want her to do such a disproportionate amount. So I suggested we hire someone to clean and she agreed. A service comes in monthly (I think annually would be sufficient) to allegedly clean an already clean house.

What I hadn't anticipated was that Sharon would have me clean more the morning of the maid service than I used to clean previously. Apparently, Sharon would be embarrassed if the maids were to find any dirt in the house. Were all customers like her, maids would have the easiest job on the planet.

But we had a more serious problem early on, which I'm happy to say is completely resolved. Sharon wanted me to stop sleeping with other women.

She took my literal "sleeping with" to be figurative. The math department at the College of Charleston used to save money by sharing hotel rooms at the national convention of the American Mathematical Society. At first, only men attended. When women were finally hired in the department, some members began pairing at conferences according to compatibility rather than gender.

I had "slept with" Bev Diamond before I met Sharon, and we agreed to share a room again at our 1991 convention, when Sharon and I were living together. Sharon, who did not know Bev well, objected strongly, but I didn't want to go back on my word to Bev. I also would have felt uncomfortable telling Bev the reason, especially when Ned Hettinger, her soon-to-be husband in the philosophy department, was perfectly comfortable with the arrangement. I also wanted to show Sharon that she could trust me. When I returned from the conference and said in my "I-told-you-so" voice, "See, nothing happened," Sharon was still angry. It took a long time for her to get over something she said would be unheard of at the software company where she was working as a technical writer.

We both learned from the experience. For me, Sharon's feelings now matter more than anyone else's. She also learned that we did indeed have a very different culture in the math department. The following year I slept with one of my favorite partners, Bob Mignone. I like him, and sleeping with him had one advantage over sleeping with Sharon. Bob has a hearing problem, so it never bothered him when I fell asleep listening to the radio. That disturbs Sharon, so my compromise with her is to set the radio timer for ten minutes. Overall, though, I'd rather sleep with Sharon than with Bob.

The next year I slept with Deanna Caveny, which was fine with Sharon since she knew and liked Deanna (Sharon also now likes Bev and her husband, Ned). As it turned out, Deanna slept her way to the top (in a manner of speaking). Our department chair was retiring and I thought Deanna might be an excellent replacement. So I asked her during pillow talk (from separate beds) if she'd be interested. She was, we discussed the position, and I mentioned our conversation to other department members. We chose Deanna as our next department chair and she did an outstanding job. Bev went on to become senior vice provost, Deanna eventually left as department chair to become associate provost, and Bob succeeded Deanna as math department chair. Despite the obvious benefits of sleeping with me, the math department now budgets single rooms for all members who attend conferences.

Sharon once taught "special education" and took me to a student senior prom, the first prom of any kind I ever attended. She knew I had trouble with small talk, which she encouraged me to do at the prom because some students were very sensitive and would be upset if I ignored them. Sharon got a little perturbed when I told her it would be helpful if she'd arrange for students to wear numbers indicating their IQs, so I'd know better how to converse. But she knew me well enough not to take my comment too seriously. As it turned out, I probably had the lowest DQ (dancing quotient) at the prom.

Sharon and I periodically argue about Chestnut Hill College, her alma mater, and a Catholic college for women (now coed) outside Philadelphia. She had attended because a nun from her high school recommended her for a scholarship. From elementary school through college, Sharon attended only Catholic schools, and she still feels cheated at having received such a narrow education. I was hoping we could go to one of her reunions for interesting conversations with her classmates about her path to atheism. Sharon continues to refuse, though each year I try a different tactic to persuade her.

Then there is the hair problem. Perhaps I was too high on champagne at our wedding on January 1, 2000, to remember one of my marriage vows, according to Sharon. It seems I must get a haircut within two weeks of when Sharon says I desperately need one. Since Sharon has been disappointed approximately 100 percent of the time by the job my barbers have done in the past, she consistently asks me to tell the next barber, "Short, but not *too* short."

When I return, Sharon always looks exasperated because my hair is too short. I argue that I tried to communicate her request, but she rightly suspects I'm lying. I justify this little white lie by reasoning that hair too short will eventually be just right for Sharon, if only for a day, but hair too long can't be made right without another barber experience. An additional reason to err on the short side is that the shorter the hair, the longer the interval between repeat ordeals. My biggest fear, however, is that a barber might counter Sharon's request with the stumper, "How short is *too* short?" Since I haven't a clue, I'd probably say, "You know, *too* short," as if such a clarification would be the least bit meaningful to anyone over the age of seven. Both "too short" and "short" are relative terms, but I wouldn't want to discuss this theory of relativity with any barber. So I just say "Short," hoping the barber will know what that means. If I have to answer *how* short, I'm prepared to respond, "Short enough so I don't have to see you again for a long time."

In a clever attempt to get me a better haircut, Sharon became a grooming pimp. She fixed me up with a high-priced establishment in downtown Charleston called Gents, where attractive young women service male clients. Based on the price differential, I expected either a five times better haircut or interesting "benefits." The benefits turned out to be big televisions tuned to ESPN and a decade's worth of *Playboy* magazines. The added cost also entitles the cutters to be called stylists instead of barbers.

My activity there consisted mainly of pretending not to stare at the stylist's well-endowed breasts, while thinking they are probably a Gents criterion for employment. When my stylist asked strange and, to me, unanswerable questions, like how I wanted my hair shaped, my typical response was, "Whatever." The stylist even shoved a mirror behind me so I could critique the hair on the back of my head. All I learned from the mirror was that I have a bald spot.

Very few people know the endearing nickname I have given my wife, though it once helped me win a "special recognition" prize in an essay contest sponsored by C-SPAN, the television network that focuses on Congress and national politics, to mark its 25th anniversary on TV. It read as follows:

C-SPAN saved my marriage! Well, not quite. But my wife and I now communicate much better, and not only because we enjoy discussing issues raised on C-SPAN. The biggest recurring argument my wife and I used to have was what to call her. She wanted me either to use her name or some mutually agreed-upon nickname. Sparse with words, I saw no need when we were alone to preface my remarks to her with any label. While watching C-SPAN together one Friday morning about five years ago, she mentioned that even TV host Brian Lamb appropriately identifies his callers. At that moment, my wife and I looked at each other and knew our "problem" had been resolved. My lovely wife (Charleston, South Carolina) and I thank you for helping us find the perfect nickname for her.

P.S. Charleston's nickname for me is the last four digits of my Social Security number (but she calls me "3" for short).

I close this chapter with two pieces of marital advice, gleaned from my personal experience in a happy marriage.

1. Argue periodically with your spouse, but always with a sense of humor. Remind your spouse that you are arguing because you respect his/her opinion, even if it's really stupid. If your spouse gets concerned about the relationship, remind her/him of all the fun times you have together. When the argument ends, do something fun to prove it.

2. Don't marry until you are at least in your fifties. Before you realize the marriage isn't working, one of you will probably be dead.

CHAPTER 21

LAST WORDS

People on deathbeds are generally incapable of long speeches. I happen to hold the all-time record for the shortest speech ever delivered about death or anything else. At one freethought conference, participants were invited to give speeches of no more than two minutes. Mine was billed, "Is There Sex After Death?" When my name and title were announced, I came to the stage, stared at the audience for thirty seconds, and shouted "NO!" I then returned to my seat, confident that nothing more could be said on the topic.

On my deathbed, I expect to say, "See? There are atheists in foxholes." If I die before Sharon does, my penultimate words will be "I love you" to her. However, my last words will serve to eliminate a cliché. I plan to be the first dying person to say, "I wish I had spent more time at the office."

INDEX

ABOUT THE AUTHOR

Herb Silverman graduated from Temple University with a bachelor's degree in mathematics and received his PhD in mathematics from Syracuse University. He is Distinguished Professor Emeritus of Mathematics at the College of Charleston. He has published more than one hundred research papers in mathematics journals and a couple of books on complex variables, and is the recipient of the College of Charleston Distinguished Research Award.

Herb ran for governor of South Carolina in 1990 to challenge its unconstitutional provision that barred atheists from holding public office. After an eight-year battle, he won a unanimous decision in the South Carolina Supreme Court, which struck down this religious test requirement. He is founder and president of the Secular Coalition for America. He founded the Secular Humanists of the Lowcountry in Charleston, South Carolina, and served as founder and faculty advisor to the College of Charleston Atheist/Humanist Alliance student group. He is a Humanist Celebrant and board member of the American Humanist Association, as well as advisory board member of the Secular Student Alliance and member of the Advisory Council of Americans United for Separation of Church and State.

Herb has participated in a number of debates with religious scholars, including one at the Oxford Union at Oxford University in England on the topic "Does American Religion Undermine American Values?" He has had many articles in freethought publications, and a book chapter titled "Inerrancy Turned Political" in *The Fundamentals of Extremism*. He also contributes weekly to "On Faith," an online forum on religion produced by the *Washington Post*. He lives in Charleston, South Carolina, with his wife Sharon Fratepietro.